Preschool Prevention of Reading Failure

Preschool Prevention of Reading Failure

Edited by
Richard L. Masland and
Mary W. Masland

York Press/Parkton, Maryland

This book was manufactured in the United States of America.
Typography by Brushwood Graphics, Inc., Baltimore, Maryland.
Printing and binding by McNaughton & Gunn, Inc., Ann Arbor, Michigan.
Cover design by Joseph Dieter, Jr.

Proceedings of a conference on preschool prevention of reading failure sponsored by The Orton Dyslexia Society held in San Francisco, California on November 4, 1988.

Library of Congress Catalog Card Number 88-50703
ISBN 0-912752-14-9

Contents

Preface vii

Contributors xi

PREDICTION OF READING FAILURE

1. Are Prelinguistic Abilities Predictive of Learning Disability? A Follow-up Study
   Rachel E. Stark, Beth M. Ansel, and Jennifer Bond 3
2. Preschool Language Processing Performance and Later Reading Achievement
   Katharine G. Butler 19
3. Speech- and Language-Impaired Three and Four Year Olds: A Five Year Follow-up Study
   S. Yancey Padget 52
4. Predicting Dyslexia in a Preschool Population
   Nathlie A. Badian 78

INTERVENTION

5. Slingerland Screening and Instructional Approaches for Children At-Risk for School
   Barbara K. Keogh, Sue Sears, and Nancy Royal 107
6. Studies of the Effects of Teaching Auditory Segmenting Skills Within the Reading Program
   Diane J. Sawyer 121
7. Rhyme Recognition and Reading and Spelling in Young Children
   Lynette Bradley 143

8. Preschool Prevention of Reading Failure: Does Training in
    Phonological Awareness Work?
    Ingvar Lundberg 163
9. Invoking Precursors of Deficient Reading
    Dirk J. Bakker 177

ONGOING STUDIES

10. The Early Identification of Developmental Language Dis-
    orders and the Prediction of the Acquisition of Reading
    Skills
    Barbara C. Wilson and Donald A. Risucci 187
11. Phonological Precursors to Reading Acquisition
    Susan A. Brady and Anne E. Fowler 204

RETROSPECT

Overview of Early Prediction and Intervention
Jeannette Jefferson Jansky 219
Discussion and Reactions to Prevention of Reading Failure
Doris J. Johnson 225

APPENDIX

Speech and Hearing Checklist 231
INDEX 235

Preface

The symposium on which this book is based was sponsored by The Orton Dyslexia Society as background for a research program to study the early recognition and remediation of deficiencies that lead to failure to learn to read. Its purpose is to evaluate the state of knowledge in respect to two fundamental questions: "What is the earliest age at which characteristics predisposing to failure to learn to read can be recognized?" and "At what age and through what means can reading failure be prevented in susceptible individuals?"

This book includes reports of a variety of approaches, but they agree on one fundamental fact. Reading is a linguistic activity. The vast majority of dyslexia-prone children have some deficiency in their basic spoken language skills. Of particular interest in this volume is the demonstration that phonological awareness and knowledge of segmentation of speech are essential to acquiring the phonological keys to a phonetic written language. As documented by R. Stark deviations of language development can be recognized at an extremely early age, even in infancy. D. J. Sawyer, L. Bradley and I. Lundberg have demonstrated in carefully controlled studies that children who have failed to develop these abilities can be recognized in the preschool years. Specific training in segmentation recognition and in rhyming to develop phonemic awareness can have a long lasting impact on subsequent acquisition of reading and spelling. However, I. Lundberg finds that those whose language skills are most severely deficient are those least responsive to this type of intervention. For those who cannot develop such skills, D. J. Sawyer suggests that a whole word (idiographic) method of learning may be required.

The importance of specific instruction may be highlighted by the report of S. Y. Padget who found that in spite of conventional speech training only 30% of a group of children whose severe language problems were diagnosed at preschool age were subsequently able to remain in regular classrooms.

Although 50–70% of variance in reading ability is attributable to lack of phonemic skills, N. Badian points out that for precise predictions, correlations are not sufficient, and other factors must be evaluated. When such factors as inheritance, school and home environment, and socio-economic level are taken into consideration a high degree of predictive accuracy can be achieved.

K. C. Butler tested 229 kindergarten children and followed them to the 11th grade. Of the screening tests used, morphology, syntax, and attention were the most predictive of subsequent reading ability. Attention showed a high correlation with reading success. The ten poorest readers had all had language problems at the time of preschool testing. However, prediction of failure was unreliable, and it was evident that the school and socio-economic environments were important variables.

B. Keogh, using a battery of predictive tests, noted that accurate identification was difficult because of the multiplicity of the factors involved. Success was more accurately predicted than failure. She found that the Slingerland tests were quite accurate in predicting success. However, many children predicted to fail were in fact successful. B. Keogh suggests that we need to study the characteristics of those children considered at risk who actually succeed.

That other factors than simply phonemic awareness must be taken into consideration is suggested by the work of D. Bakker. Using electrophysiological tests, he has demonstrated atypical patterns of localization of brain activity during word recognition tasks in dyslexic children. He has developed a method of stimulation directed toward enhancing the use of the appropriate hemisphere of the brain. His sophisticated studies, based on scientific observation, should have a better prospect of improving reading than have previous efforts based on attempts to alter handedness or eyedness.

In conclusion, the studies reported here verify that a majority of children who subsequently have problems in learning to read have demonstrable deficiencies in language skills in the preschool years. These deficiencies can be significantly overcome by specific types of instruction during the preschool years directed toward enhancing phonemic awareness. Prediction of reading success can be

achieved with considerable reliability in those who have no such deficiencies. Prediction of failure is less reliable, since many factors are
involved in failure. Unless these factors are taken into account in the
prediction, many children predicted to fail will in fact succeed.

It would be unfortunate if in our present pre-occupation with
linguistic abilities we overlook other less evident characteristics of
sub-populations of dyslexic children who might require other forms
of preschool intervention. Also of interest is the observation of both
B. Keogh and I. Lundberg that children who have received preschool linguistic instruction, while better than controls in reading,
did less well in arithmetic.

The exciting prospective studies now being undertaken by
B. Wilson and by S. Brady should provide means for early recognition of specific sub-types of dyslexia and for the development of pre-
ventative or remedial measures specific to the defect.

An area of primary interest for both of us, but especially
M. W. M., has been in the prevention of academic failure by early
identification of the oral language problems that are so frequently
the precursor of difficulty in learning to read. Aspects of auditory
awareness and memory and their relation to language development
have been particular areas for investigation. Thus, this book reflects
our lifetime interest in the early recognition of deviations of language development.

Richard L. Masland
Mary Wootton Masland

Contributors

Beth M. Ansel, Ph.D.
Department of Audiology and Speech Sciences
Purdue University
West Lafayette, Indiana

Nathlie A. Badian, Ed.D.
Holbrook Public Schools
Holbrook, Massachusetts and
Children's Hospital
Boston, Massachusetts

Dirk J. Bakker, Ph.D.
Department of Child Neuropsychology
Free University
Amsterdam, The Netherlands

Jennifer Bond, M.A.
Kennedy Institute for Handicapped Children
Baltimore, Maryland

Lynette Bradley, Ph.D.
Department of Experimental Psychology
University of Oxford
Oxford, England

Susan A. Brady, Ph.D.
Department of Psychology
University of Rhode Island

Kingston, Rhode Island and
Haskins Laboratories
New Haven, Connecticut

Katharine G. Butler, Ph.D.
School of Education
Syracuse University
Syracuse, New York

Anne E. Fowler, Ph.D.
Haskins Laboratories
New Haven, Connecticut

Jeannette J. Jansky, Ph.D.
Department of Pediatric Psychiatry
College of Physicians and Surgeons
Columbia University
New York, New York

Doris J. Johnson, Ph.D.
Department of Communicative Sciences and Disorders
Northwestern University
Evanston, Illinois

Barbara K. Keogh, Ph.D.
Department of Educational Psychology
Graduate School of Education
University of California Los Angeles
Los Angeles, California

Ingvar Lundberg, Ph.D.
Department of Psychology
University of Umea
Umea, Sweden

Mary W. Masland
Department of Pediatric Psychiatry
Columbia Presbyterian Medical Center
New York, New York

Richard L. Masland, M.D.
Department of Neurology
University of Medicine and Dentistry of New Jersey
Rutgers Medical School
Rutgers, New Jersey

S. Yancey Padget, Ph.D.
Syracuse City School District and
Syracuse University
Syracuse, New York

Donald A. Risucci, Ph.D.
Department of Surgery
North Shore University Hospital
Manhasset, New York

Nancy Royal, Ph.D.
The Prentice School
Costa Mesa, California

Diane J. Sawyer, Ph.D.
School of Education
Syracuse University
Syracuse, New York

Sue Sears, M.A.
Department of Educational Psychology
Graduate School of Education
University of California Los Angeles
Los Angeles, California

Rachel E. Stark, Ph.D.
Department of Audiology and Speech Sciences
Purdue University
West Lafayette, Indiana

Barbara C. Wilson, Ph.D.
Center for Neuropsychological Services
North Shore University Hospital
Manhasset, New York

Prediction of Reading Failure

1

Are Prelinguistic Abilities Predictive of Learning Disability? A Follow-up Study

Rachel E. Stark, Beth M. Ansel, and Jennifer Bond

INTRODUCTION

A number of retrospective studies suggest that reading impairment may be related to speech and language delay, at least in certain groups of reading-impaired children (Doehring 1968). Until recently, however, there have been few prospective studies examining this overall hypothesis. As a result, it has not been clear how early in life it is possible to detect speech and language delays or to predict reading impairment on this basis.

Some forms of early language delay appear to be overcome and are not predictive of later language or learning impairment (Morley 1965; Menyuk 1979). This reflects the considerable variability among normal children in both learning styles and learning strategies. How, then, can we determine which forms of delay

This work was supported in part by Grant Number R01 HD 11970 from the National Institute of Child Health and Human Development and in part by Grant Number 1R01 NS 24462 from the National Institute of Neurological Diseases, Communicative Disorders and Stroke.

should be taken seriously for predictive purposes and which are without clinical significance?

A recent follow-up study of children selected in an unbiased manner suggests that there may be a relationship between early language measures and the decision to provide some form of reading intervention in first and second grade (Capute, personal communication). This study has not, however, identified specific measures at preschool ages that are predictive of reading impairment in individual cases. Other recent studies of infants suggest early measures that may be useful predictors of phonological and of cognitive-linguistic development at least through the later preschool years. Menyuk, Liebergott, and Schultz (1986) state:

> There is some evidence that there may be a link between some early phonological and lexical behaviors and later ones. The early ability to shape vocalizations into syllabic structures and words is a precursor to a later ability to map sound segments accurately onto words. In particular, a child's ability to correctly map final segments onto words appears to be a strong indicator of speech *and* lexical development.

This finding is perhaps all the more important because traditional risk factors such as prematurity with low birth weight and intraventricular hemorrhaging were not found, in this study, to be predictive of language delay in the preschool years. Pre-term infants with extremely low birth weight differed from term infants in the preschool ages at which they could complete a short speech discrimination task. This difference, however, was not predictive of language delay.

Vihman (1986) also found that a relatively high use of true consonants in babbling at 6 to 9 months of age and in words at age 1 year was predictive of advanced phonological development at age 3 years. She suggests that early consonant use may reflect early maturity in both articulation skill and sensitivity to the sound structure of the language.

Menyuk and her colleagues plan to follow their cohort of premature and full-term subjects into the early school years. They suggest that early phonological and language delays may become submerged and manifest themselves only when the child's phonological knowledge is put to a later stringent test, for example, in learning to read.

The present study was designed to investigate phonatory development in normal infants in the prelinguistic period, that is, between 2 weeks and 18 months of age. Six different levels of speech motor development were proposed for this period and the objective was to find out if they emerged in an invariant order in all normal infants. A follow-up study of some of the infants in this project was conducted when they were in second grade.

Speech motor development reflects the status of development of oral musculature and the neuromotor system governing movement of the articulators during speech. Speech motor development also depends upon auditory-motor linkages and therefore reflects the status of development of the auditory system and of speech perception as well as anatomical and neurophysiological development of the speech motor system. It would not, therefore, be surprising if this development were quite highly predictive of later phonological and linguistic development and ultimately of reading ability. Although it was not the original purpose of the present project to develop a set of predictors identifying children at risk for language, speech, and reading impairment, it became apparent that the measures of speech motor development we were constructing might also have predictive value in relation to these impairments.

METHODS

The subjects of the study of speech motor development were from a larger cohort whose prespeech perception and production skills were studied. Forty-five first-born infants who had normal birth and development histories and who had normal hearing were included. Hearing of potential subjects who were three months of age or younger was assessed by means of auditory brainstem response testing. Hearing of subjects older than three months was assessed by means of behavioral audiometry; middle ear status was also assessed in all subjects by means of acoustic immittance measurements. In addition, all subjects were required to obtain a score within normal limits on the Denver Developmental Screening Test (Frankenberg and Dodds 1967).

The 45 infant subjects were studied within a mixed cross-sectional and longitudinal study design. All were studied across an age range during which marked changes in vocal behavior might be expected. They comprised the following groups:

1. Ten infants studied over an 8-week period at 2-week intervals from 2 through 10 weeks of age. Infants in this period were expected to begin to produce vowel-like sounds when they were not crying.

2. Nine infants studied over a 10-week period at 2-week intervals from 12 through 22 weeks of age. Infants in this period were expected to produce the same sound types (e.g., squealing) over and over again as though experimenting with them.
3. Eight infants studied over a 10-week period at 2-week intervals from 26 through 36 weeks of age. Infants in this period were expected to begin babbling in the accepted sense of that term, i.e., to produce syllables repeated in long strings such as /dadadada/.
4. Eight infants studied over a 14-week period at 3-week intervals from 40 through 55 weeks of age. These infants were expected to acquire new vowel types such as /u/ and /i/.
5. Ten infants studied over a 16-week period at 4-week intervals from 72 through 88 weeks of age. These infants were expected to acquire prewords or protowords with general (nonreferential) meanings or to use so called "expressive jargon."

Equal numbers of males and females were sought for each of the five age groups. A number of subjects had to be excluded, however, either because they failed the hearing assessment or the developmental assessment or because their subsequent motor or cognitive development was thought to be mildly delayed. As a result, unequal numbers (3 males, 5 females) were included in the 26 to 36-week old group. All other groups comprised at least 4 males and 4 females. The five age groups were made comparable as a result of proportional sampling with respect to race and socioeconomic status on the Hollingshead Scale (Hollingshead and Redlich 1958).

The 45 infants were video and audio recorded in their own homes. Audio and videotape recordings were made of the infants by trained speech-language pathology assistants and by a research associate at each of the age intervals selected for study (bi-weekly for the youngest infants and at 3-to-4 week intervals for the oldest infants). Two twenty-minute recordings were made on each occasion, except in the case of the youngest group. These infants were unable to remain awake for more than twenty minutes.

A standard test protocol was adopted for each recording session which included the following: (a) A five-minute period during which the mother interacted with the infant; (b) a five-minute period during which she left him/her in a comfortable setting with a visual display (mobile) or appropriate toys (the order in which these two situations were presented was random); (c) five-minute feeding period; (d) five-minute period after feeding during which the mother interacted with the infant as before; and (e) a five-minute period during which the infant was again left alone to play.

These situations were designed to elicit characteristic vocal behaviors at all of the infant subjects' developmental levels. The observers recorded general comments and any new developmental history information after the session was completed.

Subsequently, all utterances produced by these infant subjects were identified and coded in terms of their communicative context (Stark, Bernstein, and Demorest 1984). An utterance was defined as a series of vocalizations separated from all others by at least two seconds of silence. These utterances were assigned codes representing one of four categories of communicative vocal behavior, using a system that derived in part from Halliday (1973). The mean number of vocalizations per session was 142 (SD ± 51). This mean number increased with the age of the infant. For the purposes of the present study, 40 to 50 utterances were selected from the first and last recording session for each infant. The selection was such that a proportional representation was achieved for the categories of communicative vocal behavior that the infant had produced.

Computer-assisted spectral analyses were prepared for each selected vocalization. A wide band spectrogram (450 Hz bandwidth), a narrowband spectrogram (40 Hz bandwidth), and an amplitude and a pitch contour were all available. Two trained judges identified vocal segments (vocalizations within a series separated from all others by at least 50 ms of silence) and assigned to each one a code descriptive of the speech motor characteristics of the utterance. Detailed definitions for these codes were developed in a prior study of eight normal infants. They were then tested and modified in intensive study of five infants from the present study, one from each age group. The definitions made use of perceived auditory characteristics of squealing, babbling, and other types of vocalizations, as well as acoustic measurements and descriptors of acoustic phenomena (Stark and Bond in preparation).

Each code was assigned to an hypothesized level of vocal development. These levels are summarized in table I. It will be observed that the first level (0–2 months) is referred to as a Reflexive Level. This term had already been employed to describe communicative context of vocalization rather than aspects of vocal production per se. However, the correspondence between communicative context (as determined by facial gestures, movement of the limbs,

TABLE I
Level of Speech Motor Skill

Level	Descriptors	Age
1	Reflexive	0–2 months
2	Vowel Production	2–3 months
3	Expansion 1	4–5 months
	(consonant and vowel series, squeals, etc.)	
4	Marginal Babbling	6–8 months
5	Consonant-Vowel Syllables,	9–12 months
	Reduplicated Babbling,	
	Non-reduplicated Babbling	
6	Expansion 2	12–16 months
	(new syllable types, new vowel types)	
7	Jargon, Diphthongs, Prewords	16–18 months

and reactions of adult caregivers) and the acoustic/auditory features of vocalization is very high for sustained crying, fussing, and vegetative sounds.

The second level (2–3 months) is characterized by beginning vowel production. Control of phonation emerges at this level. While few continuous vowels may be produced by infants of 2 to 3 months in noncrying, nonfussing contexts, portions of cooing and neutral sounds are frequently vocalic. Uvular or epiglottic friction noises, or nasalization may be imposed upon these vocalic sounds. The consonantal quality of such sounds does not reflect a controlled closure of the vocal tract but instead is related to the restricted space within the oral cavity of the infant in this developmental period (Kent 1981; Bosma 1975) and also to the uncontrolled movements of tongue, especially those of the protrusion-retraction reflex described by Peiper (1963) that are characteristic of infants in this age range.

Level 3 (4–5 months) is characterized by expansion of the existing repertoire of sound types. True (continuous) vowels are produced singly and in series. Glides, squeals, and growls may be introduced and the consonant-like noises, previously associated with uncontrolled movements of the vocal tract, begin to be prolonged and are also produced in series. These "consonants" are more often produced at the front of the mouth than was true of the consonantal sounds at Level 2. Marginal babbling at Level 4 (6–8 months) has been characterized by Oller (1980) as a succession of consonant and vowel sounds which is poorly controlled and takes place at a slower rate than is found in mature speech. Marginal babbling has also been referred to as "primitive" and "not speech like." Three different types were described at this level in the present study.

The fifth level proposed was that of consonant-vowel (CV) syllables, reduplicated or canonical babbling, and nonreduplicated babbling incorporating CV syllables (Oller 1980; Stark 1980). Canonical babbling is easily recognized by parents and others at its onset because its timing and rhythmic characteristics are unlike those of any sound types previously produced by the infant.

Many of the infant's utterances at Levels 6 and 7 (12–18 months) have a very general meaning although a few may actually have referential meaning. New syllable types, such as CVC syllables begin to be used and high front /i/, back rounded /u/, and other vowel types appear. Some infants in this age range produce a great deal of jargon, i.e., long series of meaningless syllables with speechlike rhythms. Parents describe these sounds by saying: "It's as if he were talking a foreign language." Other infants produce very few vocalizations of this type.

It should be noted that the vocal segments within a long series might be assigned codes ranging across two or more of these levels of skill. Each series, however, was subsequently scored at the highest level to which it could be assigned on the basis of judgment of its component segments.

Two experimenters worked independently in making their judgments and subsequently compared them. Whenever disagreements arose, they were discussed by the experimenters and resolved, except in a small number of instances (2%) where there was insufficient information available to the experimenters for this purpose. In these cases, the utterances were eliminated from consideration.

RESULTS

The percent occurrence of vocalizations judged to fall at each of the seven proposed levels are shown for the five age groups in table II. This table indicates an overall increase with age in the percentage of vocalizations falling at higher levels. There is a corresponding decrease with age in percent of vocalizations falling at lower levels. These lower level vocalizations persist however, even in the oldest age group.

Data from a typical 9- to 12.5-month-old infant is shown in figure 1. If our goal were to provide a single data point characterizing this infant's developmental level at the first or last recording, we

TABLE II
Percent Occurrence of Vocalizations at Different Levels of Speech Motor Skill

Age Group	Level						
	1	2	3	4	5	6	7
2–10 weeks	87.06	9.65	3.29	—	—	—	—
(.5 to 2 months)							
12–24 weeks	56.82	18.77	15.52	8.39	.10	.40	—
(2.5 to 5.5 months)							
26–36 weeks	39.47	16.07	20.78	16.76	6.37	.55	—
(6 to 8 months)							
40–52 weeks	24.45	22.94	24.31	12.64	12.64	2.75	.28
(9 to 12.5 months)							
72–88 weeks	9.72	17.06	15.59	8.93	19.96	18.98	10.06
(16 to 20 months)							

might decide to use the highest level that this infant had attained at 9 months and at 12 months. It was decided that a pass/fail score should be applied to such data in order to determine each infant's best or highest level of functioning. If three or fewer vocalizations were classed as falling at the highest level for which an entry was made, it was considered that skills at that level were emerging but not yet fully established. If four or more vocalizations (approximately 10%) were judged as falling at that highest level, however, then it was considered that the infant's speech motor skills were established at that level.

The highest level attained, as determined in this manner, by the subjects in each of the five age groups is shown in figures 2 through 6. From these figures it can be seen that no infant regressed in the course of the study from a starting level to a lower one.

In the 2- to 10-week age group only one infant remained at

Subject ID	Level							Total
	1	2	3	4	5	6	7	
AR40								
9 months	11	11	10	7	4	—	—	43
12.5 months	9	8	9	3	11	8	—	48
Total	20	19	19	10	15	8	—	91

Figure 1.   Number of Vocalizations Judged to Fall at Each of Seven Levels of Speech Motor Skill in a 9 to 12.5 Month Infant.

Subject ID	Highest Level	
	.5 Months	2 Months
AN	1	1
JH	1	2
AA	1	2
WB	1	2
CR	1	2
JX	1	2
CT	1	2
PR	1	3
JN	1	3
KL	1	3

Figure 2.   Highest Levels of Speech Motor Skill Attained by Infants of 2 to 10 Weeks (.5 to 2 Months).

starting level (figure 2). This infant had begun to smile and to interact with adults by 10 weeks of age but she produced only "small grunts" in this interactive situation during her last video recording session.

Every infant in the 12- to 24-week age group was at least at Level 2 at the time of the first recording (figure 3), and at least at Level 3 at the time of the last recording. Two had already progressed to Level 4 (Marginal Babbling) by the time they were 12 weeks old. We suspect that there are marked acoustic and articulatory differences between the sustained vocal activity that was coded as

Subject ID	Highest Level	
	2.5 Months	5.5 Months
JN	2	3
EO	2	3
JL	3	3
DL	3	3
DN	3	3
AO	3	4
RT	3	4
AA	4	4
LL	4	4

Figure 3.   Highest Levels of Speech Motor Skill Attained by Infants of 12 to 24 Weeks (2.5 to 5.5 Months).

marginal babbling in both of these 12-week-old infants and the marginal babbling of older infants (6 to 8 months). We believe that marginal babbling needs further study and definition. In addition, there is considerable heterogeneity among normal infants with respect to the order in which different behaviors assigned to Levels 3 and 4 may manifest themselves. It may be that Levels 3 and 4 should be combined into one level with protracted duration. However, new combinations of old "expansion" behaviors may emerge toward the end of the Expansion Period and persist until the onset of Canonical Babbling; if so, these advances should be reflected in the proposed system.

Almost all of the infants in the 6- to 8-month age range had attained Level 4, that is, true marginal babbling, at the time of their second recording session (see figure 4). Indeed, more than half had attained Level 4 at their first recording. Two had progressed to canonical babbling by 8 months of age. In a third, (JE26), canonical babbling was emerging at 8 months of age and marginal babbling had begun to disappear from his repertoire, as happened in other infants at this particular transition period (see figure 7).

All but one of the 9- to 12-month-old infants had progressed to Level 5 (Canonical Babbling) at the last recording session, and two had progressed to Level 6 (see figure 5). Three infants had already advanced to Level 5 by 9 months of age. Infant EO40, whose highest level at the first recording was Level 2, cried and fussed throughout that session. Subsequent recordings including the 12.5 month recording yielded behaviors within the expected range for his age group.

The majority of the infants in the 16- to 20-month age range

	Highest Level	
Subject ID	6 Months	8 Months
JE	3	3
RR	3	4
LC	3	4
LV	4	4
MC	4	4
AE	4	4
II	4	5
JI	4	5

Figure 4. Highest Levels of Speech Motor Skill Attained by Infants of 26 to 36 Weeks (6 to 8 Months).

Subject ID	Highest Level	
	9 Months	12.5 Months
EO	2	5
SW	4	4
CM	4	5
AI	4	5
CI	4	6
CN	5	5
BT	5	5
AR	5	6

Figure 5.   Highest Level of Speech Motor Skill Attained by Infants of 40 to 55 Weeks. (9 to 12.5 Months).

had attained Level 6 or Level 7 at their last recording (figure 6). Indeed all but three were at Level 6 or 7 at the time of their *first* recording. While onset differences probably reflect the normal variability among infants in this age range, it may be that Levels 6 and 7 should be combined for the purposes of obtaining normative data. Jargon, for example, may not be found in all normal infants of 16 to 18 months or may be so infrequent that it cannot readily be sampled in recording all normal infants (see Dore 1973 and Vihman 1986 for further discussion of this phenomenon).

When the data were first examined, the status of three infants in the study appeared to be significantly lower than that of their peers, even at their final recording session. Two infants in the oldest

Subject ID	Highest Level	
	16 Months	20 Months
KF	5	5
NE	5	5
JO	5	7
LP	6	6
RR	6	6
DW	6	7
AS	7	7
EO	7	7
BF	7	7

Figure 6.   Highest Level of Speech Motor Skill Attained by Infants of 72 to 88 Weeks (16 to 20 Months).

				Level				
Subject ID	1	2	3	4	5	6	7	Total
JE 26								
6 months	26	13	9	1	—	—	—	49
8 months	14	12	12	2	3	—	—	43
Total	40	25	21	3	3	—	—	92

Figure 7.   Number of Vocalizations Judged to Fall at Each of Seven Levels of Speech Motor Skill in a 6 to 8 Month Infant.

age group (KF72 and NE72) gave rise to some initial concern on this score because they were apparently still at the canonical babbling level at 20 months of age. Individual data for these two infants is shown in figure 8. It will be seen that if the "counts" from Levels 6 and 7 were combined, these two infants would "pass" at a level higher than Level 5. As we stated earlier, it is possible that Levels 6 and 7 should be combined at present for the purpose of measuring speech motor skill.

Finally, it will be recalled that for one infant (SW40) in the 9- to 12.5-month age group, canonical babbling had still not been established by 12.5 months of age. As may be seen in figure 9, only one example of Level 5 behavior was recorded at each of the two sessions reported here (on CV at 9 months and one brief babbled series at 12.5 months). New vowel types (in particular the /u/ vowel) were beginning to emerge at 12.5 months but consonants were seldom pro-

				Level				
Subject ID	1	2	3	4	5	6	7	Total
KF72								
16 months	5	11	13	4	11	1	2	47
20 months	4	15	8	4	7	3	2	43
Total	9	26	21	8	18	4	4	90
NE72								
16 months	8	6	13	7	13	—	—	47
20 months	2	13	11	1	8	3	2	40
Total	10	19	24	8	21	3	2	87

Figure 8.   Number of Vocalizations Judged to Fall at Each of Seven Levels of Speech Motor Skill in Two 16 to 20 Month Infants.

Subject ID	Level							Total
	1	2	3	4	5	6	7	
SW40								
9 months	12	12	12	9	1	1	—	47
12.5 months	13	10	12	6	1	3	—	45
Total	25	22	24	15	2	4	—	92

Figure 9. Number of Vocalizations Judged to Fall at Each of Seven Levels of Speech Motor Skill in a 9 to 12.5 Month Infant.

duced. When the mother was questioned about this infant, she reported that, in the thirteenth month, she had just begun to observe infrequent, canonical babbling in SW40's repertoire.

When this infant was 18 months of age, the mother approached the principal author. She was concerned that the child had not yet begun to say any words. She mentioned that the child's father had had some speech problems in his school years and that this history made her particularly anxious about SW40's perceived lag in development of speech and language.

Audiological and speech and language evaluations were accordingly scheduled. The child's hearing was found to be normal, his speech and language delayed. The mother was given some advice about general language stimulation in the home and asked to contact the clinical facility again if she should continue to have concerns about the child's progress. Follow-up telephone calls elicited the information that early in his third year, this child showed a marked developmental spurt in speech and language and began to produce phrases and short sentences. He adjusted well to kindergarten.

Follow-up telephone calls were also made to the parents of infants KF72 and NE72. Both were reported as having shown normal speech and language development. Neither was said to have shown any sign of learning difficulties in first grade.

A follow-up study confined to children in such a sample who were identified as at some degree of risk could be considered inadequate. We cannot claim, on this basis, that our early findings were or were not predictive of disorder. It is quite possible that some children who appeared normal at the time of the initial study later developed speech, language, or reading problems of which we were unaware. Fortunately, we were in a position to re-evaluate a subgroup of children from the original project at a time when they were six to seven years of age. We had funding to study a group of potentially normal children in the age range of our subjects and attempted to recall as many of the original subject group as possible for this purpose. We contacted the parents of those children, 30 in all, for whom current addresses and telephone numbers could be obtained.

We employed a brief questionnaire to determine the speech and language developmental history and the academic progress in school of these 30 children at the time of follow-up. This questionnaire yielded the information shown in table III. Some children appear more than once in this table, for example, a child with a history of otitis media might also be reported as having a speech articulation delay. For the most part, the developmental problems documented in table III were mild and had resolved by the time the child entered first grade. Exceptions were found in the case of the female child with hyperactivity for whom Ritalin was still being prescribed at the time of follow-up; and the male child with difficulty in learning to read.

TABLE III

Number of Children in the Follow-Up Study with a History of Speech, Language, Hearing, Reading, or Other Developmental Problems

Speech	Language	Hearing	Reading	Other
Males				
2 Articulation delay until 5 years only. 1 Stuttering	—	6 History of otitis media with effusion one of whom had bilateral myringotomy.	1 History of difficulty learning to read in first and second grade.	1 Motor developmental problems.
Females				
2 Articulation delay resolved in first grade	1 Expressive language delay reported	6 History of otitis media with effusion, one of whom had bilateral myringotomy.	—	1 Poor fine motor skills and coordination
1 Hyponasal speech; language abilities in the low normal range.				1 hyperactive 1 poor development of socialization skills

This child was, in fact, infant SW40, whom we had considered to be at risk for speech and language delay because of demonstrated failure to develop consonant sounds in his vocal repertory in the first year of life. It will be recalled that this child manifested language delay until he was almost three years of age, at which time he showed a developmental spurt and caught up with his peers. The mother further disclosed at the time of follow-up that she herself had required special education as a child because of reading failure. It appeared from the information relayed by his parents at the latest follow-up that SW40's reading problems might also be undergoing resolution. In first grade, however, he was considered by his teachers to "lack motivation" and to show poor attention during reading instruction. It is probable that his difficulty with reading reflected his earlier problems with phonetic development. These problems might well have resurfaced as a difficulty with phonetic recoding. Lack of understanding of such a difficulty could lead to a mislabelling of such a child in the classroom and to loss of confidence and lack of self-esteem on the part of the child.

In conclusion, there were some mild speech and language problems among these 30 children at follow-up and some problems in other areas (socialization and motor skill areas) that were not predicted by our earlier measures of phonatory and speech motor skill development. Reading difficulty was reported in one child only, however. That child had been identified at the age of 12 months, on the basis of a lag in the development of speech motor skills, as being at risk for language delay and possible learning problems. There was also a reported history of difficulty in learning to read in his family.

These findings, taken together with preliminary reports from Menyuk, Liebergott, and Schultz (1986) and Vihman (1986) suggest that a significant lag in development of speech motor skills should be considered seriously as predictive of reading difficulty. It is not claimed that this is the only factor that should be considered as predictive in the case of young infants, nor that it may operate in the absence of other factors such as familial history of dyslexia. However, it is probable that such a delay is related to a lag in the development of auditory-motor linkages pertaining to speech. Evidence for the significance of these linkages in relation to reading in young children is certainly of interest, both theoretically and clinically.

REFERENCES

Bosma, J. F. 1975. Anatomic and physiologic development of the speech apparatus. *In* D. B. Tower (ed.) *The Nervous System, Vol 3; Human Communication and its Disorders.* New York: Raven Press.

Doehring, D. 1968. *Patterns of Impairment in Specific Reading Disability*. Montreal: McGill University Printing Services.

Dore, J. 1973. A developmental theory of speech act production. *Transactions of the New York Academy of Sciences* 35:623–630.

Frankenberg, W. K., and Dodds, J. B. 1967. Denver Developmental Screening Test. *Journal of Pediatrics* 71:181-191.

Halliday, M. A. K. 1973. *Learning How to Mean: Explorations in the Functions of Language*. London: Edward Arnold.

Hollingshead, A. B., and Redlich, F. C. 1958. *Social Class and Mental Illness: A Community Study*. New York: Wiley.

Kent, R. D. 1981. Articulatory—acoustic perspectivés on speech development. *In* R. E. Stark (ed.) *Language Behavior in Infancy and Early Childhood*. New York: Elsevier-North Holland.

Menyuk, P. 1979. The measurement of linguistic competence over the first five years of life. *In* R. Kearsley and I. Sigel (eds.) *Infants at Risk: Assessment of Cognitive Functioning*. Hillsdale, N.J.: Lawrence Erlbaum Associates.

Menyuk, P., Liebergott, J., and Schultz, M. 1986. Predicting phonological development. *In* B. Lindblom and R. Zetterstrom (eds.) *Presursors of Early Speech*. New York: Stockton Press.

Morley, M. E. 1965. *The Development and Disorders of Speech in Childhood*. London: Livingstone.

Oller, D. K. 1980. The emergence of the sounds of speech in infancy. *In* G.H. Yeni-Komshian, C. Ferguson, and J. Kavanagh (eds.) *Child Phonology Vol I: Production*. New York: Academic Press.

Peiper, A. 1963. *Cerebral Function in Infancy and Early Childhood*. New York: Consultant's Bureau.

Stark, R. E. 1980. Stages of speech development in the first year of life. *In* G. H. Yeni-Komshian, C. Ferguson, and J. Kavanagh (eds.) *Child Phonology Vol I: Production*. New York: Academic Press.

Stark, R. E., Bernstein, L. E., and Demorest, M. E. 1984. Assessment of vocal communication in young children. *ASHA* 25:56.

Vihman, M. M. 1986. Babbling and early speech: Predicting to age three. *In* B. Lindblom and R. Zetterstrom (eds.) *Precursors of Early Speech*. New York: Stockton Press.

2

Preschool Language Processing Performance and Later Reading Achievement

Katharine G. Butler

INTRODUCTION

The importance of preschool language acquisition to later academic achievement is well documented (Aram and Nation 1980; King, Jones, and Lasky 1982; Wallach and Butler 1984). Over the past two decades, evidence has been mounting that preschool language impairment may be reflected later in reading, writing, and spelling difficulties during the school years (Forell and Hood 1985; Lee and Shapero-Fine 1984; Stark, Bernstein, and Condino 1984). More recent evidence indicates that oral language problems as well as reading problems may continue into adulthood (Johnson 1980; Stominger and Bashir 1977), with a few exceptions (Finucci, Gottfredson, and Childs 1985).

Language, whether spoken or read, is a complex and dynamic system of conventional symbols (Butler 1986) and language learning and its use are determined by biological, cognitive, psychosocial, and environmental factors (ASHA 1983, p. 44). The interaction between spoken and written language, particularly in literate societies, is best demonstrated by the knowledge transfer from the former to the latter within the context of the schools. A child's task early in life is to learn language; later, the child's task is to use language to learn.

Almost a decade ago, Satz et al. (1987) reviewed a number of studies that attempted to follow up on the progress of reading-disordered children. They noted that reading disabilities often persisted into late childhood and appeared to lead to secondary emotional and behavioral disturbances (Satz et al. 1978, p. 315). The authors emphasized the need for early identification of children at risk for reading disorders at the beginning of formal schooling and the concomitant need for well-controlled long-term longitudinal studies. In their view, developmental reading disorders stem from delays in early sensory-perceptual and later conceptual-linguistic skills, and are considered to be disorders in central processing (p. 320). Satz et al. based their study of white male kindergarten pupils in a Florida school system on an early detection battery that included some language measures as well as a larger number of nonlanguage tasks. Of interest to the study to be reported here is the importance of socioeconomic status in the Satz et al. (1978) study. SES ranked highest in prediction of reading disorders on both language and nonlanguage variables.

Silver (1978) recommended the use of a scanning procedure (i.e., a survey of entire populations of children) to predict or detect those children who will fail in reading in the early school years. He points out that an instrument to predict such failure must actually be able to predict reading difficulty, provide for few false positives and false negatives, be suitable for rapid and economical administration to large numbers of subjects following a brief personnel training period, be able to identify children who will need further diagnosis, be statistically acceptable, and appropriate for the population studied (p. 353). While noting the difficulties encountered by researchers attempting to scan kindergarten children, Silver also indicated that there is general agreement that the incidence of potential reading failure is 8 to 10 percent for severe failures and "perhaps 25 percent of entire kindergarten classes classified as vulnerable to later reading failure" (p. 376). Finally, Jansky (1978) reported on the work of de Hirsch, Jansky, and Langford in the 1960s which essentially found that oral language skills in kindergarten contributed most to reading and spelling performance at the end of second grade.

Since the longitudinal studies reported above, speech-language pathologists have come to realize that a continuum may well exist between early oral language disorders and later reading deficits. Bashir et al. (1983) refer to such children as exhibiting developmental language disorders and note that they represent a heterogeneous group whose preschool language problems may become submerged, only to resurface once more as learning problems. The assumptions of Bashir et al. were based on a study by Strominger and Bashir (1977) who re-evaluated 40 children they had assessed and treated during their preschool years when they were 9 to 11 years of age. No child was found without residual deficits, while 38 of the 40 children continued to demonstrate difficulties in both written and spoken language. Even the two children reported to be at grade level continued to have some difficulty with recalling names of objects, sequencing sounds, and spelling.

Over the past decade there has been an increased emphasis on the linguistic basis for reading (Lerner 1972; Mattingly 1972; Vellutino 1979), resulting in an emerging awareness that disordered oral language may be causally linked to reading disorders (Gleitman and Rozen 1977; Liberman 1982; Liberman and Shankweiler 1979; Perfetti 1985; Perfetti and Lesgold 1979, Vellutino 1979). A recent study by Kamhi and Catts (1986) throws additional light on the reciprocal relationship between developmental oral language problems and developmental reading impairments. They studied the similarities and the differences between these two presumably different groups of children. While the primary purpose of their research was to compare the phonological processing abilities of these two groups of children and a normal control group, another purpose was to compare language-impaired and reading-impaired children's awareness of lexical and morphological information. To their surprise, they found that the language-impaired children did as well as the reading-impaired children although neither did as well as the normal control group. Kamhi and Catts question whether the groups are truly distinct from each other since school-age children with a history of developmental language impairments and poor readers with no history of developmental speech-language problems reveal considerable similarity, both demonstrating significant academic difficulties in elementary school, particularly in reading (Aram, Ekelman, and Nation 1984). Conversely, reading-impaired children exhibit deficits in higher level language forms (e.g., narrative discourse and figurative language) in much the same manner as do language-impaired children (Feagans and Short 1984; Liles 1985; Nippold and Fey 1983; Roth and Spekman 1986). Kamhi and Catts hypothesize that while there may be a continuum of performance by language- and reading-impaired children, there may also be subgroups, with "children [being] differentiated by some other factor, such as phonological processing abilities, short-term memory, or performance IQ" (p. 345).

Swanson (1982) points out that since "information-processing difficulties [e.g. memory, reading comprehension, problem solving, and selective attention] clearly differentiate learning-disabled students from their normal counterparts" (p. 312), multilevel, multidirectional assessment is required. Among the areas to be assessed is language competence, which Swanson defines as including sensory representation, working memory, linguistic structure (e.g. socialized speech, language regulation, language function, metalinguistic variables) pragmatics, and semantic output (p. 318). Further evidence of the importance of language disabilities in older elementary poor readers is reported by Leong (1987) and of auditory processing disorders among learning-disabled children by van Kleeck and Richardson (in press), and of memory (Liberman et al. 1982; Siegal and Linder 1984; Torgeson 1984; Wolf 1984) and attention (Ackerman et al. 1986; Ackerman and Dykman 1982; Dykman, Ackerman, and Holcomb 1985; Swanson and Obrzut 1985).

In summary, there is evidence, emanating from research grounded in the extant theories of the 1960s and 1970s, and confirmed by increasingly sophisticated designs of the 1970s and 1980s, that oral language and reading problems co-exist, and in fact, that the overlap may be greater than researchers previously anticipated. Subtyping and subgrouping has been a matter of great interest among dyslexia researchers (Denckla 1985; Satz, Morris, and Fletcher 1985), and is gaining prominence in allied disciplines (Johnson in press; Kamhi and Catts 1986). Attentional deficits appear to be involved in both language and reading difficulties and may have an impact on both selective and sustained attention (Dykman, Ackerman, and Holcomb 1985). The demonstrated linkages between early oral language skills and reading are now more clearly evident, as is the interaction of language, memory, and attention. The following report of a study of 229 preschool children's performance on an experimental language processing test and their later reading performance in primary and secondary school (3rd, 6th, and 8th grades), with continued follow-up at the 12th grade level of a selected sample of poor and good readers, may serve to provide further insight into such interactions.

THE STUDY: TIME 1

Subjects

The total population of entering kindergarteners in a medium-sized unified school district in northern California, made up of 229 preschool children (125 male, 104 female), age 58 to 78 months (mean, 74.6), was administered an experimental language processing (LPI) instrument prior to school entry in 1974. Of the children in the sample, 46.3% were Caucasian, 24.5% were Black, 12.7% were Asian and 6.6% were Hispanic. They were screened for speech, language, and/or hearing problems. Socioeconomic status, as represented by the California Assessment Program (1974) occupational ranking, was predominately skilled or unskilled labor for fathers and unskilled labor for mothers (table I). In this particular community, tourism plays an important role in the local economy, having replaced fishing as the primary industry of several decades ago.

Experimental instrument (Form A)

The language processing instrument was designed to assess the auditory comprehension of children, ages 3–6, through presen-

TABLE I
Standardization Sample (N = 229) by Age, Sex, Ethnicity
and Father's and Mother's Occupation

Item	Mean	S.D.	Percentage of Normative Population by Item
Age in Months	58–68	3.6	
Sex: Male			55.0
Female			45.0
Ethnicity:			
White			46.3
Black			24.5
Asian			12.7
Hispanic			6.6
Occupational Groups:*			
Fathers:			
Executive/Professional			7.4
Semi-Professional			13.5
Skilled Labor			25.8
Unskilled Labor			22.3
Unemployed			5.2
Unknown			25.8
Mothers:			
Executive/Professional			.9
Semi-Professional			8.7
Skilled Labor			7.4
Unskilled Labor			13.5
Unemployed			65.9
Unknown			3.5

*California Assessment Program (California State Department of Education 1974)

tation of linguistic stimuli within a competing message format. A series of carefully controlled background linguistic and nonlinguistic stimuli, ranging from −15 dB to +5 dB are utilized in various combinations throughout the four sections of the screening instrument. An examiner provides 120 seconds of pre-training and training (described below), followed by audiotaped instructions over the remaining 6 minute 20 second interval of the actual test. Thirty-four items, divided into four tasks, require that the child respond nonverbally for periods of 90 seconds to 145 seconds. Responses include placing blocks in a box, on a piece of paper, and in the examiner's hands, as well as raising one hand in response to an intermittent nonlinguistic stimulus (a dog barking).

It should be noted that Form A of this language processing instrument is the first of three versions that were administered to large groups of three, four, and five-year-old children in metropolitan and suburban areas in the San Francisco Bay region over an extended period. While this report deals primarily with Form A of the instrument, later forms (B and C) reduced the time required to administer the test and increased the number of tasks and items. Later forms and their utilization in language processing research will be briefly summarized as they relate to the findings of this longitudinal study. In each case, the language processing instrument was designed to complement, not replace, the language comprehension and expression tasks (sometimes formal, sometimes informal) typically administered by speech-language pathologists as part of multidisciplinary preschool screenings in many educational settings prior to school entrance.

Such screenings are designed to identify for further assessment children who may have handicapping conditions, but are also designed to identify children who may be at risk for academic failure due to unidentified language or learning disorders (Butler 1981b). As is often the case, Time 1 subjects were screened for hearing loss by a qualified audiologist and were administered several rapid language screening measures, including Form A of the language processing instrument in a one-to-one quiet setting. As noted above, Form A calls for a 120 second pretraining session in order to orient the preschool child to the tasks and to the required responses. Forms B and C reduced this time period to 30 seconds, based upon the normative data collected on Form A which revealed that the 120 second pretraining and training could safely be reduced to 30 seconds.

Equipment

Material needed for the administration of the language processing instrument, in addition to the audiotaped test, includes a high-quality audiotape playback unit, 12 1' × 1' × 1' wooden blocks of a solid color, a box the size of a shoe box, a standard size paper plate, an 8½' × 11' piece of colored paper, plus a stopwatch. Cardboard or paper products are utilized in order to diminish the potential for extraneous noise caused by the subject's handling or throwing of the wooden blocks. Since this is a free-field test, the quietest available location should be selected for administration of the instrument. A headset has not been utilized in this standardization sample, since in 1974–75 they were not yet as commonplace as they are today.

Procedure

Section 1. The subject is seated at a child-sized table across from the examiner, who places the tape recorder on the right, and the other equipment to the left on the examiner's side of the table. The examiner begins:

> Step 1. "We are going to play a game today. Here are some blocks and a box. Put the block in the box WHEN I ask you to do so. Be sure to WAIT until I ask you. Watch me first. (Examiner puts a single block in the box.) Now you do it. (Whether or not child succeeds, examiner continues): Watch me again. I'm putting the block in the box. Now you do it."
>
> Step 2. (Whether or not the child succeeds, the examiner then turns on the player. The tape commences with the verbal identification of the instrument, while kindergarten "classroom chatter" is established −5 dB below the recorded speaker's voice. The remainder of Section 1 requires the examiner to continue the training session with the classroom chatter as background.) The examiner continues: "Remember, wait until I ask you and then put a block in the box. (Waits 3 seconds) Put a block in the box." (Eight trials take place under kindergarten chatter condition in order to establish mastery and automaticity under divided attention conditions. As noted earlier, this time is reduced to 30 seconds for Forms B and C of the instrument.)

Three beeps signal that the taped portion of the actual testing is to begin. Any adjustment of the signal strength of the auditory stimuli on the tape to the child's Most Comfortable Loudness Level (MCL) should be done at this time. All items on the remainder of the taped portion are to be administered in one sitting, unless significant deviations in the ambient noise conditions require stopping the tape and reinstating its use following cessation of extraneous noise.

The remainder of the audiotaped processing instrument is composed of four sections, presented in Form A in the following sequence, all four of which require that the child now respond to the speaker on the audiotape. The examiner continues to interact with the child throughout, observing the child's reactions and recording passage or failure of items, as well as evaluating the child's ability to attend to the "wanted verbal message," i.e., the taped speaker's directions against linguistic or non-linguistic distractors. An optional five point scale (1–5) is used to estimate overall subject attentiveness with 1 representing little or no attention to task; 2, some attention to task; 3, normal attention to task; 4, good attention to task and 5, excellent attention to task. The substantive portion of the instrument follows:

Section 2. *Following Directions Against Natural Environmental Background.* Child places a block in, or takes a block out of, the box at the direction of the taped voice which is heard against the "kindergarten chatter." Loudness of background linguistic/non-linguistic stimuli increases over the ten items from −15 dB to +10 dB, at increments of 5 dB over items, for a period of 2 minutes.

Section 3. *Following Directions Against Music and Lyric Background.* Child gives a block to the examiner, or takes away one or two blocks, at the direction of the taped voice. "Radio music" with lyrics is held stable at −5 dB for 6 items over a period of 90 seconds.

Section 4. *Following Directions Against Verbal Rhyming.* Examiner places paper plate to the right of the child, within easy reaching distance, and a piece of colored construction paper to the left (equidistant) with the blocks centered between the plate and the paper. The child is required to put a block on either the plate or the paper over 10 trials as indicated by the taped voice. The background stimulus (−10 dB to −5 dB) is a rhyme about a child and his shadow, and continues for 90 seconds.

Section 5. *Following Directions Against Narrative Discourse.* The last task requires that the child raise one hand whenever a foreground non-linguistic stimulus (a single dog bark) is heard against a background (−5 dB to −10 dB) of a discourse that invites a child to prepare for bed so that a story may be read. Since the task requires a different motoric response, the examiner establishes the child's ability to attend to the "wanted signal," i.e., the dog bark, by raising his/her hand to indicate that the stimulus had been noted. Two training items are provided and monitored by the examiner. The wanted signal is provided for a total of ten times over the 90 second duration of the narrative, on an intermittent reinforcement schedule, after the child has succeeded on the two training items.

This 34 item language processing instrument was designed to provide some measure of auditory comprehension, selective listening, and auditory attention or vigilance (Butler, in Johnson 1976). Clinical experience has shown that while an audiotaped instrument such as this may be used by trained paraprofessionals, the optional use of the more qualitative Attention Scale requires the observational skills of fully trained and qualified personnel.

Results

The 229 preschool subjects constituted the normative sample for the experimental Form A of the language processing instrument. The mean and standard deviations for 4 scored sections, excluding the pretraining and training (Section 1), are reported in table II. As noted above, mean performance on Sections 2, 3, and 4 was less than 1 point from the ceiling of the test (Section 2: 9.25 out of a possible 10 points; Section 3: 5.82 out of a possible 6 points; Section 4: 9.13 out of a possible 10 points.) Only Section 5 deviated from this pattern, with performance ranging from 0 to 8 points. The mean performance was 5.68, with a S.D. of 2.96, and performance on this Section contributed 60% to the total variance of the test. The data indicate that the task of attending to the non-linguistic stimuli against interesting conversational discourse, while easily accomplished by almost 50% of the subjects, provided substantial difficulty to 24% of the normative sample. The pattern of performance on Section 5, wherein the child is to provide a motor response to an intermittent non-linguistic stimulus in the presence of background narration (-5 dB to -10 dB) is reported in table III.

Approximately one half of the subjects (N = 109) responded without error to all items in Section 5, but 18 subjects who responded appropriately to the pretraining trials were unable to carry out the task once the background narrative was initiated. In addition, 37 children were unable to respond to more than one or two of

TABLE II
Performance of 229 Subjects in the Normative Sample on Four Subtests and Total Score on Language Processing Instrument, Form A

Section Number	Possible Range	Actual Range	Mean	Standard Deviation	Standard Error
Two	0–10	5–10	9.25	.87	.77
Three	0–6	2–6	5.82	.04	.28
Four	0–10	3–10	9.13	1.30	.09
Five	0–8	0–8	5.68	2.96	.20
Total Score	0–34	16–34	29.89	3.74	.25

TABLE III
Performance of the 229 Subjects on Section 5
of the Language Processing Instrument

Number of Items in Section 5	Number of Subjects Successfully Completing Items	Percentage of Normative Sample Successfully Completing Items
Succeeded in Pre-Training & Failed Item 1	(18)	(7.9)
Item 1	25	10.9
Item 2	12	5.2
Item 3	7	3.1
Item 4	5	2.2
Item 5	9	3.9
Item 6	15	6.6
Item 7	29	12.7
Item 8	109	47.6

the foreground stimulus items on this divided attention task. In fact, examiners frequently report that within the group whose performance yields low scores, there are a significant number whose comments indicate that within the 90 second interval of the test's duration, the children's absorption in the background narrative is documented by the conversations the children attempt to hold with the narrator on the audiotape, and by such comments at the end of the 90 seconds as, "Why is the dog barking?" and "Can he come to my house to read me a story?"

The Attention Scale, which attempts to measure observable behaviors reflective of the subject's attending to, and following of, the directions, as first provided by the examiner, and then the taped instructions, reveals that of the 229 Ss in the normative sample, 113 were recorded as being very attentive. Only 12 subjects were reported as falling below the mid-point of the scale. The mean performance is 4.13 on a 5.0 scale. While this is an informal measure, the scores accurately reflect the general level of the children's expressed interest and attention (table IV).

Among the dependent variables measured (but not reported in detail here), no significant differences were found between age, sex, ethnicity, parental occupation, school attended, and performance on the language processing instrument (utilizing the Statistical Package for the Social Sciences for Pearson's R) with the excep-

TABLE IV
Performance of 229 Subjects on the Attention Scale
of the Language Processing Instrument

Percentage of Subjects	Number of Subjects Falling Across the Scale's Continuum								
	1.0	1.5	2.0	2.5	3.0	3.5	4.0	4.5	5.0
3.1%	7								
1.7%			4						
5.7%				13					
15.7%					36				
3.5%						8			
10.0%							23		
10.9%								25	
49.3%									113

Mean: 4.13
Median: 4.72
S.D.: 1.67

tion of <.0027 for the total test performance and age. As noted earlier, children's performance was most variable on Section 5.

Other Related Studies Using the Language Processing Instrument

It may be pertinent to include additional information gathered on this instrument during or shortly following the testing of the 229 subjects in the study reported here. A modified form of the instrument (Form B) was administered along with the Preschool Language Scale (PLS) (Zimmerman, Steiner, and Evatt 1974) and another language processing test, to 60 preschool children in a neighboring rural area. The sample was composed of 29 males and 31 females, with a mean age of 4:2 (range: 3:0 to 4:11). Sixty five percent of the subjects were Caucasion, 13.3% were Black, 6.7% were Asian-Americans and 1% were Mexican-Americans (Butler 1981b). Of the 21 preschoolers aged 3:0 to 4:0 (mean age, 3:6) and the 39 subjects with ages between 4:0 and 5:0 (Mean 4:5), there was a significant difference (t test, df = 20, 38) at the .05 level between 3 and 4 year olds on the language processing test. The reader will recall that, similarly, there was a significant difference on Form A for age on the total test score (p < .02). In addition, the total test score was significantly related to the Verbal Ability Subscale of the PLS at the .01 level of confidence, a rather surprising finding since the language processing instrument requires no verbal responses on the part of the child (Butler 1981b).

In another study utilizing Form A of the language processing instrument, hereafter identified as Study A-2, 84 normal kindergarten children without demonstrable speech, language, or hearing difficulties following kindergarten screening, and who reside in a middle class suburban school district in a large metropolitan area of Northern California, were tested. While ethnic data are not available, 15% of the subjects reported that another language was spoken in the home. In contrast to the 229 subjects in the normative sample (Form A-1), 31% of the families were employed as professionals, another 31% as semi-professionals, and still another 31% were classified as skilled or semi-skilled, and the remainder unknown. None was unemployed. It is obvious that the SES composition of this group (Study A-2), is significantly different from that of the families of the 229 subjects first discussed in this paper (Study A-1). Analysis of variance revealed differences in performance by the 84 students in Study A-2 by sex at the .05 level of significance (F ratio 4.97, 3.96) and by age (N = 43) for Ss aged 5:0 to 5:7 and those subjects (N = 42) aged 5:8 to 6:3 (F ratio: 4.80, 3.96). These 84 Ss' mean performance on the language processing test, Form A, was 31.12 (S.D. 3.37, range 23 to 34). Performance on the total test and on each of the sections is somewhat higher, but not significantly so, than the 229 subjects in the standardization sample. There was a significant difference by school attended, although this did not appear to reflect socioeconomic status for this group of 84 students, according to an analysis of variance between and within groups.

Finally, 117 kindergarten children from the same school district as noted in Study A-2 above, but who had been identified as at risk for learning disabilities, were administered Form B of the language processing instrument. Of relevance to the current discussion is that performance on Section 5 (Form A) (in Form B labeled as Section 4) was significantly below (p < .01) that of the 229 Ss in the normative group, and significantly below the performance of the 84 normal subjects from the same school district. These students identified as high-risk also displayed speech and language difficulties. For example, on Section 4 these high-risk children had a mean of 3.88 with a standard deviation of 3.49, well below the performance of their age mates in the same school district (M: 6.06; SD 2.93), and that of the standardization sample (M: 5.68; SD 2.96), as noted in table V.

In each case Section 4 is the only section to reveal such diversity of performance (SDs ranging from 2.52 to 3.49). The performance of the "high risk" kindergarten group is more like the preschool three- and four-year-old population's performance than that of the entering kindergarten children in the other samples.

TABLE V
Performance on Section Related to Non-Linguistic Foreground Stimuli and
Narrative Discourse Background Stimuli by Three Groups of Normal Children and One Group of High-Risk Children

Sample	Age-Range	SES Status	Demographics	Mean on Section	S.D.	Other
Normative Sample (229 Ss)	58–68 (Mos.)	Skilled & Unskilled Labor	Multi-ethnic Small City	5.68	3.74	Form A (Study A-1)
Study B-1 (60 Ss)	36–59 (Mos.)	—	Multi-ethnic Rural	2.97	2.52	Form B* (Study B-1)
Study A-2° (84 Ss)	60–70 (Mos.)	Professionals/ Semi-Professional	Large City Primarily Caucasian	6.06	2.93	Form A (Study A-2)
Study B-2° (117 Ss) "High-risk"	59–73 (Mos.)	Semi-Professional Skilled Labor	Large City Primarily Caucasian	3.88	3.49	Form B* (Study B-2)

°Normal and High Risk Ss drawn from same school district
*Form B contains identical Section 4, but placed earlier in the administration of the Sections

RESULTS OF FOLLOW-UP STUDY IN
THIRD, SIXTH, AND EIGHTH GRADES

The Comprehensive Test of Basic Skills (CTBS) was administered to the subjects in the normative sample in subsequent years. Of interest to this report was the performance of the children who remained within the school district at third (Time 2), sixth (Time 3), and eighth (Time 4) grade (and a subportion of such children followed at Time 5 at the 11th and 12th grade level in 1987–1988).

Subjects

Of the original 229 entering-kindergarten children in the normative sample, 113 subjects remained in the school district when the CTBS was administered at third grade, 103 at sixth grade, and 107 at eighth grade. Subject characteristics of the initial 229 may be found by referring to table I, and their performance on the Language Processing instrument may be found on table II.

Description of the CTBS Test

Form Q of the CTBS was utilized at the 3rd and 6th grade levels, and Form S was used at the 8th grade level in this retrospective study. The CTBS: *Bulletin of Technical Data* (1968) notes that the tests are clearly limited to the measurement of basic skills as "evidenced by the understanding and effective use of language and number" (p. 5). The CTBS: *Examiner's Manual* Form Q, Level 1 (1968) also notes that "the emphasis in the process dimension is on the measurement of comprehension and application of concepts and principles as generally understood by school personnel, rather than on the measurement of knowledge per se" (p. 5).

Form Q was standardized on some 18,000 students from Grades 2 through 10, randomly selected from all regions and states of the United States, and an educational-economic index was applied to the selection of subjects. There was no breakdown of the standardization sample by race, although the authors insist that the sampling techniques should provide for proportionate representation of minority populations.

Various reviewers have praised the content validity of the CTBS based on Bloom's taxonomy, and the levels of difficulty of test items across grade levels. However, the use of grade equivalents rather than other normative data was not recommended (Ahmann 1972; Brown 1972). Brown suggested that the test was more appropriate at early grade levels, and that higher-order intellectual skills were not sufficiently tapped at the upper levels. All reviewers

(Ahmann 1972; Brown 1972; Taylor 1972) commented on the lack of validity data, but responded favorably to the conscientious construction procedures and certain internal measures, e.g., percent passing items at each grade level. Subsequent reviews (Findley 1978; Nitko 1978) also questioned the usefulness of grade equivalents in later forms of the battery (Forms S and T). The CTBS correlates highly with both the California Achievement Test and the California Short-Form Test of Mental Maturity.

The CTBS is a timed test, although the emphasis is "on the measurement of skills rather than speed" (CTBS: *Bulletin of Technical Data* Form Q 1968, p. 48). Of the 7 subtests of Form Q given to the children who had previously been administered the language processing test, only the Reading Vocabulary and Reading Comprehension Subtests will be reported here. All subtests are timed with Reading Vocabulary having 40 items, with the time permitted to answer these items ranging from 15 to 11 minutes. Reading Comprehension has 45 items, and time alloted ranges from 34 to 30 minutes, with time being reduced at older age levels for both Reading Vocabulary and Reading Comprehension.

The Reading Vocabulary (Test 1) permits the student to choose from among four alternatives the word that means *the same* or *about the same* as the underlined word used in context in the stem of the item. The Reading Comprehension (Test 2) assesses "the child's ability to recognize symbols, and sound and symbol correspondences; to recognize directly stated details; to comprehend the meaning of ideas by simple rewording; to interpret what is read by identifying the main idea, perceiving relationships and drawing conclusions; and to extend interpretation beyond stated information." (CTBS *Manual* 1968, p. 8). The primary content consists of the reading of sentences, paragraphs, stories, letters, and poems.

Results

Children in the normative sample of the language processing instrument performed at grade level or above overall, e.g. at 3rd grade, mean performance was 4.23 (SD 1.78), at 6th grade, the mean was 6.68 (SD 1.97) and at 8th grade, mean performance was 8.10 (SD 2.56).

In an effort to determine whether the students who were no longer in the school district (the "drop-outs") were significantly different from those who remained in the sample at the various grade levels (N = 113 at 3rd grade; 103 at 6th; 107 at 8th grade), performance on the language processing instrument of the two groups was analyzed. Those who left the district did not differ from those who remained, according to their performance on the language processing instrument ($t = -0.74$, df $= 227$, p $< .45$), nor did they differ on parental occupation ($t = -0.12$, df $= 166$, p $< .90$), or on school attended ($t = -0.43$, df $= 277$, p $< .66$).

Conversely, performance on the language processing instrument was significantly correlated with reading achievement, as reflected by the subjects' performance on CTBS Tests 1 and 2 at 3rd, 6th, and 8th grade levels and with the Attention Scale of the Language Processing Instrument (LPI) itself. Highly significant ($.001$) correlations were found between the total LPI and Section 5; between the LPI and reading achievement at third grade; between the LPI total score, the Section 5 score and the Attention Scale; and between reading achievement scores at all three grade levels. As can be seen in table VI, other significant, but more modest correlations (p $< .01$), exist between the LPI total score and reading achievement at 6th grade and with age, and at 8th grade, between school site and parental occupations (SES). Finally, very modest correlations (p $< .05$) exist between the Attention Scale and 3rd and 6th grade reading achievement. Other correlations occurring at the .05 level of confidence are (a) those between age and Section 5 of the LPI, Third Grade Reading Achievement and the Attention Scale; (b) between school site and the Attention Scale and parental occupation, and (c) between Section 5 of the LPI and Third and Sixth Grade Reading Achievement.

Stepwise regression of all variables onto Third Grade Reading Achievement resulted in an equation containing only total LPI scores and school sites. This model has an R^2 of .1481, which is significant at the .01 level ($F = 5.735$ with df 2 and 66).

A simple linear regression of LPI scores (x) onto Third Grade Reading Achievement scores (Y) resulted in an R^2 of .0838. The R^2, although small, is significant ($F (1,97) = 9.95$, p $< .005$). A prediction equation based on this model was derived as $\hat{Y} - .0851 + .1439$ (x) where y is the predicted score for any individual. The regression coefficient (.1439) has a 95% confidence interval of (0.0850, 0.2028). In order to further determine the relative importance of this finding, a determination of the practical significance of the probability of .005 was conducted.

The threshold value of one-third of a standard deviation was selected since it was the largest value for which a clear determination of practical significance could be made from the data at hand; i.e., if the "true" value of the regression coefficients is captured by the region of no practical importance, it results in an increase in predictive accuracy, beyond simply predicting the means of less than one-third of a standard deviation of the achievement score itself.

TABLE VI

Pearson Intercorrelations between the Language Processing Instrument (LPI) Total Scores, Section 5, Reading Achievement at Three Grade Levels, Attention, Sex, Parental Occupation (SES), School Site, and Age

	Reading Achievement by Grade Level			Attention Scale	Sex	SES	Age	School	Section 5 of the LPI
	3rd	6th	8th						
LPI Total Score	.29***	.28**	.19*	.63***	NS	NS	.15**	NS	.86***
Section 5 of the LPI	.17*	NS	NS	.53***	NS	NS	.13*	NS	
Read. Achieve.:									
Third Grade		.77***	.78***	.16*	NS	NS	−.21*	NS	.21*
Sixth Grade			.84***	.17*	NS	NS	NS	NS	.20*
Eighth Grade				NS	NS	−.31**	NS	.26**	NS
Attention Scale					NS	NS	.14*	.12*	
Sex						.17*	NS	NS	
SES							NS	−.14*	
Age							NS		

*p.05, one tailed
**p.01, one tailed
***p.001, one tailed
°All correlations with Bilingual Status were NS
N of Ss varied: LPI Original Normative: 229
Later Grade Levels: 106 at Grade 3
94 at Grade 6
99 at Grade 8

As can be noted above, the region of no practical importance on the regression coefficient was computed as ±.0833. The 95% confidence interval lies completely outside of this region of no practical importance, leading to the conclusion that the LPI scores are of both statistical and practical significance in predicting third grade reading achievement.

Similarly, a simple linear regression of LPI scores (x) onto Sixth Grade Reading Achievement scores (Y) resulted in an R^2 of .0832 and an adjusted R of .0737. The R^2 is significant (F (1,97) = 8.799, p < .0005). The prediction equation is $\hat{Y}$ = 2.171 + (.1529) (x). The 95% confidence interval on the regression coefficient (.1529) is (0.0863, 0.2194). Assuming again a threshold of practical importance of one-third of a standard deviation, a region of no practical significance was computed for the coefficient as ±.0833. Again, the 95% confidence interval lies completely outside of the region of no practical significance, leading once more to the conclusion that the LPI scores are both statistically and practically significant in predicting achievement scores, this time at the sixth grade level as noted above.

The same procedure was followed on the eighth grade achievement scores, but in this case the scores fell just short of statistical significance (F = 3.651, p = .0590).

Thus, LPI scores appear to have some practical significance in predicting reading achievement, at least through the elementary school years.

ANOVAs were run on School × LPI Total, School × Third Grade Reading Achievement, School × Sixth Grade Reading Achievement, and School × Eighth Grade Reading Achievement. There was no effect of school on LPI scores, an expected result,

TABLE VII
Analysis of Variance Between Groups and Within Groups According to School and Third, Sixth, and Eighth Grade Reading Achievement Levels

Source	SS	df	MS	F	P
3rd Grade:					
Between Groups	70.23	4	17.56	6.60	.0001
Within Groups	287.26	108	2.65		
6th Grade:					
Between Groups	43.13	4	10.78	2.98	.0226
Within Groups	353.99	98	3.61		
8th Grade:					
Between Groups	90.50	4	22.62	3.80	.0064
Within Groups	607.09	102	5.96		

since children were given the LPI just prior to entrance into a school setting. There was, however, a significant effect of school on third, sixth, and eighth grade reading achievement scores. Subjects attending Schools #4 and #5 consistently achieved higher scores at all three grade levels (3rd, 6th, and 8th) while subjects attending School #1 had the lowest achievement scores across grade levels (table VII).

THE STUDY: TIME 5

Following the analysis of group data over Times 1, 2, 3, and 4, an attempt was made to collect data on those children from the original cohort (Time 1, LPI scores and Times 2, 3, or 4, Reading Achievement Scores) who were at the extremes of the distribution 13 years later (Time 5). Two periods are represented with Time 5. The first period was the close of the 1986–1987 school year (June, 1987) in which data on the poorest readers (N = 10) were collected, and continuing school placement for the 14th year was determined. The second period was at the beginning of the 1987–1988 school year (September, 1987, the commencement of the subjects' 14th year) at which time the "best readers'" (N = 17) school placement and data were gathered.

An a priori decision was made to select those subjects who fell two years or more below grade level on reading achievement at the close of eighth grade, since this was the last year for which CTBS reading scores were gathered by the school district. A similar decision was made in terms of good readers, that is, those scoring two years or more above grade level on reading achievement at the close of eighth grade were selected. While grade level reading achievement scores are often thought to be less stringent criteria than other indices, such scores constituted the only available information on the subjects who entered the school system 14 years previously and upon which the Language Processing Instrument was standardized.

Of the 229 subjects who were enrolled in the school district at Time 1, 10 were found to be among those who were reading two or more years below grade level when tested in eighth grade. This constitutes approximately 10% of the 99 students whose reading performance was measured in Year 9 of the study, and who remained in the school district at Time 5 (the 13th year of the study). Table VIII indicates the current outcomes for these students as they enter their final years of secondary education.

It is of some importance that all 10 (100%) had received speech-language pathology services for delayed or disordered speech and language during the kindergarten and early school years. Unfortunately, it was not possible to identify the specific parameters of the speech/language difficulty, since such records are removed from cumulative files at the close of the elementary school years. However, some documentation remains in the special education files in which all of these subjects are currently enrolled. In addition, data gathered from the speech-language pathologists who both assisted in the collection of the LPI normative data and also provided speech/language services to these children during Times 1, 2, and 3, indicates that, in general, phonological, syntactical, and semantic processing disorders constituted the major areas of difficulty.

A retrospective analyses of the individual students' files revealed that these children had been identified as handicapped under federal law and had been the recipient of special education services from some time during their elementary school years to the present (Time 5). Inspection of table VIII reveals that 100% were currently in either self-contained special education classrooms at the secondary level (70%) or in resource rooms (30%) in more integrated secondary educational settings. Within this group of poor readers, 80% were minority students and 20% were Caucasian. The normative population (Time 1) was composed of approximately 40% minority students and 60% Caucasian students. As can be noted in table VIII, three of the five schools of the district were represented in this sample. It should be recalled that there existed a correlation of $-.31$ (significant at the .01 level of confidence) between eighth grade reading achievement and school site (table VI) and that significant correlations at the .05 level also existed between school site and the Attention Scale and parents' occupation. ANOVAs reported in table VII also identified a significant effect of school on third, sixth, and eighth grade reading achievement scores, although there was no effect of school on LPI scores.

Turning now to the mean performance of good readers ($N = 17$), as displayed in table IX, a very different order of events may be seen. Of those subjects from the kindergarten normative sample remaining in the school district in the fall of 1987, who are enrolled in their 13th year of public education, 5 are in self-contained gifted classrooms, 7 are in regular 12th grade classrooms, one is in 10th grade, and one is in 11th grade. One of the 17 subjects displayed an articulation disorder upon entry into kindergarten while 16 others displayed no speech or language disorder. Two had not registered for their senior year at the time of data collection (four weeks after school commenced). In this case, the majority of good readers (53%)

TABLE VIII

Mean Performance of Poorest Readers (N = 10) Scoring Two Years or More Below Grade Level at Eighth Grade (Range 2nd–6th Grade) and Educational Placement at C.A. 17–18 by School, LPI Total Score, Attention Scale, SLP Services, Placement in Special Education

School	N	LPI Total Score at Kgn. Entry	Attention Score at Kgn. Entry	Reading Performance			SLP*	EMR SCC**	LH SCC**	Resource Room***
				3rd Gr.	6th Gr.	8th Gr.		Special Services		
#1	4	27.5 ($\overline{X}$) 30.1 ($\overline{X}$)°	3.2 ($\overline{X}$)	2.2 ($\overline{X}$)	4.2 ($\overline{X}$)	4.0 ($\overline{X}$)	100%	1	2	1
#2	3	24.5 ($\overline{X}$) 29.4 ($\overline{X}$)°	3.7 ($\overline{X}$)	1.9 ($\overline{X}$)	3.3 ($\overline{X}$)	4.3 ($\overline{X}$)	100%	1	1	1
#3	3	25.6 ($\overline{X}$) 29.8 ($\overline{X}$)°	3.0 ($\overline{X}$)	1.7 ($\overline{X}$)	2.8 ($\overline{X}$)	4.4 ($\overline{X}$)	100%	1	1	1

*Speech-Language Pathology Services in Kindergarten and early years of school
**Self-Contained Classroom—from elementary school through secondary school
***Resource Room–½ day or less from elementary through secondary school
°Mean for School as a whole
Note: Composition of Poor Readers by Race: 5 Black, 3 Asian, 2 Caucasian

TABLE IX

Mean Performance of Good Readers (N=17) Scoring Two Years or More Above Grade Level
at Eighth Grade (Range 10.0 to 12.9) and Educational Placement at 12th Grade Level at C.A. 17 to 18
by School, LPI Total Score, Attention Scale, Early Speech-Language Services and Current Services/Placement

| School | N | LPI Total Score at Kgn. Entry | Attent. Score Kgn. | Performance | | | SLP* | Gifted SCC** | Special Services or Regular Class Placement | | |
				3rd Gr.	6th Gr.	8th Gr.			10th Gr.	11th Gr.	12th Gr.
#1	4	32.0 ($\overline{X}$)	4.7 ($\overline{X}$)	7.0 (X)	9.4 ($\overline{X}$)	11.5 (X)	33%	1	1	1	1
		30.1 ($\overline{X}$)°									
#2	3°°	28.0 ($\overline{X}$)	5.0 ($\overline{X}$)	4.7 (X)	8.5 ($\overline{X}$)	11.7 (X)	0%				2
		29.4 ($\overline{X}$)°									
#3	3	31.7 ($\overline{X}$)	5.0 ($\overline{X}$)	NA	NA	11.1 (X)	0%	2			1
		29.8 ($\overline{X}$)°									
#4	3	29.0 ($\overline{X}$)	3.7 ($\overline{X}$)	6.8 (X)	8.8 ($\overline{X}$)	12.8 (X)	0%	1			2
		30.5 ($\overline{X}$)°									
#5	4°°	31.5 ($\overline{X}$)									
		29.5 ($\overline{X}$)°	4.5 ($\overline{X}$)	8.3 (X)	10.4 ($\overline{X}$)	12.1 (X)	0%	1			2

*Speech-Language Pathology Services in Kindergarten and Early Years of School
**Self-Contained Classroom At Data Gathering Time, Fall, 1987
°Mean for the school as a whole
°°One student not registered for Fall, 1987
Note: Composition of Best Readers by Race: 9 Black, 8 Caucasian

were from minority groups, while 47% of the good readers were Caucasian. It should be noted that this study reflects *only* the course of events related to children who began their education in the school district as kindergarten children and were still enrolled at 8th grade (Reading Achievement) and as a subsample of poor and good readers at the equivalent of 12th grade. No attempt was made to identify how this original normative group (every kindergarten child entering school in this district, Time 1) or the subsequent groups from that normative sample as measured at Times 2, 3, 4, or 5, differed from, or were the same as, the current school population of the school district. Ethnicity data for the original normative LPI sample, and for the "poor" and "good reader" groups in their 13th year of school attendance, may be found in table X. Again these data reflect the performance by ethnicity of the longitudinal study, not the current ethnic make-up of the school district, or the current parental occupation/SES status of the families.

Caution must be exercised in reviewing table X, which identifies the follow-up of the poorest and best readers from the original normative sample in their final year(s) of secondary education, since these groups of readers were not compared with other poor and good readers who were not in the normative sample, but are now part of the total school population. However, it is instructive to note that the best readers of the original sample come from all five elementary schools in approximately equal numbers, although these schools reflect varying socioeconomic and ethnically balanced settings. While poor reading continues to reflect significant correlations between school site and performance in the 13th year, the good readers represent all schools within the district. As noted by the ANOVA summary table, subjects attending schools 4 and 5 consistently revealed higher achievement scores at all three grade levels (3rd, 6th, and 8th), while subjects attending school 1 consistently scored lowest in reading achievement scores at the same grade levels. Thus, 12th grade documentation differs from 8th grade documentation in relation to good readers, but not poor readers.

Case Studies of Poor Readers

A perusal of the records of the 10 poorest readers at Time 5 (the 13th year of school for all subjects) provides some further clues to their early spoken language difficulties and their later performance in reading and writing. Limited English proficiency or bilingualism does not appear to have been a pivotal factor, although a significant number of both the normative population (Time 1) and of the subsamples studied throughout the thirteen years were minor-

TABLE X
LPI Normative Population's Ethnic Diversity at Time 1, and Poor and Good Readers'
Elementary School Placement Between Times 1 and 3 (throughout the Elementary School years)

School #	Ethnic Diversity of Standardization Population at Kindergarten By Percentage				Ethnic Diversity of "Poor Readers" (N = 10) at Time 4				Ethnic Diversity of "Good Readers" (N = 17) at Time 5			
	A	B	C	D	A	B	C	D	A	B	C	D
1	25%	47%	25%	3%	—	66.3%	33.3%	—	33.3%	66.3%	—	—
2	25%	25%	15%	10%	—	75.0%	25.0%	—	66.3%	33.3%	—	—
3	82%	3%	9%	6%	75%	—	25.0%	—	33.3%	66.3%	—	—
4	80%	—	15%	5%	—	—	—	—	33.3%	66.3%	—	—
5	84%	12%	2%	2%	—	—	—	—	75.0%	25.0%	—	—
Totals	59.2%	21.8%	13.2%	5.2%	20%	50.0%	30.0%	0%	47.0%	53.0%	—	—

A = Caucasian
B = Black
C = Asian
D = Mexican-American

ities. Student and parent reports of a second language in the home revealed that 38 out of the 229 subjects came from homes where another language was spoken by at least one parent. Review of the cumulative files of both the good and poor readers provide no mention of bilingualism.

All poor readers (N = 10) had been evaluated by a qualified school psychologist utilizing primarily the Wechsler Intelligence Scale for Children (WISC), the Wide Range Achievement Test (WRAT), the Bender Visual-Motor Gestalt Test (BVMG), and the CTBS. Less frequently the Test of Written Language (TOWL), the Spencer Memory for Sentences Test, and the Brigance Inventory of Basic Skills (BIBS) were administered. WISC Full Scale Scores ranged from the low 70s to the mid 90s, with several failing to reflect the expected low Verbal/higher Performance Subscale scores. While grade placement varied from 9th grade onward, 7 of the 10 were in special education full-day classes, while three were enrolled in regular education and were being provided with two or more hours per day of resource room assistance by a teacher of the learning handicapped. Mathematical scores typically were as depressed as reading and spelling scores, with only 1 of the 10 revealing a relative strength in arithmetic. Two of the 10 reports identify visual perceptual processing as a deficit area.

As indicated earlier, detailed records of speech and/or language assessment and intervention had been largely eliminated from the children's records over time. Even so, a number of comments testified to the early, and frequently continuing, comprehension and production problems. Short- and long-term memory difficulties were also frequently implicated. Verbal concept formation and poor spelling and writing were almost universally cited as current weaknesses at the secondary level.

Finally, difficulty in attending to task, absenteeism, and multiple departures and returns to the school district were recurring themes. This triad of inability to ignore distractions, of irregular attendance, and of movement in and out of the school district was noted in approximately one third of the records of the poorest readers.

It may be recalled that parental mobility was a continuing factor, with more than 50% of the school population having moved out of the school district between the subjects' entrance to kindergarten and grade 3. Of the original 229 children who formed the kindergarten cohort, 106 remained at grade three, 94 at grade six and 99 at grade eight. A perusal of the records of the poorest readers revealed such statements as "This child has bounced back and forth between this district and _____ District," or "The family moved south to _____ two years ago and has recently returned."

From this review it is not possible to identify a specific constellation of factors contributing to the difficulties encountered by this subsample of the poorest readers from the normative sample, although those identified above may contribute in some measure. Since all subjects in this subsample revealed early speech and language disorders, and all continue to exhibit significant difficulties in reading and writing, the language component seems to play an important role, although it may be influenced by other factors as noted above.

DISCUSSION

Results of this retrospective study suggest that performance on a measure of auditory comprehension, i.e. following directions against variable background stimuli, may serve as a predictor for later developing academic skills, such as reading. The experimental language processing instrument (LPI) was standardized on 229 preschool children prior to the entrance to kindergarten classrooms. A brief audiotaped instrument, Form A, was designed to assess listening comprehension in children three through six. An examiner provided pretraining (Section 1) and the audiotaped instructions presented four tasks (Sections 2–5) ranging from 90 to 145 seconds in length. Nonverbal responses included manipulation of blocks and raising a hand in response to foreground verbal instructions against background linguistic and non-linguistic stimuli.

This 34-item language processing instrument constitutes a brief initial screening device to assess auditory comprehension, selective listening, and auditory attention or vigilance. A numerical Attention Scale (1 to 5) was also used, requiring the examiner to observe overt behaviors and to record a holistic score for the entire 7 to 8 minute period of testing. Of particular interest was the statistically significant Section 5, wherein a background narrative and a foreground nonlinguistic stimulus were presented. This section was correlated with the total score of the LPI at the .001 level, and with reading at third grade at the .05 level. In addition, the total LPI Score was correlated with reading at the third grade at the .0001 level, at sixth grade at the .01 level, and at eighth grade at the .05 level. Finally, the Attention Scale was correlated with both the total LPI score and Section 5 score ($p < .0001$) and with reading at the third and sixth grade ($p < .05$).

Related studies indicated that the LPI was useful with younger children (mean age of 4:2, range of 3:0 to 4:11) and that the total LPI score was significantly related (p < .01) to the Verbal Ability Subscale of the Preschool Language Scale (Zimmerman, Steiner, and Evatt 1974). These studies also revealed a steadily increasing total score as children became older; the total LPI score was significantly higher for four year olds than for three year olds (p < .05) and for five year olds than four year olds in the study reported here (p < .01). Other studies with the LPI have reported similar results, suggesting that a developmental perspective may be applied to this processing task.

Equally important was the relationship between the total LPI Score and the reading achievement component of the Comprehensive Test of Basic Skills (CTBS). While children in the normative sample of the LPI performed at grade level or slightly above on Reading Achievement at grades three, six, and eight overall, differences emerged when children's performance was analyzed at the tails of the distribution, i.e., poor and good readers' performance on the LPI at school entry and later failure or success in reading. Statistical analysis indicates that both listening comprehension and auditory attention were significantly related to performance on the LPI as well as to reading achievement in the later years. Reading success or failure at the third grade level accurately predicts achievement at the sixth and eighth grade level (p < .001) for the entire normative population as well as for the tails of the distribution, at least as measured by CTBS. It must be recalled that the CTBS has been criticized for being more appropriate for use at early grade levels, but that it may not sufficiently measure higher-order intellectual skills at the upper levels and that the use of grade equivalents was not recommended (Ahmann 1972; Brown 1972).

A more fine-grained analysis of the poorest and the best readers of the normative sample was conducted during Time 5 (the equivalent of the twelfth grade, i.e., the thirteenth year of school attendance). The poorest readers (10% of the original sample) scored two years or more below grade level (range: less than third grade to sixth grade) at eighth grade. The current records of these poor readers at Time 5 indicate significantly depressed LPI Total Scores and Attention Scores at school entry, speech-language disorders of both comprehension and production at school entry and subsequent intervention during the early school years, and concomitant reading difficulties throughout their school careers, extending into middle and high school. These children entered school at approximately the same time the Public Law for Education of All Handicapped (P. L. 94-142) was enacted. Most of the poor readers entered special education classrooms during their elementary school years, and all of them have remained in either EMR (educably mentally retarded) or LH (learning handicapped) self-contained classrooms (70%) or in LH Resource Rooms/General Education classrooms (30%). This may well reflect a continuum that begins with speech and language disabilities in the early years of life, followed by reading difficulties that surface during the early and middle years of elementary school, and continues, even with the advent of special education services throughout the remaining years in school.

Conversely, an overview of the most successful readers provides evidence of normal early speech and language development, reading success in the early elementary school years leading to mean reading grade levels of 11.1 to 12.8 at eighth grade, and to possible placement in classrooms for the gifted (30% of the Good Reader sample of 17) and/or normal progression through the secondary school to Senior status at the 13th year of schooling (K–12th). However, 8% (N = 2) of this group of good readers were retained one or two years. Investigation revealed that one of these students had experienced emotional and behavioral difficulties resulting in retention; no information was available on the second student.

A significant effect of specific schools on reading achievement was found at all grade levels through eighth grade, with schools 4 and 5 producing readers who consistently achieved higher scores at all levels. School 1 had the lowest achievement scores across grade levels. School 1 accounted for 26.2% of the normative population while schools 4 and 5 accounted for 34.1% of the sample. School 1 had a minority representation of 75%, while school 4 had a minority representation of 20% and school 5, 16%. School site 1 is located in the poorest socioeconomic area of the school district, while sites 4 and 5 were located in middle class areas. School site 2 is close to both school 1 and an army base is nearby, contributing to considerable mobility of the surrounding families and children. School site 3 is a mixture of lower and upper middle class families. All schools are described as "melting pots" in terms of the financial, ethnic, and intellectual status of the students who attended them in the 1970s and early 1980s. A number of these schools have now closed, and the district attendance patterns reconfigured.

As noted in the introduction, there is a need for early identification of children at risk for reading disorders (Satz et al. 1978; Silver 1978). This retrospective study provides some evidence that early identification of oral speech and language disorders as well as early screening for auditory comprehension and attentional skills can serve this purpose. It also tends to support Jansky's (1978) report that oral language skills in kindergarten contribute to reading performance at the end of second grade. In fact, this study supports extension of that finding well beyond the second grade. It also supports the development perspective offered by Bashir et al. (1983) and Kamhi and Catts (1986) in which a reciprocal relationship between oral language problems and reading impairments was hypothesized and the presumed difference between language-impaired and reading-impaired children was questioned.

Swanson (1982) and Margolis and Keogh (1974) among others, have noted the importance of selective attention in differentiating learning-disabled and reading-impaired children from their normal counterparts. Support for this position is found in the performance of the normative group on the LPI and the Attention Scale and later performance on the CTBS reading subscales. Margolis and Keogh also reported that auditory vigilance was correlated with school success and reading. Performance by kindergarten subjects in this study revealed a similar pattern, i.e., poor performance on the LPI was significantly correlated with later reading performance at the third and sixth grade levels. However, the data also suggests that many other factors come into play as children move through the school years as evidenced by the diminution of significance of some of the dependent variables and the ascendancy of others (see tables VI, IX, and X). The extent to which external factors (such as socioeconomic status and parental occupation, school site, etc.) and the children's internalized processing strategies, neurological status, and other intrinsic variables are related or are modified over the school years cannot be ascertained from the extant data of this study.

SUMMARY

The emerging evidence of the causal linkages between oral language disorders and reading disabilities (Liberman 1982, Liberman and Shankweiler 1979, Perfetti 1985, Vellutino 1979) appears to be supported by the study reported here. Indeed, a recent review of a number of longitudinal studies (Tallal 1987) led to the conclusion that developmental language disorders and developmental reading disorders do indeed co-occur. Tallal noted that developmental dysphasia (i.e., language disorders) and dyslexia, (i.e., reading disorders) are consistently linked in such studies and raised a central issue: are dysphasia and dyslexia two distinct disorders or are they, rather, "a single developmental disability affecting specific processing constraints or specific aspects of the language learning system at different ages"? (p. 164).

Although consensus appears to be growing that oral language problems and reading difficulties are inextricably intertwined, there remains to be discovered the specific relationships between events in early life and the problems encountered later in school life (Butler and Wallach 1984), as well as the possible intrinsic versus extrinsic variables that contribute to a dysfunctional language-learning system. Although research has moved forward since the studies of the 1960s and 1970s, and the linguistic basis for reading appears to be firmly established, the exact nature of the relationship between oral language and reading has yet to be defined. However, the literature also suggests, and this study supports, the notion that research currently in progress will increase our ability to identify children, possibly in the pre-school years, who may be at risk for language learning problems and potential school failure. It may be that the next decade will provide an answer to the question of the possible degree of overlap between previously considered-to-be-distinct groups of children: those with oral language disorders and those with reading disorders.

REFERENCES

Ahmann, J. S. 1972. [Review of] California Test of Basic Skills. *In* O. K. Buros (ed.) *The Seventh Mental Measurement Yearbook* (pp. 18–21). Highland Park, NY: The Gryphon Press.

American Speech-Language-Hearing Association. 1983. Committee on Language Report. *Asha* 25:44.

Ackerman, P. T., Anhait, J. M., Dykman, R. A., and Holcomb, P. J. 1986. Effortful processing deficits in children with reading and/or attention disorders. *Brain and Cognition* 5:22–40.

Ackerman, P. T., and Dykman, R. A. 1982. Automatic and effortful information processing deficits in children with learning and attention disorders. *Topics in Learning and Learning Disabilities* 2:12–22.

Aram, D., Ekelman, B., and Nation, J. 1984. Preschoolers with language disorders: 10 years later. *Journal of Speech and Hearing Research* 27:232–245.

Aram, D. M., and Nation, J. E. 1980. Preschool language disorders and subsequent language and academic difficulties. *Journal of Communication Disorders* 13:159–170.

Bashir, A. S., Kuban, K., Kleinman, S. N., and Scavuzzo, A. 1983. Issues in language disorders: Considerations of cause, maintenance and change. *In* J. Miller, D. E. Yoder, and R. Schiefelbusch (eds.) *Contemporary Issues in Language Intervention* (ASHA Reports) 12:92–106. Rockville, MD: American Speech-Language Hearing Association

Brown, F. G. 1972. [Review of] California Test of Basic Skills. *In* O. K. Buros (ed.) *The Seventh Mental Measurement Yearbook,* (pp. 21–23). Highland Park, NJ: The Gryphon Press.

Butler, K. G. 1986. *Language Disorders in Children.* Austin, TX: PRO-ED.

Butler, K. G. 1981a. Language disorders: Assessment of certain comprehension factors. *In* B. Sigurd and S.J. Svatvik (eds.) *AILA'81 Proceedings I*, (pp. 371–373). Lund, Sweden: Wallin and Dalhom.

Butler, K. G. 1981b. Language processing and its disorders. *In* P. S. Dale and D. Ingram (eds.) *Child Language: An International Perspective.* Baltimore, MD: University Park Press.

Butler, K. G. and Wallach, G. 1984. From theory to therapy. *In* K. G. Butler and G. Wallach (eds.) *Language Learning Disabilities in School-Age Children*, (pp. 360-365). Baltimore, MD: Williams and Wilkins.

California Assessment Program: Reading Test Manual. 1974. Sacramento, CA: California State Department of Education.

Comprehensive Test of Basic Skills: Examiner's Manual. 1968. Monterey, CA: CTB/ McGraw-Hill.

Comprehensive Test of Basic Skills: Bulletin of Technical Data. 1968 Monterey, CA: CTB/ McGraw-Hill.

Denckla, M. B. 1985. Issues of overlap and heterogeneity in dyslexia. *In* D. B. Gray and J. F. Kavanagh (eds.) *Biobehavioral Measures of Dyslexia.* Parkton, MD: York Press, Inc.

Dykman, R. A., Ackerman, P. T., and Holcomb, P. J. 1985. Reading disabled and ADD children: Similarities and Differences. *In* D. B. Gray and J. F. Kavanagh (eds.) *Biobehavioral Measures of Dyslexia.* Parkton, MD: York Press, Inc.

Feagans, L., and Short, E. 1984. Developmental differences in the comprehension and production of narratives by reading disabled and normally achieving children. *Child Development* 55:1717–1737.

Findley, W. J. 1978. [Review of] California Test of Basic Skills, Expanded Edition. *In* O. K. Buros (ed.) *Eighth Mental Measurement Yearbook*, (pp. 40–43). Highland Park, NJ: The Gryphon Press.

Finucci, J., Gottfredson, L. S., and Childs, B. 1985. A follow-up study of dyslexic boys. *Annals of Dyslexia* 35:117–136.

Forrell, E. R., and Hood, J. 1985. A longitudinal study of two groups of children with early reading problems. *Annals of Dyslexia* 35:97–116.

Gleitman, L. R., and Rozen, P. 1977. The structure and acquisition of reading: Relations between orthographies and the structure of language. *In* A. S. Reber and D. L. Scarborough (eds.) *Toward a Psychology of Reading: The Proceedings of the CUNY Conference.* Hillsdale, NJ: Lawrence Erlbaum Associates.

Jansky, J. J. 1978. A critical review of "some developmental and predictive precursors of reading disabilities." *Dyslexia: An Appraisal of Current Knowledge.* New York: Oxford University Press.

Johnson, D. 1980. Persistent auditory disorders in young dyslexic adults. *Bulletin of The Orton Dyslexia Society* 30:268–276.

Johnson, O. G. 1976. *Tests and Measurements in Child Development, Handbook II* (pp. 899–900). San Francisco, CA: Jossey-Bass.

Kamhi, A. G., and Catts, H. W. 1986. Toward an understanding of developmental language and reading disorders. *Journal of Speech and Hearing Disorders* 51:33.

King, R. R., Jones, C., and Lasky, E. 1982. In retrospect: A fifteen-year follow-up report of speech-language disordered children. *Language, Speech and Hearing Services in the Schools* 13:24–32.

Lee, A. D., and Shapero-Fine, J. 1984. When a language problem is primary: Secondary school strategies. *In* G. Wallach and K. G. Butler (eds.) *Langauge Learning Disabilities in School Age Children.* Baltimore: Williams and Wilkins.

Leong, C. K. 1987. Metalinguistic and specific language abilities in nine- and eleven-year old good and poor readers. Paper read at the Third World Congress on Dyslexia, June 1987, Crete, Greece.

Lerner, J. 1972. Reading disability as a language disorder. *Acta Symbolica* 3:39–45.

Liberman, I. Y. 1982. A language-oriented view of reading and its disabilities. *In* H. Myklebust (ed.) *Progress in Learning Disabilities.* Vol. 5. New York: Grune and Stratton.

Liberman, I. Y., and Shankweiler, D. 1979. Speech, the alphabet and teaching to read.

In L. Resnick and P. Weaver (eds.) *Theory and Practice of Early Reading*, Vol. 2. Hillsdale, NJ: Lawrence Erlbaum Associates.

Liberman, I. Y. Mann, V. A., Shankweiler, D. 1982. Children's memory for recurring linguistic-non-linguistic material in relation to reading ability. *Cortex* 18:367–375.

Liles, B. 1985. Cohesion in the narratives of normal and language-disordered children. *Journal of Speech and Hearing Research* 28:123–133.

Margolis, J. S., and Keogh, B. K. 1974. School achievement and ability to maintain attention to task: A vigilance model applied to school learning. A paper presented at the Annual Meeting of the Western Psychological Association, San Francisco, CA, April 1974.

Mattingly, I. 1972. Reading, the linguistic process and linguistic awareness. *In* J. Kavanagh and I. Mattingly (eds.) *Language by Ear and by Eye*. Cambridge, MA: MIT Press.

Nippold, M., and Fey, S. 1983. Metaphoric understanding in preadolescents having a history of language acquisition difficulties. *Language, Speech and Hearing Services in Schools* 14:171–180.

Nitko, A. J. 1978. [Review of] CTBS, Expanded Version. *In* O. K. Buros (ed.) *The Eighth Mental Measurement Yearbook*, pp. 43–45. Highland Park, NJ: The Gryphon Press.

Perfetti, C. A. 1985. *Reading Ability*. New York: Oxford University Press.

Perfetti, C. A., and Lesgold, A. M. 1979. Coding and comprehension in skilled reading and implications for reading instruction. *In* L. B. Resnick and P. A. Weaver (eds.) *Theory and Practice of Early Reading*, Vol. 1. Hillsdale, NJ: Lawrence Erlbaum Associates.

Roth, F., and Spekman, N. 1986. Narrative discourse: Spontaneously generated stories of learning-disabled and normally achieving students. *Journal of Speech and Hearing Disorders* 51:8–23.

Satz, P., Morris, R., and Fletcher, J. 1985. Hypotheses, subtypes, and individual differences in dyslexia: Some reflections. *In* D. B. Gray and J. Kavanagh (eds.) *Biobehavioral Measures of Dyslexia*. Parkton, MD: York Press, Inc.

Satz, P., Taylor, H. G., Frield, J., and Fletcher, J. 1978. Some developmental and predictive percursors of reading disabilities: A six year follow-up. *In* A. L. Benton and D. Pearl (eds.) *Dyslexia: An Appraisal of Current Knowledge*. New York: Oxford University Press.

Siegal, L., and Linder, B. 1984. Short-term memory processes in children with reading and arithmetic learning disabilities. *Developmental Psychology* 20:200–207.

Silver, A. A. 1978. Prevention. *In* A. L. Benton and D. Pearl (eds.) *Dyslexia: An Appraisal of Current Knowledge*. New York: Oxford University Press.

Stark, R. E., Bernstein, L. E., and Condino, R. 1984. Four-year follow-up study of language-impaired children. *Annals of Dyslexia* 34:29–48.

Stominger, A. Z., and Bashir, A. S. 1977. A nine-year follow-up of language-delayed children. Read at the annual meeting of the American Speech-Language-Hearing Association, November 1977, Chicago, IL.

Swanson, H. L. 1982. A multidirectional model for assessing learning disabled students' intelligence: An information-processing framework. *Learning Disability Quarterly* 5:312–326.

Swanson, H. L., and Obrzut, J. E. 1985. Learning disabled readers' recall as a function of distinctive encoding, hemispheric processing and selective attention. *Journal of Learning Disabilities* 18:409–417.

Tallal, P. 1987. Developmental Language Disorders. In *Learning Disabilities: A Report to the U. S. Congress*. Washington, D. C. Interagency Committee on Learning Disabilities.

Taylor, P. A. 1972. [Review of] CTBS. *In* O. K. Buros (ed.) *Seventh Mental Measurement Yearbook*, pp. 23–24. Highland Park, NJ: The Gryphon Press.

Torgeson, J. K. 1985. Memory processes in reading disabled children. *Journal of Learning Disabilities* 18:350–357.

van Kleeck, A., and Richardson, A. In press. Language delay in children. *In* N. Lass, L. McReynolds, J. Northern, and D. Yoder (eds.) *Handbook of Speech-Language Pathology and Audiology*. New York: Academic Press.

Wallach, G. P., and Butler, K. G. (eds.) 1984. *Language Learning Disabilities in School Age Children*. New York: Williams and Wilkins.

Wolf, M. 1984. Naming, reading and the dyslexias: A longitudinal overview. *Annals of Dyslexia* 34:87–116.

Zimmerman, I. L., Steiner, V. G., and Evatt, R. L. 1974. *Preschool Language Scale*. Columbus, Ohio: Merrill Publishing.

Vellutino, F. R. *Dyslexia: Theory and Research*. Cambridge, MA: MIT Press.

3

Speech- and Language-Impaired Three and Four Year Olds: A Five Year Follow-up Study

S. Yancey Padget

Although it has been assumed that there is a link between early speech and/or language problems and later acquisition of academic skills, there have been relatively few studies that have focused on this issue. It has also been widely assumed that intensive speech and language intervention during the preschool years will have a positive effect on later academic achievement. Again, there has been only minimal investigation of this issue. This follow-up study was conducted to investigate both of these questions. What is the long-range prognosis for academic success for children diagnosed as speech- and language-impaired during the preschool years? If speech/language-impaired children are provided with therapy during the preschool periods, what reasonable outcomes can be expected?

Two early studies were reported in England that provided follow-up data on children who had been diagnosed as severely delayed in speech or language. However, in the study conducted by Griffiths (1969) the children were not intially diagnosed until ages 5 to 8 and in the study reported by Garvey and Gordon (1973) no information was included regarding the ages of the subjects when initially diagnosed. Both studies also included multiply handicapped students and significant numbers of children with intellectual functioning measured as more than one standard deviation below the mean. Considering the multiple handicapping conditions of these samples it was not surprising that more than half of the students in each study attended a special class or school at the time of the follow-up contact.

Since 1977 there have been several studies in the United States that have investigated communication skills and academic abilities of students who had been diagnosed initially as speech- and language-impaired during their preschool years. The procedure in these studies typically has been to collect data from parent and teacher questionnaires regarding current functioning. Hall and Tomblin (1978) followed 36 students who initially had been evaluated at a university clinic; half of their sample had been diagnosed as language-impaired with the other half having articulation problems only. Although the two groups were comparable on many background variables it was evident that the sample as a whole was more socioeconomically advantaged than a random selection of the general population. That this factor influenced the educational progress of the sample seems reflected in the fact that the articulation-impaired students as a group were scoring one-half to three-fourths of a standard deviation above the mean on the school-administered achievement tests. Although the language-impaired group performed significantly below the articulation-impaired group they were still close to the national mean in all subjects except reading where they scored as a group only one-half a standard deviation below the mean. In this study, the time of follow-up was approximately 15 years after diagnosis, and almost all of the sample had completed high school and many were involved in post-secondary education programs.

Another study using a similar method was conducted by Aram and Nation (1980). They assessed current functioning of 63 students four or five years after they had been diagnosed at preschool age in an urban clinic as language-disordered. Based on parent and teacher questionnaires they determined that at least 40% of the students continued to exhibit speech and language problems and 40% of the students were either not in regular classrooms or had repeated a grade. Based on school-administered achievement tests, 50% of the students were at or above grade level norms in reading, spelling, and math while the other students were below grade level in one or more achievement area. King, Jones, and Lasky (1982) used parent questionnaires to evaluate current communication abilities of a sample of 50 individuals, 13 to 20 years old, who had been diag-nosed 15 years earlier as having speech and language problems. In their sample, 42% were reported by their families to be still experi-encing communication difficulties. In an unpublished study by Strominger and Bashir (cited in Maxwell and Wallach 1984) current data were collected through parent and teacher ratings. They evalu-ated 40 students between the ages of 9 and 11 who had been diag-nosed prior to age 5 as having delayed language. On the follow-up evaluation only two of the students demonstrated reading or writ-ing skills that were on or above grade level.

These studies indicate that speech and language impairments diagnosed in early childhood typically persist for years and are also linked to problems with written language. Reviewing such studies led Snyder (1980) to entitle her article "Have We Prepared the Lan-guage Disordered Child for School?" This is a valid question; however, in the studies cited above which were conducted in this country many of the children who were diagnosed as speech- language-impaired during their preschool years did not receive any therapeu-tic intervention prior to school and, in some cases, not even as a part of their educational program. Aram and Nation (1980) reported for their sample of 63 students that "even though all these children had been diagnosed as language disordered during the preschool years, 23.9% received no therapy during their preschool years and 38.1% received no therapy during their school years" (p. 165). Their data also indicate that of the children who received preschool therapy, in 20 cases this intervention lasted less than one year, so that of the sample of 63 students only 44% received preschool services for more than one year. For their sample of 36 students, divided between lan-guage-impaired (LI) and articulation-impaired (AI), Hall and Tomb-lin (1978) report "15 of the 18 LI subjects reportedly received remedi-ation as youngsters, as had 13 of the 18 AI subjects. The remediation was conducted primarily within the school setting. . ." (p. 231). Since they also indicated that 8 students received no therapy and only "several" children received services outside the school setting through private therapists or university clinics, the majority of stu-dents in their sample appear not to have received intervention ser-vices at the preschool level. Aram and Nation concluded that

> . . . children receive, or do not receive, therapy as preschoolers for reasons other than the severity of the presented disorder. Some of these reasons are likely to be the money, time, and inconvenience required to obtain the services, the lack of priority given preschool speech and language disorders by both parents and certain profes-sionals and the failure to provide speech and language services that meet community and parent requirements and restrictions. (p. 167)

The follow-up studies to date have indicated that children who evidence speech and language disorders during their preschool years are highly at risk for later academic problems. This link between oral language and written language has generally been accepted. The follow-up studies to date, however, have been only minimally helpful in answering the questions about the effects of early intervention in this sequence. Snyder's (1980) question regarding whether we have prepared the language-disordered child for academics is valid but the studies that have been conducted contribute very little toward answering this question.

The present study was undertaken to follow up a sample of students who were diagnosed as speech/language-impaired during their preschool years and who then received intensive therapeutic intervention. All of the children were diagnosed initially at ages 3 or 4 and received both individual speech therapy 5 days per week and a daily preschool program that included peers with normal language development. Follow-up data were collected over a $6\frac{1}{2}$ year period from school records and include periodic individual psychological, speech, and academic evaluations.

PRESCHOOL YEARS

The 27 students in this study were born in 1976, 1977, and 1978 and therefore constitute three groups. They attended a prekindergarten program between 1979 and 1984 and were there identified as speech/language-impaired. The pre-kindergarten program served approximately 800 economically disadvantaged 3- and 4-year-old children each year. When students in the program exhibited speech and/or language problems they were referred by their classroom teachers for a comprehensive evaluation. This evaluation included observation and testing by a speech/language pathologist and a psychologist as well as complete social, medical, and developmental histories. On the basis of such an evaluation all of the students in this study were diagnosed as severely speech/language-impaired and they received individual speech/language therapy for 30 minutes, 5 days per week, for at least one year prior to kindergarten.

The funding for the prekindergarten program included federal and state sources as well as local school district support. Children who were 3 or 4 years old were eligible to participate if the economic resources of their families indicated they qualified for free school lunches. The number of children diagnosed as severely speech/language-impaired in any year ranged from 7 to 13 for the three year period and therefore represents a very small percentage of the 800 children served each year. All of the children who were diagnosed as severely speech/language-impaired have been included in this follow-up study. There were additional children in the prekindergarten program who evidenced mild speech problems or language delays of less than one year. These students received speech/language therapy one day per week and they have not been included in this follow-up study.

The students in this study formed three groups according to the year in which they were eligible to begin kindergarten. Because children were required to be 5 years old by December 1 to enter kindergarten, the groups consist of children born between December 1 of any year and November 30 of the following year. The number of males and females identified as severely speech/language-impaired for each school year are presented in table I.

For the sample as a whole there were 14 males and 13 females and this represents a somewhat higher proportion of girls than is typically found in a sample of speech/language-impaired students. The unequal division of males and females each year may also be unusual and does not seem to have an explanation.

Preschool Diagnostic Profile

In most cases an intelligence test was administered while these students were in prekindergarten. Because of their severe speech and/or language impairments non-verbal measures of intelligence were considered most appropriate. Twelve of the children had been evaluated with the Arthur Adaptation of the Leiter International Performance Scale (1950) and their IQs ranged from 72 to 121 with a mean IQ of 102. Eight of the students were evaluated with the Performance Scale of the Wechsler Preschool and Primary Scale of Intelligence (1967) and their average Performance IQ was 89 with a range from 76 to 104. Therefore 20 of the children had been evalu-

TABLE I
Subjects Grouped by Sex

Date of Birth	Subjects		
	Boys	Girls	Total
12-1-75 to 11-30-76	1	6	7
12-1-76 to 11-30-77	2	4	6
12-1-77 to 11-30-78	11	3	14

ated with non-verbal intelligence tests and their mean IQ was 97. The Stanford Binet, form L-M (Terman and Merrill 1973) had been administered to four additional students and on this test (which combines verbal and non-verbal tasks) their IQs ranged from 82 to 122 with a mean of 96. In all cases the school psychologist who evaluated the students judged their intelligence to be above the retarded range. In several cases the IQ scores were within the borderline range but the pattern of performance indicated scattered abilities with functioning in the average range in some areas tested. In considering the intelligence of this group of 27 speech/language-impaired children, it would appear that their cognitive ability is within the average range, particularly when considered in the context of their economically disadvantaged status.

The specific speech and language problems diagnosed for each child at age 3 or 4 years are presented in table II. In all cases language comprehension was measured by the Peabody Picture Vocabulary Test (Dunn and Dunn 1981), the Auditory Comprehension Scale of the Zimmerman Pre-School Language Scale (Zimmerman, Steiner, and Evatt 1969) and responses to "Wh-questions." In many cases the Assessment of Children's Language Comprehension (Foster, Giddan, and Stark 1972) was administered also. Expressive language abilities were evaluated by the Verbal Abilities Scale of the Zimmerman Preschool Language Scale and by analyzing a spontaneous language sample both for mean length of utterance (MLU) in morphemes and also for Brown's (1973) Stages of Grammatical Morphemes. Pragmatic use of language was judged by determining the various purposes for which the child used oral communication.

Specific diagnostic data from preschool records were missing in 4 cases, but it was known that the students were diagnosed as speech/language-impaired and they had received speech therapy. Of the 23 remaining students 2 had mild hearing losses, 5 had fluctuating hearing and frequently, but not consistently, failed hearing tests, and 2 others had a history of repeated otitis media with effusion (OME). Only 3 children exhibited no articulatory difficulties and the remaining 20 experienced problems that ranged from mild (N = 5), to moderate (N = 7), to severe (N = 8), as judged by their speech clinician. One child was diagnosed as a moderate stutterer but none of the other children exhibited fluency problems during their preschool years. Five children had developed average language comprehension skills. The remaining 18 children exhibited language comprehension problems across several measures and they were functioning from 3 to 24 months below their chronological age on receptive language tasks. All of the children were judged to

TABLE II
Speech and Language Problems Diagnosed at Ages Three and Four Years

Student	Speech and Language Problems					
	Hearing	Articulation	Fluency	Language Comprehension	Expressive Language	Pragmatics
TC	N	mild	N	−14 mo.	−20 mo.	N
RN	fluctuating	moderate	N	−12 to 24 mo.	−24 mo.	N
TB	fluctuating	severe	N	N	−12 mo.	N
RH	N	severe	N	N	−18 mo.	N
TE						
TJ	N	moderate	N	−14 mo.	−20 mo.	N
TBr						
AP	N	mild	N	−24 mo.	−24 mo.	N
SB						
KL	fluctuating	moderate	N	−18 mo. Laotian −32 mo. English		N
MDL	N	N	N	−17 to 21 mo.	−16 mo.	−12 mo.
BM	N	N	N	−24 mo.	−24 mo.	−24 mo.
NP						

ML	fluctuating	severe	N	−8 mo.	−15 mo.	N
CH	N	mild	N	−12 mo.	−20 mo.	N
CL	mild loss	severe	N	N	−18 mo.	N
RH	fluctuating	severe	N	−3 to 6 mo.	−6 mo.	
DB	N	severe	N	N	−6 mo.	N
CR	N	moderate	N	−12 mo.	−12 mo.	N
TP	N	severe	N	N	−6 mo.	N
JC	frequent ear infections	mild	N	−12 mo.	−24 mo.	
TC	N	moderate	N	−12 mo.	−12 mo.	N
CS	N	severe	N	−8 mo.	−12 mo.	N
FT	mild loss	moderate	N	−12 mo.		N
PT	frequent ear infections	moderate	N	−12 mo.	−22 mo.	N
SP	N	mild	N	−15 mo.	−12 mo.	N
MC	N	N	moderate stuttering	−12 mo.	−12 mo.	N

Note: N = normal range

have expressive language deficits and were functioning 6 to 24 months below age level in their verbal abilities. Most of the children had no difficulty with the pragmatic aspects of language and used language to request information, to direct activities, to describe aspects of the environment, to comment on experiences, to express individuality, and for social interaction. However, two students were diagnosed as having moderate or severe problems with the pragmatic aspects of language and they demonstrated very limited uses of communication.

All of these 24 children received individual speech therapy five days a week for either one or two years while in preschool. In addition their classroom programs emphasized oral language activities. The speech/language clinicians consulted regularly with the classroom teachers and with the parent(s) of each child to encourage carry over of language skills from therapy to other settings.

Initial Educational Placement

As each child approached school age decisions were made regarding educational placement. These decisions were the result of a two-step process. As the first step there was a meeting of the prekindergarten support staff, psychologist, speech/language pathologist, nurse, and social worker, and each child's teacher and parent(s), to discuss placement alternatives. After a decision regarding an appropriate program had been reached, the second step was for this group to meet with the school district Committee on Special Education (then referred to as the Committee on the Handicapped). At this meeting the child was officially classified as handicapped and educational placement decisions were made. The possible placements or programs available included the following: an additional year in prekindergarten; combining prekindergarten and kindergarten; regular kindergarten; integrated kindergarten which included handicapped and non-handicapped students; regular kindergarten plus special education resource services; and self-contained developmental special education classes. The developmental special education classes were cross-categorical programs for handicapped children ages 5 to 8. Although many of the students in these developmental self-contained classes were classified as speech/language-impaired these classes also included children with a variety of handicapping conditions.

For the seven students who were eligible to begin kindergarten in the 1981–1982 school year the following educational placements were made. One student remained in prekindergarten an additional year and another student was placed in a self-contained special education class. The other five children were assigned to regular kindergarten classes in the school their parents selected. All of the students were classified as speech-impaired and they were all scheduled to receive speech therapy as a related service.

The following school year there were six children who were eligible to begin kindergarten and three of them attended a regular kindergarten class. Of these three, two attended parochial schools and one received supplemental services through the English as a Second Language Program. The remaining three students were assigned to self-contained special education classes. Again, all of these students were scheduled to receive speech therapy.

There were 14 students who were school age as of September 1983 and 10 of them were enrolled in a regular kindergarten program. One more student was assigned to a regular kindergarten for one-half of the day and also attended prekindergarten for the other half day. One student was assigned to an integrated special education kindergarten which served 6 handicapped students and 12 nonhandicapped students. One student was placed in a self-contained special education class and another student would also have been assigned to this type of class but his family moved to another school district prior to the beginning of school.

Within the school district many different educational programs were available to be considered in recommending the most appropriate school placement for each child. For a significant number of children, 6 out of 27, it was decided that special education services of some type were necessary. However, the placement of the majority of the children, 19 out of 27, in regular kindergarten classes reflected careful selection from among a range of available options.

Therefore, when these 27 speech- and language-impaired children were eligible to begin school, regular kindergarten was determined to be the most appropriate program for the majority of them. It was anticipated that the educational needs of these students could be met within the typical classroom with the addition of speech therapy sessions. It was with some optimism that the majority of these children entered the school program. They had attended a comprehensive preschool program and they had received intensive, individual therapeutic intervention at an early age. This early intervention program was believed to have provided a careful foundation for academic progress.

ELEMENTARY SCHOOL YEARS

Diagnosis

All of the students in this sample entered school in 1981, 1982, or 1983 classified as speech/language-impaired. They attended many different elementary schools within one district and subsequent decisions regarding their diagnostic classifications were made by the district's Committee on Special Education (CSE) based on the recommendations of the Pupil Services Team in each building. The Pupil Services Team consists of an administrator, a school psychologist, a social worker, a school nurse, and a special education teacher; the team's recommendations are based on individual evaluations. All handicapped students, including those classified as speech/language-impaired, are re-evaluated every three years as legally mandated. In addition, students are referred to the Pupil Services Team at any point when there is serious concern regarding their educational progress.

The diagnostic classifications for the students during their elementary school years are presented in table III.

During their kindergarten year all of the students remained classified as speech/language-impaired. At the end of their next year in school, which was the end of first grade for most of the students, the diagnostic classification of six students was changed. One student was declassified and has not received any special services since. One student was classified as hard of hearing. One student's classification was changed by the CSE to mentally retarded. (In this case the school psychologist's report stated that the student was not mentally retarded and recommended that the student be classified as learning disabled.) Three students were classified as learning disabled. The diagnosis of learning disabled was based on New York State guidelines which require a discrepancy of approximately 50% between intellectual potential and academic achievement—a pattern of deficits in basic psychological processes that is consistent with a learning disability—and the absence of other handicaps or environmental factors that could explain the lack of academic progress.

By the end of the following year, their third year in school, an additional five students had their handicapping condition changed from speech/language-impaired to learning disabled. During their fourth year, the diagnosis of learning disabled was made for three more students and also for the student who had previously been designated as mentally retarded. Another student moved out of the district and was subsequently classified as mentally retarded in a

TABLE III
Diagnostic Classifications by Committee on Special Education

Student	School Year					
	81–82	82–83	83–84	84–85	85–86	86–87
TC	SI	SI	SI	SI	LD	LD
RM	SI	LD	LD	LD	LD	LD
TB	SI	SI	SI	SI	SI	SI
RH	SI	SI	SI	SI	SI	SI
TE	SI	SI	SI	SI	SI	LD
TJ	SI	SI	SI	MR	MR	LD
TBr	SI	SI	LD	LD	LD	LD
AP	—	SI	SI	SI	LD	LD
SB	—	SI	MR	MR	LD	LD
KL	—	SI	SI	SI	SI	LD
MDL	—	SI	SI	LD	LD	LD
BM	—	SI	SI	SI	SI	SI
NP	—	SI	LD	LD	LD	LD
ML	—	—	SI	SI	SI	LD
CH	—	—	student left district			
CL	—	—	student left district			
RH	—	—	SI	HOH	HOH	HOH
DB	—	—	SI	Declassified		
CR	—	—	SI	SI	LD	LD
TP	—	—	SI	SI	LD	LD
JC	—	—	SI	SI	LD	LD
TC	—	—	SI	SI	SI	SI
CS	—	—	SI	SI	SI	SI
FT	—	—	SI	SI	LD	LD
PT	—	—	student left district			
SP	—	—	student left district			
MC	—	—	SI	SI	SI	SI

Note: SI = Speech Impaired, LD = Learning Disabled, HOH = Hard of Hearing, MR = Mentally Retarded

new school district. An additional two students were classified as learning disabled during their fifth year in school. During their sixth year in school one more student was diagnosed as learning disabled and the student who had been classified as mentally retarded in another school district returned, was evaluated, and the classification was changed to learning disabled.

In summary, 4 of these 27 students left the district within two years and have not re-entered. Of the remaining 23 students, 16

TABLE IV
Educational Placement

Student	School Year								
	79–80	80–81	81–82	82–83	83–84	84–85	85–86	86–87	87–88
TC		Pre-K	K	1st	1st	2nd	2nd	Sp.Ed.	Sp.Ed.
RM		Pre-K	Sp.Ed.	Sp.Ed.	Sp.Ed.	2nd & R	2nd	Sp.Ed.	Sp.Ed.
TB		Pre-K	Pre-K	K	1st	2nd	2nd	3rd	4th
RH		Pre-K	K	Sp.Ed.	Sp.Ed.	1st	2nd	3rd	4th
TE		Pre-K	K	½ K & ½ 1st	1st	2nd[a]	2nd[a]	Sp.Ed.	Sp.Ed.
TJ	Pre-K	Pre-K	K	1st	2nd	Sp.Ed.[a]	Sp.Ed.[a]	3rd & R	left
TBr	Pre-K	Pre-K	K	1st	2nd	2nd & R	3rd & R	4th & R	5th & R
AP			Pre-K	Sp.Ed.	Sp.Ed.	Sp.Ed.	Sp.Ed.	3rd & R	Sp.Ed.
SB			Pre-K	K	K	Sp.Ed.	Sp.Ed.	Sp.Ed.	Sp.Ed.
KL			Pre-K	K & ESL	1st & ESL	1st	2nd	3rd	Sp.Ed.
MDL			Pre-K	Sp.Ed.	Sp.Ed.	Sp.Ed.	2nd[a]	Sp.Ed.[a]	Sp.Ed.
BM		Pre-K	Pre-K	Sp.Ed.	Sp.Ed.	1st & R	2nd & R	3rd & R	4th
NP			Pre-K	K	1st	1st & R	Sp.Ed.	2nd & R	Sp.Ed.

ML		Pre-K	Pre-K	K	1st	1st	2nd & R
CH	Pre-K	Pre-K	½ Pre-K & ½ K	left district			
CL	Pre-K	Pre-K	K	left district			
RH	Pre-K	Pre-K	K	1st	Sp.Ed.	Sp.Ed.	Sp.Ed.
DB	Pre-K	Pre-K	K	declassified			
CR		Pre-K	K	1st	1st & R	2nd & R	Sp.Ed.
TP	Pre-K	Pre-K	K	1st	1st	Sp.Ed.	Sp.Ed
JC		Pre-K	IK	IK	Sp.Ed.	Sp.Ed.	Sp.Ed.
TC	Pre-K	Pre-K	K	1st	1st	2nd & R	Sp.Ed.
CS	Pre-K	Pre-K	K	1st	2nd	3rd	4th
FT	Pre-K	Pre-K	Sp.Ed.	Sp.Ed.	Sp.Ed.	Sp.Ed.	Sp.Ed.
PT	Pre-K	Pre-K	K	left district			
SP		Pre-K	left district				
MC	Pre-K	Pre-K	K	1st[a]	1st[a]	2nd	3rd

Note. Sp.Ed. = Self-contained Special Education Class. R = 1 to 2 hours per day in Special Education. ESL = English as a Second Language. IK = Integrated Kindergarten.
[a]placement in another district

(70%) are currently classified as learning disabled, 5 remain classified as speech impaired, 1 is categorized as hard of hearing, and 1 has been declassified and is no longer considered handicapped.

Educational Placement

Outlined in table IV are the educational placements for the students in the sample from the year they entered prekindergarten to their present placement. Of the 23 students who remained within the district, 19 (83%) have at some point received special education services in addition to speech therapy. Table IV indicates that some students have been placed in self-contained special education classes throughout their school career to date. Other students began in regular classes with speech therapy services also provided, then repeated one or two grades and were subsequently placed in special education classes. A few students received special education services in their initial few years in school and now are in regular classes.

For the 1987–1988 school year, 14 of the students are assigned to self-contained special education classes. Two students attend regular classes and receive special education services through the resource program; one other student received resource services last year but left the district prior to beginning this school year. Five students receive speech therapy as their only special service and 12 other students receive speech therapy in conjunction with their other special education services. Therefore, 17 students still receive speech therapy.

Children entering kindergarten in 1981 would now be either 10 or 11 years old and would be expected to be in sixth grade. From the students in this study, seven are in this cohort. Of these, three are in ungraded special education classes, two are in fourth grade and an additional student would also have been in fourth grade if still in the district. The final student is in fifth grade. All of these students are either in ungraded programs of have repeated one or more grades.

There are six students in the study who entered kindergarten in 1982 and are now 9 or 10 years old and therefore would be expected to be in the fifth grade. Of this group five students are in ungraded special education classes and the sixth is in fourth grade having repeated one grade.

In 1983 14 students in the sample began school and are now 8 and 9 years old and should be in fourth grade. Of this group four students left the district within two years of entering kindergarten and one was declassified at the end of first grade. Of the remaining nine students, six are placed in ungraded special education classes, one is in fourth, one is in third, and one is in second grade

Academic Progress

Considering the proportion of students in the sample who are now designated learning disabled it is not unexpected that this sample has shown very slow educational progress. Their academic skills have been evaluated with individual achievement measures such as the Kaufman Test of Educational Achievement (Kaufman and Kaufman 1985), the Peabody Individual Achievement Test (Dunn and Markwardt 1970), the Diagnostic Achievement Battery (Newcomer and Curtis 1983), and the Woodcock-Johnson Psycho-educational Battery (Woodcock 1978). If only those students who are now classified as learning disabled are considered, their progress in reading forms a fairly consistent pattern. Many of the students were evaluated toward the end of their third year in school when they were 7 years old. When they were tested at that point they all had achieved at a first grade level. Although the grade equivalents ranged from 1.0 to 1.8 almost all of the students scored in the early part of first grade. The reading achievement scores for 8 year olds ranged from 0.6 to 2.9; however, almost all of the students' scores fell at the mid- to late first grade level. Students who were tested at age 9, during their fourth year in school, typically achieved between the mid-first and early second grade levels, with the actual scores ranging from 1.4 to 2.4. In general, these students required four years in school to acquire first grade reading skills. The results of the most recently administered reading achievement test for each student are included in table V.

The math achievement for this group of students now classi-fied as learning disabled has not followed as consistent a pattern. Most of the students demonstrated math skills that were one-half to one year above their reading grade equivalents, but some students' math achievement was lower than their reading achievement. The results of the most recent math achievement tests are also presented in table V.

Evident from table V is the stronger achievement of students who are still classified as only speech/language-impaired compared to the achievement of the learning disabled group. Although one of these students is significantly below grade level the other four are much closer to grade level than any of the learning disabled students.

TABLE V
Most Recent Achievement Grade Equivalent

Student	Age at Evaluation	Evaluation Results	
		Reading	Math
TC	9	2.4	1.9
RM	9	1.8	2.7
TB[a]	9	2.6[a]	2.7[a]
RH[a]	10	1.8[a]	2.6[a]
TE	10	1.2	2.2
TJ	9	2.0	2.4
TBr	10	4.3	4.6
AP	8	2.9	1.1
SB	8	1.1	1.6
KL	9	1.4	3.1
MDL	9	2.2	2.4
BM[a]	9	4.0[a]	3.7[a]
NP	8	1.8	2.5
ML	8	0.6	
CH		student left district	
CL		student left district	
RH	7	1.4	2.0
DB		declassified	
CR	9	1.5	2.3
JC	8	1.8	2.2
TP	7	1.3	2.6
TC	8	1.8	2.2
CS[a]	8	3.2[a]	3.8[a]
FT	7	1.0	1.6
PT		student left district	
SP		student left district	
MC[a]	9	3.6[a]	3.0[a]

[a]student classified only as Speech Impaired.

DISCUSSION

Most other follow-up studies have attempted to identify patterns in the data from the preschool years that related to patterns in the data collected during the follow-up period. Both Hall and Tomblin (1978) and King, Jones, and Lasky (1982) compared students with language deficits to students with articulation problems only. Aram and Nation (1980) also considered the preschool diagnostic data, but they rated the children in their sample for severity level for seven types of hearing, speech, and language problems. They also investigated the duration of preschool therapy as a variable. Strominger and Bashir (1977) suggested that the pattern of intelligence test scores for language-disordered children who later achieve average academic skills might be different from scores of those who do not. Various follow-up studies have frequently examined the relationship between specific types of preschool speech and language disorders and later academic and communication abilities. To a lesser degree the duration of preschool intervention and patterns of scores on intelligence tests have been considered. Each of these factors will be considered using the data from the current study.

Early Diagnostic Features Related to Current Educational Status

The diagnostic patterns at the time of the initial speech and language evaluation for each child in the present study are presented in table II. As previously noted, for 4 of the students no detailed information was available because records are missing; it is only known that they were diagnosed as speech/language-impaired and received daily therapy services. Of the remaining students, 4 subsequently left the district so there is no current data available. This leaves only 19 comparisons for which there are both current data and detailed preschool records.

In considering the early diagnostic pattern for these 19 cases it is evident that a significant number, 7 children or 37%, experienced hearing problems ranging from a history of frequent ear infections (OME), to fluctuating hearing, to a mild hearing loss. In the Aram and Nation (1980) study information on hearing was available for 41 students and, of these, 20 had normal hearing and 21 had auditory reception problems that ranged from mild to severe. In both studies, then, a significant proportion of the children experienced some degree of hearing problems. When Aram and Nation looked at the correlations between the early diagnostic features and later classroom placement however, hearing problems were the only feature, out of seven diagnostic areas, that did not result in a significant correlation. In the current study there were six students who either remained classified as speech/language-impaired and are now attending regular classes or were declassified, and of these students only one experienced early hearing problems. As with the Aram and Nation study, this relationship was not statistically significant.

Only two of the children were found to have problems with the pragmatics of language. Of these, one student is currently classified as learning disabled but the other is still diagnosed as speech-impaired and after 5 years of special education services is now placed in a regular class and demonstrates reading skills within the average range. Only one child was diagnosed as having a fluency problem and this student currently attends regular class and receives only speech therapy.

The distinction that has most frequently been made in follow-up studies has been between the students with language impairments and those who had articulation problems only. In the current study five children evidenced articulation problems only, with no significant delays in language comprehension. Two of these children did have delayed vocabulary development and another child evidenced a 3 to 6 month delay in comprehension, but none of these were considered significant. Of the five students with articulation problems only, three are now in the group who receive only speech therapy or no services at all. However, of the other 14 children who exhibited receptive language deficits there are now 3 students who also are receiving either no services or only speech therapy. For this sample then there was no statistically significant relationship between current class placement and the diagnostic distinction of articulation problems only versus language comprehension problems. It should be noted, however, that of the three students with preschool language delays but who are now in regular classes, two demonstrated delays of less than one year, and the other student is now in a regular class after five years of special education services. If we had had a larger sample of students with only articulation problems this relationship might have been statistically significant. This relationship has been quite consistent in other follow-up studies.

Intelligence Measures

In the present study the mean IQ for the sample during their preschool years was 96, with a range from 72 to 122, based on non-verbal measures whenever possible and on the results of the Stanford Binet, Form LM (Terman and Merrill 1973), when necessary. To determine the current IQ level of the sample, only the results of the most recently administered intelligence test were considered for each student. The WISC-R (Wechsler 1974) Full Scale (FS) IQ or the K-ABC (Kaufman and Kaufman 1983) Mental Processing Composite (MPC) were used as the most accurate estimate of intelligence in all cases except those where there was a discrepancy of 15 points or more. In these cases either the Performance IQ or the Simultaneous

Standard Score was considered the more appropriate estimate of intelligence. Following this procedure the mean WISC-R FS IQ for 12 students was 89 and the mean K-ABC MPC for 4 students was 86. The mean WISC-R Performance IQ for 5 students was 102.5 and the mean Simultaneous Score for 2 students was 94.5. Using these intelligence scores for each student yields a mean of 92 for the whole sample with a range of scores from 74 to 112. The mean IQ for the sample during their preschool years was based more heavily on non-verbal measures of intelligence than the later mean IQ. If the decision were made to estimate the IQ of the group based on the WISC-R Performance IQ or on the higher K-ABC score in all cases, rather than using the WISC-R FS IQ or K-ABC MPC, then the mean IQ would be 95 with a range from 80 to 118. In either case the data indicate that the children in this sample continued to test above the mentally retarded range and the mean IQ continued to be within the average range. It appears that the non-verbal IQs for the 3 and 4 year olds were reliable estimates of functioning 5 or 6 years later, on both non-verbal and verbal measures of intelligence.

Although two of the students in the sample were classified as mentally retarded for a period during their school career, in both of these cases the diagnosis was subsequently changed to learning disabled. It is not a new problem for students with severe language deficits to be misdiagnosed as retarded and, unfortunately, it does not seem to be a problem that has been entirely eliminated. In both of the cases in this study, the students had tested within the borderline range on non-verbal measures in preschool and they continued to achieve WISC-R Performance IQs in the mid-80 range but their WISC-R Verbal IQs were in the mid 70s. It became evident that, although these students had significant learning problems, their abilities and disabilities did not conform to patterns seen in students typically classified as mentally retarded but were more similar to students classified as learning disabled. Two other students who subsequently continued to be classified as speech impaired only and to attend regular class also consistently had IQs in the 74 to 84 range. Even considering the several students in the sample who consistently tested with IQs in the 75 to 85 IQ range, low intelligence does not seem a likely basis for the lack of academic progress of the group of students in this sample.

Of the follow-up studies cited, only Strominger and Bashir's research (cited in Maxwell and Wallach 1984) considered intelligence test results in any detail. In their study of 40 students they found that 30 children had a Verbal-Performance IQ discrepancy of 10 to 15 points on the WISC-R (Wechsler 1974). In his statistical analysis of the WISC-R standardization sample, Kaufman (1979) found that 24% of the individuals in the national standardization sample demonstrated a Verbal-Performance discrepancy of 10 to 15 points. This suggests that approximately twice as many students in the Strominger and Bashir study had a discrepancy of this magnitude as compared with what would be expected from the national standardization sample. Kaufman also indicated that to be significant at the .01 level the Verbal-Performance difference must be greater than 15 points.

In the current study all of the students were tested at least once with the WISC-R (Wechsler 1974) or the K-ABC (Kaufman and Kaufman 1973). Using Kaufman's (1979) criteria for .01 level of significance on the WISC-R and also on the K-ABC the discrepancies for this sample were examined. Of the 23 students, 13 (57%) of them, never exhibited a Verbal-Performance or Sequential-Simultaneous difference that was 15 or more points. However, five students did demonstrate a statistically significant discrepancy on all of the intelligence tests administered; one of the five students was administered three measures over the six-year period, one was administered two tests, and three were each tested once. An additional five students demonstrated a significant discrepancy on at least one test but not on other IQ tests administered; all together these five students were administered 14 intelligence tests and 6 of these produced significant discrepancies. These figures suggest that standard score differences between scales on intelligence measures are not consistent when students are tested at different times and that the diagnostic or predictive significance of such discrepancies should not be exaggerated. Considering this caution and also Kaufman's data on the occurrence rate in the general population it seems that a somewhat higher proportion of students who have significant speech and language problems evidence discrepancies on IQ measures that are significant at the .01 level than would be expected from the general population.

Strominger and Bashir (cited in Maxwell and Wallach 1984) also stated that from their sample of 40 students the 2 students who were on grade level had a Verbal-Performance difference of less than 5 points. In the present study there were five students who were in regular classes and receiving only speech therapy and one student who had been declassified. Of these six students, four had never exhibited a Verbal-Peformance or Sequential-Simultaneous discrepancy, one had shown very large discrepancies on all three intelligence tests, and one had exhibited a significant discrepancy on one test but not on another. The results of this study do not seem to support Strominger and Bashir's suggestion that a lack of a discrepancy may suggest a better prognosis for speech/language-impaired students.

Duration of Early Intervention

Unlike other follow-up studies, the present one investigated only students who had received preschool therapeutic services. When Aram and Nation (1980) considered the relationship between the duration of preschool speech services and current speech, language, and academic functioning they found there was no correlation. However, the duration of school speech services was related to current functioning levels and the authors concluded that "when therapy is readily available, requiring no additional financial or time commitments by the family, duration of therapy related considerably to the severity of the problem" (p. 168). In the current study, speech therapy was available to preschool students in much the same way it is available to school populations, at least in terms of the family responsibility required. However, it was necessary for the family to enroll the preschool child in the preschool program for the diagnostic and therapeutic services to be available. All of the children who were identified as speech/language-impaired received intervention but the duration of preschool therapy was determined by the age at enrollment rather than by the severity of the presenting problems. Of the 23 students who have remained in the district, 11 received therapy for only one year and 12 of them participated for two years. Of the six students now in regular classes and receiving either no services or speech therapy only, five received two years of preschool intervention. This relationship was not statistically significant but it could be characterized as a strong trend.

IMPLICATIONS

All of the follow-up studies emphasize that children diagnosed as speech- and language-impaired during their preschool years are at risk for developing serious learning problems during their school careers. In the present study all of the children identified as speech/language-impaired as 3- and 4-year-olds received daily individual speech therapy in addition to a group preschool program. Even with this intervention during early childhood, 70% of these students are now classified as learning disabled and are receiving special education services. Only 30% of the students attend a regular class and they receive either resource services and/or speech therapy and all except one student have repeated either one or two grades. Of these speech-impaired students, the majority were judged to be most appropriately placed in regular classes when they entered school, however, for these students this is now their fifth, sixth, or seventh year in school and all but two of them have experienced major problems acquiring academic skills. Considering these data, as well as the results of other follow-up studies, children diagnosed as severely speech/language-impaired during their pre-school years appear to have a 40% to 70% probability of evidencing learning disabilities during elementary school. Can this academic failure be prevented?

It is difficult to question seriously whether early intervention can eliminate or significantly minimize learning disabilities, but it seems appropriate at least to ask what are reasonable expectations for the long-range effects of early intervention programs. To a great degree this question is avoided by having separate service delivery systems for preschool children and school students. The preschool programs have goals and objectives that are primarily based on research regarding normal developmental milestones prior to ages 4½ or 5. The assumption is that if a child approximates the measurable skills of a normal population then that child will be "ready" to learn academic skills when school begins. The fact that there are almost no follow-up studies of early intevention programs for severely speech/language-impaired children is a strong clue that such programs seldom investigate the long-range effects of their intervention.

On the other hand, school systems have also kept a distance from the question of what are reasonable expectations for early intervention programs. One reason for this may be that school systems typically have programs for students who are experiencing a wide range of learning problems; some of these students attended preschool programs while others did not, but this distinction is not particularly relevant for school systems that nonetheless have the responsibility for providing current programming.

In this retrospective study three groups of students were traced from diagnosis at ages 3 or 4 years, through an early intervention program, and on through elementary school. The early intervention program was based on the frequently used model of adding intensive individual speech/language therapy to a group preschool program. The results of this study indicate that this early intervention model was not effective in preventing reading failure.

From 1960 to 1975 there was a rapid accumulation of data on the progression of normal language development and on the identification of the more typical patterns of deviation from normal language acquisition. Much of the content, and many of the techniques, of speech and language therapy are still based on theoretical models developed from these data. More recently, research has focused on language skills within communicative contexts and on the complex relationships between language development and academic skill development. There has been considerable research on metalinguistic skills and their role in beginning reading (Blachman 1984; Liberman 1973; van Kleeck 1984). Researchers have investigated the language of instruction and its effects on academic functioning (Berlin, Blank, and Rose 1980; Carlson, Gruenewald, and Nyberg 1980; Nelson 1984; Silliman 1984). Other researchers have looked at language skills that contribute to comprehension of written language, such skills as semantic mapping (Bauer 1979; Freedman and Carpenter 1976; Leonard, Bolders, and Miller 1976; Israel 1984), story grammar (Applebee 1978; Kintsch 1977; Rumelhart 1977; Stein and Glenn 1979; Westby 1984), narrative discourse (deBeaugrande 1979; Westby 1984) and schema development (Anderson 1977; Pearson and Spiro 1980; Rumelhart 1981; Spiro 1977).

Considering this recent research it seems reasonable to ask if current early intervention programs have been modified to include more emphasis on the oral language skills that correlate with acquisition of beginning written language abilities. Are the clinicians who provide speech therapy for preschool and kindergarten children aware of the high probability of future significant reading and writing problems for children classified as speech/language-impaired? If they were aware that follow-up studies indicate that 40% to 70% of speech/language-impaired children develop academic deficiencies that are significant enough to be considered learning disabilities, would there be changes in the focus of early intervention programs?

Should we continue the practice of classifying preschool children, like those in the present study, as speech/language-impaired and providing primarily speech/language therapy? This model may be adequate for children who evidence mild to moderate speech/language-impairments, but it does not appear adequate for children who are moderately to severely impaired. Definitive answers are not yet available to questions regarding long-range outcomes and reasonable expectations for early intervention programs and to some degree these questions are circular in nature. However, there appears to be evidence that the fields of early childhood, speech and language, and learning disabilities will need to work together to develop a more integrated, and ideally a more effective, model for early intervention. To highlight this necessary shift in focus it may be wise to re-classify, or re-conceptualize these preschool children with severe communication problems as learning disabled in language rather than to continue to regard them as speech and language impaired only.

REFERENCES

Anderson, R. 1977. The notion of schema and the educational enterprise. In R. Anderson, R. Spiro and W. Montague (eds.). *Schooling and the Acquisition of Knowledge*. Hillsdale, NJ: Lawrence Erlbaum Associates.

Applebee, A. 1978. *The Child's Concept of Story*. Chicago: University of Chicago Press.

Aram, D., and Nation, J. 1980. Preschool language disorders and subsequent language and academic difficulties. *Journal of Communication Disorders* 13:159–170.

Arthur, G. 1950. *The Arthur Adaptation of the Leiter International Performance Scale*. Chicago: C. H. Stoelting.

Bauer, R. 1979. Memory, acquisition, and category clustering in learning disabled children. *Journal of Experimental Child Psychology* 24:365–383.

Berlin, L., Blank, M., and Rose, S. 1980. The language of instruction: The hidden complexities. *Topics in Language Disorders* 1:47–58.

Blachman, B. 1984. Language analysis skills and early reading acquisition. In G. Wallach and K. Butler (eds.). *Language Learning Disabilities in School Age Children* (pp. 271–287). Baltimore: Williams & Wilkins.

Brown, R. 1973. *A First Language: The Early Stages*. Cambridge: Harvard University Press.

Carlson, J., Gruenewald, L., and Nyberg, B. 1980. Everyday math is a story problem: The language of the curriculum. *Topics in Language Disorders* 1:59–70.

deBeaugrande, R. 1979. The pragmatics of discourse planning. *Journal of Pragmatics* 3:15–42.

Dunn, L., and Dunn, L. 1981. *Peabody Picture Vocabulary Test-Revised*. Circle Pines, MN: American Guidance Service.

Dunn, L., and Markwardt, F. 1970 *Peabody Individual Achievement Test*. Circle Pines, MN: American Guidance Service.

Foster, C., Giddan, J., and Stark, J. 1972. *Assessment of Children's Language Comprehension*. Palo Alto: Consulting Psychologists Press.

Freedman, P., and Carpenter, R. 1976. Semantic relations used by normal and language impaired children at stage 1. *Journal of Speech and Hearing Research* 19:784–795.

Garvey, M., and Gordon, N. 1973. A follow-up study of children with disorders of speech development. *British Journal of Disorders of Communication* 8:17–28.

Griffiths, C. 1969. A follow-up study of children with disorders of speech. *British Journal of Disorders of Communication* 4: 46–56.

Hall, P., and Tomblin, B. 1978. A follow-up study of children with articulation and language disorders. *Journal of Speech and Hearing Disorders* 43:227–241.

Israel, L. 1984. Word knowledge and word retrieval: Phonological and semantic strategies. In G. Wallach and K. Butler (eds.). *Language and Learning Disabilities in School-age Children* (pp. 230–250). Baltimore: Williams & Wilkins.

Kaufman, A. 1979. *Intelligent Testing With the WISC-R*. New York: John Wiley & Sons.

Kaufman, A., and Kaufman, N. 1983. *Kaufman Assessment Battery for Children*. Circle Pines, MN: American Guidance Service.

Kaufman, A., and Kaufman, N. 1985. *Kaufman Test of Educational Achievement*. Circle Pines, MN: American Guidance Service.

King, R., Jones, C., and Lasky, E. 1982. In retrospect: A fifteen year follow-up report of speech-language disordered children. *Language, Speech, Hearing Services in the Schools* 13:24–32.

Kintsch, W. 1977. On comprehending stories. *In* M. Just and P. Carpenter (eds.). *Cognitive Processes in Comprehension*. Hillsdale, NJ: Lawrence Erlbaum Associates.

Leonard, L., Bolders, J., and Miller, J. 1976. An examination of the semantic relations reflected in the language usage of normal and language disordered children. *Journal of Speech and Hearing Research* 19:371–392.

Liberman, I. 1973. Segmentation of the spoken word and reading acquisition. *Bulletin of The Orton Society* 23:65–77.

Maxwell, S., and Wallach, G. 1984. The language-learning disabilities connection: Symptoms of early language disabilities change over time. *In* G. Wallach and K. Butler (eds.). *Language Learning Disabilities in School Age Children* (pp. 15–34). Baltimore: Williams & Wilkins.

Nelson, N. 1984. Beyond information processing: The language of teachers and textbooks. *In* G. Wallach and K. Butler (eds.). *Language and Learning Disabilities* (pp. 154–178). Baltimore: Williams & Wilkins.

Newcomer, P., and Curtis, D. 1983. *Diagnostic Achievement Battery*. Austin, TX: PRO-ED.

Pearson, P., and Spiro, R. 1980. Toward a theory of reading comprehension instruction. *Topics in Language Disorders* 1:71–88.

Rumelhart, D. 1977. Understanding and summarizing brief stories. *In* D. LaBerge and S. Jay (eds.). *Basic Processes in Reading: Perception and Comprehension*. Hillsdale, NJ: Lawrence Erlbaum Associates.

Rumelhart, D. 1981. Schemata: The building blocks of cognition. *In* R. Spiro, B. Bruce, and W. Brewer (eds.). *Theoretical Issues in Reading Comprehension*. Hillsdale, NJ: Lawrence Erlbaum Associates.

Silliman, E. 1984. Interactional competencies in the instructional context: The role of teaching discourse in learning. *In* G. Wallach and K. Butler (eds.). *Language and Learning Disabilities* (pp. 288–317). Baltimore: Williams & Wilkins.

Snyder, L. 1980. Have we prepared the language disordered child for school? *Topics in Language Disorders* 1:29–45.

Spiro, R. 1977. Remembering information from text: The "state of scheme" approach. *In* R. Anderson, R. Spiro, and W. Montague (eds.). *Schooling and the Acquisition of Knowledge*. Hillsdale, NJ: Lawrence Erlbaum Associates.

Stein, N., and Glenn, C. 1979. An analysis of story comprehension in elementary school children. *In* R. Freedle (ed.). *New Directions in Discourse Processing*. Hillsdale, NJ: Ablex.

Terman, L., and Merrill, M. 1973. *Stanford-Binet Intelligence Scale*. Chicago: Riverside Publishing Company.

van Kleeck, A. 1984. Assessment and intervention: Does "meta" matter? *In* G. Wallach and K. Butler (eds.). *Language Learning Disabilities in School Age Children* (pp. 179–198). Baltimore: Williams & Wilkins.

Wechsler, D. 1967. *The Wechsler Preschool and Primary Scale of Intelligence*. Cleveland: Psychological Corporation.

Wechsler, D. 1974. *Wechsler Intelligence Scale for Children-Revised*. New York: Psychological Corporation.

Westby, C. 1984. Development of narrative language abilities. *In* G. Wallach and K. Butler (eds.). *Language and Learning Disabilities in School-Age Children* (pp. 103–127). Baltimore: Williams & Wilkins.

Woodcock, R. 1978. *Woodcock-Johnson Psychoeducational Battery*. Hingham, MA: Teaching Resources Corporation.

Zimmerman, I., Steiner, V., and Evatt, R. 1969. *Preschool Language Manual*. Columbus, OH: Charles Merrill Publishing.

4

Predicting Dyslexia in a Preschool Population

For many years researchers have spent considerable time, effort, and money attempting to predict which young children are at risk for later learning disabilities. The general mood has been one of optimism: If we could pinpoint the children at risk, and give them early and appropriate help, we could prevent, or at least reduce, the frequency and/or severity of reading disability or dyslexia. Some researchers, however, have expressed disillusionment with the efficacy of early prediction (e.g. Lindquist 1982; Lindsay and Wedell 1982; Rubin et al. 1978; Schaer and Crump 1976). Lindquist (1982) concluded that the screening program used in her study (Denver Developmental Screening Test) had very little value in identifying children with learning problems, in spite of the statistically significant correlation of the measure with later reading. Lindsay and Wedell (1982) reported that over 50% of children who failed reading at age seven were missed by their British predictive measure (Infant Rating Scale).

The main objective of many predictive studies has been to demonstrate statistically significant correlation coefficients between early childhood measures and later school achievement. It is apparent to most clinicians, however, that even a statistically significant correlation does not guarantee that individual children at risk for dyslexia will be identified. Even if correlation coefficients between predictive and achievement measures reach or exceed .7, accuracy in predicting for individual children may be limited. A further problem is that it is easier to predict which children will be good readers, than which will be dyslexic (Feshbach, Adelman, and Fuller 1974; Horn and O'Donnell 1984; Rubin et al. 1978; Satz et al. 1978). A high correlation coefficient may, therefore, merely reflect accuracy in prediction of good reading. Satz et al. (1978) found that between grades 2 and 5 accuracy in prediction of good reading increased from 75% to 95%, but accuracy in prediction of poor reading decreased from 78% to 39%.

As an alternative, or in addition to the correlation coefficient, researchers have increasingly made use of a 2×2 matrix to demonstrate the number and percentage of subjects for whom prediction was correct or incorrect (Meehl and Rosen 1955). Researchers who have reported predictive accuracy in this way include Badian (1982, 1986, 1988), Feshbach et al. (1982), Satz et al. (1978), Wilson and Reichmuth (1985). Wilson and Reichmuth point out, however, that the method is deceptively simple, and the data can be interpreted or misinterpreted in a number of ways. Satz and Fletcher have demonstrated errors in the use of the 2×2 matrix (Fletcher and Satz 1984; Satz and Fletcher 1979).

With few exceptions, reading is the aspect of school achievement that has been the focus of predictive studies. An apparent assumption in many studies is that a child who scores below a designated cutoff score on a predictive measure is at risk for later reading disability. Many preschool batteries, however, include a variety of tasks (e.g. fine motor, gross motor, personal-social, language), some of which may not be closely linked to any aspect of reading. A low score on a screening battery may merely reflect low intellectual functioning. Silver (1978) reported that kindergarten children scoring low on SEARCH, a scanning instrument to identify potential learning disability (Silver and Hagin 1976), were usually below 80 on the full scale WPPSI. Other children may score low because of emotional problems or cultural deprivation. Horn and O'Donnell (1984) pointed out the confusion in the literature caused by the fact that some researchers equate the prediction of low achievement with the prediction of learning disabilities. They carried out a longitudinal predictive study to compare results based on an unadjusted raw score, with those results based on a regression-discrepancy criterion. They believed that use of an unadjusted raw score would lead to misdiagnosing a number of children as learning disabled, and also would leave unidentified some children who were learning disabled.

So-called "reading readiness" tests, which are generally administered in kindergarten or early first grade, are designed to maximize the predictive relationship with reading. The content of other predictive batteries is often determined by researchers' theoretical positions with regard to the skills underlying the reading process. Examples are: the ability to retrieve stored symbols (Jansky and de Hirsch 1972), spatial and temporal organization (Silver 1978), phonological awareness (Mann and Liberman 1984), naming ability (Wolf 1984). The more the predictive battery incorporates elements closely related to the reading process, the more confidence one can have in the ability of the battery to predict reading skills, rather than generally low achievement.

In all predictive studies, the cutoff points to define both high risk status in early childhood and poor reading skills at follow-up are problematic. Lowering the predictive cutoff point can reduce the number of false positives, but will increase the number of false negatives, while raising the cutoff will have the opposite effect. Whether the better option is to classify too many children as being at risk, or to fail to identify many who really are at risk is a matter for debate.

The cutoff point for determining poor reading achievement is usually based on the researcher's definition of reading disability or dyslexia. Finucci (1978) provided an excellent discussion of the problems in specifying reading scores to define dyslexia. Eisenberg (1978) discussed whether national norms, or norms for a child's school or social class, should determine cutoff points to define reading disability. Different geographical areas do tend to be characterized by different mean levels of reading achievement. As an example of this, Rutter and his colleagues, in their British epidemiological studies, found that specific reading retardation was more prevalent in inner London than on the Isle of Wight (Rutter 1978; Yule and Rutter 1976). The importance of base rate, defined as the incidence of a particular condition within a given population, has been pointed out (Satz and Fletcher 1979; Wilson and Reichmuth 1985). Wilson and Reichmuth, quoting Meehl and Rosen (1955), stress that validity data from one population with a given base rate cannot be generalized to populations with markedly different base rates.

Some researchers have used more than one classification to circumvent the problems associated with a single cutoff point to define poor reading or dyslexia. For example, Colligan and Bajuniemi (1984) used four indices of reading disability, and Satz classified poor readers into severe and mild groups in his longitudinal Florida studies (Satz et al. 1978). It is unlikely that the poor readers in a study are a homogeneous group (Jansky 1978). Silver (1978) also pointed out that, even controlling for age, sex, intelligence, socioeconomic status, and educational experience, it cannot be assumed that the defects associated with reading failure in one child are the same as in any other child who fails in reading. The single cutoff score to indicate that a child is at risk for reading failure also fails to take into account the heterogeneity of children who are dyslexic and the volume of recent research demonstrating that there are several subtypes of dyslexia. (For reviews see McKinney 1984; Satz and Morris 1981.)

The use of a cutoff point to classify children as high or low risk probably contributes to the inefficiency of prediction. Badian (1986) demonstrated that accuracy of prediction could be improved through retrospective classification of poor readers into groups, using both preschool screening and biographical data. Significantly more children were correctly classified as good or poor readers by this method, than by using a cutoff score to define risk status.

The current study is a follow-up of all the children in a community from preschool to late grade 6. The general purpose of the study was to investigate the long-term prediction of reading achievement, in relation to preschool test scores. More specific aims were: (1) to determine the number of poor and dyslexic readers in the community after six years of reading instruction, (2) to attempt to improve the accuracy of prediction of poor reading for the individual child, (3) to examine the preschool characteristics and later reading achievement of children considered to be at risk at age four, and (4) to determine the amount and type of early intervention and other help received by high-risk children and poor readers.

METHOD

Subjects

The subjects were all the children born in 1971–1975 in a small suburban community, who had been tested with the Holbrook Screening Battery (HSB) approximately six months before kindergarten entry, and who were still attending the schools in the community seven years later. Virtually all preschool children in the community are tested each year, since testing is state-mandated.

The population of this community is predominantly white. According to the most recent figures available, based on the 1980 census data (Gibney 1984), ethnic composition is: white–96.9%, black–1.9%, and other–1.2%. The leading single ancestry groups are Irish–41.6%, Italian–14.0%, and English–13.4%. The median number of school years completed by the adult population is 12.5. Occupational make-up is: professional, managerial, technicians etc.–22.0%, sales and clerical–30.3%, services, crafts, operatives etc.–43.3%, and cleaners, laborers–4.5%. The median family income in 1980 was $23,354.

The original number of children who were administered the HSB was 738 (364 boys, 374 girls). After seven years there were 480 children living in the community and attending school there. Two children were attending special schools for the handicapped outside the community. Thirty-six of the 480 (7.5%) were excluded from the study for the following reasons: 8 were bilingual (1.7%), 10 were adopted (2.1%), 17 had no questionnaire filled out by parents at the time of screening (3.5%), 1 had emotional problems (0.2%). The adopted children, and those for whom no questionnaire was completed, were excluded because of insufficient information about their backgrounds. The total number of subjects was 444 (220 boys, 224 girls).

All but nine of the subjects were followed up seven years after the preschool testing. Eight were followed up after eight years, seven of them because they had repeated preschool or kindergarten, and one (a first grade repeater and a very poor reader) because he was absent for testing after seven years. One girl (an excellent reader) was followed up after six years, because she had skipped a grade. At the time of the study all but the last two subjects just described had received six years of reading instruction. Most subjects were completing grade 6, but 43 (9.7%) were in grade 5, because they had repeated a grade other then kindergarten. Just over two-thirds (67.4%) of the 43 repeaters were boys. Grades repeated were: grade 1, 37.2%; grade 2, 18.6%; grade 3, 20.9%; grade 4, 16.3%; grade 5, 7.0%. Six subjects were screened twice, the second time approximately one year after the first. For these children the second screening score was the one used, unless the child was outside the normal age range the second time (2 subjects).

At the time of screening the subjects ranged in age from 51 months to 67 months, with 94.4% falling between 51 and 63 months. Sixty percent were between 51 and 59 months old.

Predictive Measures

Holbrook Screening Battery. The 14 subtests of the Holbrook Screening Battery (HSB) were administered individually to each child by a team of five trained kindergarten teachers and school specialists. The examiners also rated each child on such characteristics as speech intelligibility, attention, activity level, and distractibility. Handedness, based on three pencil and paper tasks, use of scissors, and ball throwing, was recorded as right, left, or both.

For scoring purposes the HSB subtests are divided into four groups:

Verbal:
> WPPSI Information, Sentences, Similarities.
> Language Sample: Telling a story about a picture.

Readiness:
> Naming 8 colors, 5 shapes, 13 upper case letters.
> WPPSI Arithmetic.

Fine Motor:
> Name Writing.
> Copy Forms: Pencil copying of 5 geometric shapes.
> Pencil Use (3-point rating).
> Draw-a-Person (scored as in Koppitz 1968).
> Cutting: Cutting along a horizontal line (3-point rating).

Gross Motor:
> Throwing, catching, kicking, dribbling a ball.
> Walking: heel-to-toe, backward, on tiptoe.
> Balancing on preferred foot, walking a balance beam.
> Hopping, skipping, broad jump.

A factor analysis of the HSB scores of the original 738 children tested (born 1971–1975) indicated that the HSB consists of three factors, accounting for 53.7% of the variance. The four subgroup divisions listed above predated the factor analysis. The three factors yielded by the factor analysis are: (1) Verbal (Information, Sentences, Similarities, Language Sample, Arithmetic); (2) Visual-Motor (Cutting, Copy Forms, Pencil Grasp, Gross Motor); and (3) Naming or Readiness (Letters, Shapes, Colors, Name Writing, Draw-a-Person). Name Writing has a substantial secondary loading on factor II, and Copy Forms and Arithmetic, on factor III.

Means and standard deviations of the 14 HSB subtests, based on the original 738 children tested and including all the subjects of this study, are shown in table I.

Parent Questionnaire. At the time of screening all parents were asked to fill out a detailed questionnaire about their child. Only a small percentage of parents failed to comply with this request (3.5% of children available were excluded from the study because no questionnaire was filled out).

The questionnaire included information on family constella-

TABLE I

Means and Standard Deviations of the Subtests of the Holbrook Screening Battery

	Boys (N = 364)		Girls (N = 374)		Total (N = 738)*	
Subtest	Mean	SD	Mean	SD	Mean	SD
Information	11.04	2.62	11.51	2.78	11.27	2.71
Sentences	10.68	2.87	11.37	3.00	11.03	2.96
Similarities	11.09	2.86	11.52	3.11	11.31	3.00
Language Sample	9.71	2.23	10.20	2.26	9.96	2.26
Arithmetic	10.79	2.59	11.35	2.47	11.07	2.54
Colors	7.00	1.80	7.53	1.29	7.27	1.59
Letters	8.29	4.79	9.21	4.44	8.75	4.64
Shapes	3.02	1.19	3.20	1.15	3.11	1.17
Name Writing	2.39	1.64	2.82	1.63	2.61	1.65
Copy Forms	4.50	2.03	4.84	1.84	4.67	1.94
Pencil Grasp	2.62	0.66	2.79	0.51	2.71	0.60
Draw-a-Person	4.64	1.69	4.51	1.48	4.57	1.59
Cutting	2.34	0.79	2.44	0.78	2.39	0.79
Gross Motor	27.51	4.89	28.84	4.73	28.18	4.85

*All children born between 1971 and 1975.

tion, parental occupation, birth and medical history, developmental milestones, family history of learning problems, and behavioral characteristics of the child as an infant and as a preschooler.

Follow-Up Measure (Reading criterion)

Stanford Achievement Test. All subjects were tested in late March with the Stanford Achievement Test (SAT), Intermediate 2 level, 1983 edition. Form F was administered to the majority of subjects, who were in grade 6, and Form E to the 9.7% in grade 5. The reading criterion was the Total Reading score, which is derived from two subtests: Word Study Skills and Reading Comprehension. Scaled scores were used as individual measures of achievement, because they are equivalent across forms and levels of the same subtest (SAT Norms Manual). The mean scaled scores of boys, girls, and the total group were converted to grade equivalent scores and percentile ranks, extrapolating when necessary.

Procedures

Screening (HSB) criterion. An earlier study of this community (550 children born from 1968 to 1971, and studied in the late grades 3 to 6) found that 6.7% of children were poor readers (Badian 1984). Using 6.7% as the base rate for poor reading in this community, it was predicted that 6.7% of the subjects in the current study would be at risk for poor reading. This percentage translates to 30 of the 444 subjects. Thus, the 30 children who scored lowest on the HSB total score were considered to be at risk for poor reading.

Reading criterion. Poor reading was defined as a Total Reading (SAT) score ≤20 percentile on national norms (as in Badian 1984). For the 1983 edition of the SAT this cutoff corresponds to a grade equivalent score ≤4.2, which is 2.5 years below the expected grade placement of the group, after six years of reading instruction (grade 6.7).

An additional criterion was that both reading subtest scores must be < grade 5.0. This criterion was not included in the 1984 study, but was added to exclude subjects who showed low-average to above-average ability in one aspect of reading.

A dyslexic subject was defined as a poor reader, with Wechsler Intelligence Scale for Children—Revised (Wechsler 1974) (WISC-R) verbal or performance IQ ≥90 (i.e. 25 percentile), who had no other handicapping condition, and who had attended school regularly. The WISC-R criterion was that used by Vellutino (1979) in his research. Poor readers not meeting the WISC-R criteria were termed "slow learners." If WISC-R scores were not available, the criterion was SAT grade 6 Listening Comprehension and vocabulary ≥25 percentile.

Accuracy of prediction. Using the HSB criterion and the criteria for poor reading delineated above, the accuracy rate of the HSB Total Score in predicting poor reading was determined by means of a 2 × 2 matrix, showing the number of subjects for whom prediction of reading was valid or false.

Improving accuracy of prediction of reading achievement. An attempt to improve the accuracy of the HSB Total Score in predicting individual reading achievement was made by retrospective visual inspection of all data for each subject (HSB scores, information from parent questionnaires). The visual inspection began with a search for characteristics shared by poor readers, and was based on an earlier study of third grade boys in this community (Badian 1986). Subjects were classified into subgroups, so as to include as many poor readers, and as few good readers, as possible.

Analysis of biographical information. The information provided by parents through questionnaires was analyzed for dyslexic subjects, slow learners, total poor readers, good readers, boys, girls, and the total group. Additional groups investigated were false positives (low on HSB, but good readers later), and subjects with the poorest birth history.

Information examined included: prenatal and birth history, neonatal problems, birth weight, food sensitivity, high fever (>105°), serious illness, convulsions, surgery (excluding tonsillectomy and minor superficial procedures), speech development (i.e. late speech and/or poor intelligibility at age four), attention deficit disorder (ADD) at preschool age, family history of learning disability (LD), birth order, and socio-economic status (SES). Handedness, as recorded on the relevant HSB subtests, was also examined. SES was defined by a five-category occupational classification: (1) professional and technical, (2) managerial, clerical, sales, (3) skilled workers, (4) operatives and service workers, (5) laborers (McCarthy 1970).

Early intervention and other special help received by poor readers and high-risk children. In the community studied, a low HSB score usually leads to an evaluation, which is followed by special help for most children. Help available includes a special preschool class (ages 3–5), a full-day language acquisition class (ages 5–7), a half-day special, small kindergarten (ages 5–6), and, at all grades (k–6) tutorial help in a resource room or through Title I services, and speech and/or language therapy. More recently, a special class for older children (ages 8–12) with severe learning disability was added.

The groups of subjects for whom the type and amount of special help received was investigated were: false positives (low on HSB, but good readers later), valid positives (low on HSB and poor readers later), false negatives (high on HSB, but poor readers later).

RESULTS

Reading Achievement at Grade 6

The mean scores of boys, girls, and the total group for the two SAT reading subtests and Total Reading are shown in table II. Mean chronological age of the subjects was 11.78 years (SD 0.33, range 10–11 to 13–2).

Boys scored at the 61 to 63 percentile on the two reading subtests and Total Reading; girls were approximately 10 percentile rank points higher. The total group of subjects scored 1.8 years above grade placement in Total Reading.

Incidence of Poor Reading and Dyslexia

Poor reading. Twenty-four subjects (5.4%) met the criteria specified for poor reading. Eighteen (8.2%) were boys and 6 (2.7%) were girls. The mean reading scores of the 24 poor readers were:

TABLE II
Means and Standard Deviations on the Stanford Achievement Test, Intermediate 2, Reading Subtests and Total Reading

Subtest	Boys (N = 220) Stand. Score Mean	SD	G. =*	%ile	Girls (N = 224) Stand. Score Mean	SD	G. =	%ile	Total (N = 444) Stand. Score Mean	SD	G. =	%ile
Word Study	656.3	34.2	7.7	62	667.4	34.7	9.0	72	662.0	34.9	8.5	68
Reading Comprehension	671.3	42.7	8.1	61	687.6	41.2	9.7	72	679.5	42.9	8.8	66
Total Reading	665.2	38.3	7.9	63	677.2	32.0	9.3	74	670.6	32.5	8.5	68

*G. = stands for grade equivalent score.

Total Reading—grade 3.5, standard score 600.1 (boys), grade 3.6, standard score 601.2 (girls); Word Study Skills—grade 3.5, standard score 599 (boys), grade 3.2, standard score 592 (girls); Reading Comprehension—grade 3.4, standard score 595 (boys), grade 3.7, standard score 607 (girls). The poor readers were about 2 standard deviations below the group mean for Total Reading, and more than three years below actual or expected grade placement.

Dyslexia. Twenty-one poor readers were given the WISC-R. Mean full scale IQ was 95.8 (range 82–111) for boys. Verbal IQ was 94.7 and performance IQ 97.9. For girls, scores were: Full scale IQ 81.0 (range 72–85), verbal IQ 79.6, performance IQ 84.8. Two of the three subjects who had not taken the WISC-R (both boys[1]) were above the 25 percentile on the SAT Listening Comprehension (mean = 70 percentile) and Vocabulary (mean = 47 percentile). The third subject, a girl, scored below the 25 percentile on both subtests.

Sixteen of the 18 boys who were poor readers met the criteria for dyslexia, but only two of the six girls did so. Mean full scale IQ for dyslexic boys was 97.5. Full scale IQ of the two dyslexic girls was 84 and 85. None of the 24 poor readers had a sensory deficit, or any other handicapping condition, and all had attended school regularly. Twenty-three were white and one was black. If the WISC-R criterion for dyslexia had been a full scale IQ ≥85 (as in Badian 1984), the number of dyslexic subjects would have been the same as with the current criteria, but 17 of the 18 would have been boys.

In this small group of 24 poor readers the distinction between dyslexic subjects and slow learners was not always clear. With the IQ criterion of WISC-R verbal or performance IQ of at least 90, several children would have been classified differently at different times between approximately 5 and 11 years. One of the two male slow learners would have been classified as such each of the three times he was tested, but the other male slow learner had a verbal or performance IQ of at least 90 the first two times he was tested, but not the third, and most recent, time. However, for male poor readers mean IQ was stable, with changes in verbal, performance, and full scale IQ of only 1.1 to 1.9 points from age 5 to 11 years. By contrast, girls showed considerable variability. Their mean verbal IQ dropped nearly 15 points (94.2 to 79.6), although performance IQ decreased only about 4 points. Four of the six slow learners in this follow-up were girls, but at age 5 only one girl would have been defined as a slow learner by the IQ criterion, and this girl was one of the two classified as dyslexic in this grade 6 follow up.

---

[1]One boy had an earlier WPPSI full scale IQ of 104.

TABLE III
Accuracy of the Holbrook Screening Battery (HSB) Total Score Cutoff of ≤88 at
Age Four in Predicting Stanford Achievement Test (SAT) Total Reading at Grade 6

	Boys Total Reading (SAT)				Girls Total Reading (SAT)		
	Poor	Good	Total		Poor	Good	Total
	n	n	n		n	n	n
Screening (HSB)				*Screening (HSB)*			
Low	7	16	23	Low	3	4	7
High	11	186	197	High	3	214	217
Total	18	202	220	Total	6	218	224

When the criteria to differentiate poor readers into dyslexic and slow learning subgroups were used, 4.1% of the total group of 444 subjects met the criteria for dyslexia, and a further 1.4% were slow learners. The male-to-female sex ratio for poor reading was 3:1, but for dyslexia it was 8:1, and for slow learning it was 0.5:1.

Accuracy of Prediction of Poor Reading

The mean HSB total score of the 444 subjects was 118.8 (SD 19.1)[1]. The 6.7% who were lowest on the HSB total scored 88 or lower (1.6 standard deviation below the mean). Of the lowest 6.7%, 23 were boys and 7 were girls. The accuracy of the HSB cutoff score of 88 in predicting good and poor reading seven years later, and after six years of reading instruction, is shown by sex in table III.

The overall accuracy rate for boys was 87.7% (193/220) and for girls, 96.9% (217/224). However, 61% of the boys and 50% of the girls who were poor readers were not identified by the screening cutoff (i.e. they scored above the cutoff), although 95% of good readers were correctly identified. In addition, there were 20 false positives: 16 boys and 4 girls, who scored below the HSB cutoff, but were good readers in grade 6. The least satisfactory result, however, from this use of a single cutoff score on a screening test to predict later reading achievement, was that only 42% of poor readers scored below the cutoff.

Biographical Information

Biographical information, obtained from questionnaires filled out by parents at the time of preschool screening (except for

---

[1]The mean HSB score of subjects no longer in the town was 119.3 (SD 19.97).

handedness, which was observed on screening tests), is shown in table IV, for poor and good readers, boys, girls, and the total group.

There were three significant sex differences: (1) Boys were more often of large birth weight (chi square = 6.28, p<.025); (2) Boys were considered to have an attention deficit disorder (ADD) as preschoolers more often than girls (chi square = 11.78, p < .001); (3) Boys were more frequently delayed in speech or had poor speech articulation at age 4 (chi square = 9.54, p < .005).

No statistical analysis was made for other groups shown in table IV because of the small size of the groups of poor readers. Characteristics that occurred at least twice as frequently among dyslexic subjects and slow learners than among good readers are listed below, with the increase in frequency in parentheses: Dyslexic subjects—large birthweight (2.7), surgery (2.9), family history of learning disability (2.4), birth order 4+ (2.4); slow learners—prenatal problems (2.1), birth problems (2.5), food sensitivity (2.1), family history of learning disability (2.2), SES 4–5 (2.2), surgery (4.4).

The characteristics of children low on the HSB total who were good readers later (false positives) were also examined. Compared with all other subjects, they showed a two-fold or more increase in: low birth weight (3.0), convulsions (6.7), high fever (2.4), surgery (5.6), ADD (2.4). Unlike the poor readers, they did not show a two-fold or more increase in a family history of learning disability. The majority of the false positives were average readers for their grade placement (mean Total Reading score, grade 6.5). Although they were three years ahead of the poor readers, they were two years below the mean of the total group.

The reading scores of the 71 subjects (16%) with the most serious and numerous pregnancy, birth, and neonatal problems were examined. The mean Total Reading score of these subjects was grade 8.5 (SD 2.8). This score is exactly at the mean of the total group.

Improving the Prediction of Reading

Because the use of a cutoff on the HSB resulted in too high a false negative and false positive rate, and in failure to identify more than half the poor readers, a visual inspection of all data (screening scores, biographical information) was made. The search for common characteristics of poor readers was based on an earlier study of 208 third-grade boys, born 1970–1973, including 135 boys of the current study (Badian 1986). In this study the visual inspection method was used for all subjects, but in the earlier study it was used only for boys scoring above the HSB cutoff (115 of whom were also in this study).

TABLE IV
Biographical Information Shown as Percentages, for Good and Poor Readers (Dyslexics, Slow Learners), Boys, Girls, and the Total Group

	Group						
Characteristic	Dyslexic N 18	Slow Learners 6	Poor Readers 24	Good Readers 420	Total Boys 220	Total Girls 224	Total Group 444
Prenatal Problems	27.8	33.3	29.2	16.2	17.7	16.1	16.9
Birth Problems	16.7	33.3	20.8	13.3	13.6	13.8	13.7
Neonatal Problems	38.9	33.3	37.5	20.0	20.9	21.0	20.9
Birth Weight ≤5.5 lbs.	5.6	0	4.2	5.4	4.5	5.8	5.6
Birth Weight ≥8.9 lbs.	27.8	0	20.8	10.2	14.5	7.1	10.8
Food Sensitivity	11.1	16.7	12.5	7.9	9.1	7.1	8.1
Convulsions	5.6	0	4.2	2.9	3.2	2.7	2.9
Fever >105°	11.1	0	8.3	6.9	7.3	6.7	7.0
Serious Illness	22.2	16.7	20.8	19.5	23.2	16.1	19.6
Surgery*	11.1	16.7	12.5	3.8	4.1	4.5	4.3
ADD at age 4	44.4	50.0	45.8	29.3	37.7	22.8	30.2
Speech Delay	38.9	50.0	41.7	27.1	34.5	21.4	27.9
Family History LD	72.2	66.7	70.8	30.0	32.3	32.1	32.2
Nonright-handed	16.7	0	12.5	12.6	12.7	12.5	12.6
SES 4–5	33.3	50.0	37.5	22.4	20.9	25.4	23.2
Birth Order 4+	44.4	33.3	41.7	18.8	21.8	18.3	20.0

*Excluding tonsillectomy and minor external procedures.

TABLE V
Predictive Group Criteria to Differentiate Poor Readers from Good Readers

Essential Criteria	Additional Criteria
Group 1 (boys)	
	At least 2 of:
1. Letters ≤4/13	1. Birthweight ≥9lbs.
2. Fine Motor Total ≥30%ile (Raw ≥14)	2. Birth order 4+
3. Family history (LD or speech disorder)	3. No ADD at age 4
Group 2 (boys)	
	At least 4 of:
1. WPPSI* Arithmetic ≤9	1. WPPSI Information ≤8
2. Fine Motor Total ≤36%ile (raw ≤15)	2. Difficult birth, neonatal problems
3. Letters ≥5/13, Colors ≥6/8,	3. Birth order 1–2
Shapes ≥3/5 (At least 2 of 3)	4. No family history of LD
	5. ADD at age 4
Group 3 (boys)	
1. Speech delay	
2. Family history of LD	
3. Pencil grasp poor (rated 1 or 2)	
4. Language Sample ≤8	
5. Copy Forms ≤4	
6. No pregnancy or birth problems	
7. Birth weight: 5lbs.9ozs.–8lbs.15ozs.	

The visual inspection of data yielded five groups of boys, who were poor readers. None of the six female poor readers exactly met the criteria for any of the boys' groups; but five of the six met a different set of criteria. Each of the 18 boys met the criteria for one of the five groups, and so also did three other boys, who were good readers. Subjects who met group criteria were: Boys: Group 1. Five poor readers (all dyslexic); Group 2. Three poor readers (two dyslexic, one slow learner), one good reader; Group 3. Four poor readers (all dyslexic), two good readers. Group 4. Four poor readers (three dyslexic, one slow learner); Group 5. Two poor readers (both dyslexic)[1]. Girls: Group 6. Five poor readers (two dyslexic, three slow learners).

By using the group criteria shown in table V to differentiate poor readers from good, rather than using a screening test cutoff score, accuracy of prediction of reading improved significantly (chi

---

[1]A severely dyslexic boy who had moved a year before also met these criteria.

TABLE V *continued*

Group 4 (boys)

At least 3 of:

1. Letters ≤4/13, Colors ≤5/8,	1. WPPSI Similarities ≤8
Shapes ≤2/5 (At least 2 of 3)	2. Fine Motor Total ≤22%ile (raw ≤13)
2. WPPSI Information ≤8	3. Gross Motor Total ≥30%ile (raw ≥26)
3. Family history of LD	4. SES 3–5

Group 5 (boys)

At least 5 of:

1. Letters ≤3/13	1. Language Sample ≥10
2. WPPSI Information ≥10	2. Difficult birth, neonatal problems
	3. Birth order 1–3
	4. Serious illness
	5. Ear infections
	6. No ADD at age 4

Group 6 (girls)

At least 3 of:

1. Draw-a-Person ≤4 (Koppitz scoring)	1. WPPSI Arithmetic ≤8
2. Family history of LD	2. WPPSI Sentences ≤7
3. ADD at age 4	3. WPPSI Similarities ≤9
	4. Language Sample ≤8
	5. Gross Motor Total ≤7%ile (raw ≤20)
	6. SES 4–5

*WPPSI scores are given as scaled scores. All other scores are raw scores, unless otherwise specified.

square = 24.74, $p < .001$). The improvement in accuracy is shown, separately by sex, in table VI.

Table VI shows that accuracy in predicting poor reading, by use of group criteria, increased from 42% to 96%, and accuracy in predicting good reading increased from 95% to 99%. The three good readers who met the poor readers' criteria had been referred for evaluation, two as preschoolers, and one in grade 3. One of the three had been defined as a poor reader in the grade 3 follow-up (Badian 1986), and was still a very poor speller (grade 3.3). Another boy, who began to receive special education support at age 3, and who was below the HSB cutoff, still showed a weakness in reading comprehension and language. The third boy was a poor speller (grade 4.1), and had a history of math disability and ADD.

The one girl who was not classified as a poor reader appeared quite different in her characteristics from the other five female poor readers. She was a slow learner who had never been referred for

TABLE VI
Improving Accuracy in Predicting Stanford Achievement Test (SAT) Total Reading
at Grade 6 by Formation of Groups Based on Preschool Screening Scores and
Biographical Data

	Boys Total Reading (SAT)				Girls Total Reading (SAT)		
	Poor	Good	Total		Poor	Good	Total
	n	n	n		n	n	n
Group Criteria				*Group Criteria*			
Meeting Criteria	18	3	21	Meeting Criteria	5	0	5
Not Meeting	0	199	199	Not Meeting	1	218	219
Total	18	202	220	Total	6	218	224

evaluation. Her general slowness in learning was the reason given by one of her teachers for not referring her. No good readers among the girls met the criteria for the girls' group of poor readers.

Early Intervention and Other Special Help
Received by Poor Readers and High-Risk Children

The type of special help received by false positives (low on HSB, but good readers later), valid positives (low on HSB and poor readers later), and false negatives (high on HSB, but poor readers later) is shown in table VII.

As table VII shows, the false negatives were more likely to have received special preschool help than the valid positives. Possibly as a result of the preschool intervention the false negatives scored higher on the HSB and were only about half as likely to be in special early childhood classes in their first two years in school, as either the false or valid positives. However, the majority of children in all three groups (approximately 80% of false positives and negatives, and 90% of valid positives) did receive some type of special help, beginning no later than grade 1. By the time of follow-up, at grade 6, 90% of valid positives and approximately 80% of false negatives were still receiving academic help, but only 20% of false positives still received such help. However, a substantial proportion of the false positives were still receiving speech and/or language therapy (usually one hour per week). Almost all children were integrated into regular classes at grade 6, and the amount of resource room help for reading and related subjects varied from 2½ to 10 hours per week.

TABLE VII

Special Help Received by Poor Readers (Valid Positives, False Negatives) and by Subjects Who Scored Low on the Holbrook Screening Battery Total, but were Good Readers Later (False Positives)

	Group		
	False Positives (n = 20)	Valid Positives (n = 10)	False Negatives (n = 14)
Type of Help	%	%	%
Special Preschool	20.0	10.0	28.6
Starting Grades K–1			
Special Class: 1 year	30.0	40.0	7.1
Special Class: 2 years	30.0	20.0	21.4
Mainstreaming + Tutorial*	20.0	30.0	50.0
Starting After Grade 1			
Mainstreaming + Resource Room	5.0	10.0	14.3
No Help Grades K–5	15.0	0	7.1
Grade 6 Help			
Special Class (LD)	0	10.0	7.1
Mainstreaming + Resource Room (Including Reading)	5.0	80.0	71.4
Mainstreaming + Resource Room (No reading)	15.0	0	0
Speech Therapy Only	35.0	10.0	0
No help	45.0	0	21.4

*Includes academic tutoring, and speech and language therapy.

DISCUSSION

Poor Reading and Dyslexia: Incidence

In this follow-up study of all children born from 1971 through 1975 living in a small suburban community, who were tested as pre-schoolers and were still attending schools in the community seven years later, 4.1% of the 444 subjects were found to be dyslexic, and 1.3% to be slow learners, with poor reading skills. This rate of 4.1% for dyslexia is almost the same as that found in an earlier study of all the children in this community, who were in grades 3–6 in 1980 (Badian 1984).

Although different labels have been used by different re-searchers, and different methods and criteria have been used to de-fine a serious reading disability, recent studies of populations of

English-speaking children in Britain (Rutter 1978; Yule and Rutter 1976), Australia (Jorm et al. 1986), New Zealand (Silva, McGee, and Williams 1985), and the United States (Satz and Morris 1981) have been remarkably consistent in reporting a prevalence of reading disability or dyslexia of 4 to 5 percent.

Dyslexia is reported to be several times more frequent among boys. By contrast, poor reading associated with low intellectual functioning, tends to be more evenly distributed among the sexes. Rutter found the sex ratio to be 3.3:1 for specific reading retardation, but only 1.3:1 for general reading backwardness (Yule and Rutter 1976). The corresponding sex ratios among New Zealand children were 7:1 and 3:1 (Silva et al. 1985). In the current study, the sex ratio for dyslexia was 8:1, and for slow learning 0.5:1.

There has been research linking left-handedness and dyslexia (e.g. Geschwind 1983). In this study, the incidence of non-right-handedness (left- and mixed-handedness) was 12.6%, equally distributed by sex. There was no significant increase in nonright-handedness among dyslexic subjects (16.7%), or among total poor readers (12.5%). The Isle of Wight studies also failed to find an excess of left-handedness among poor readers (Yule and Rutter 1976).

Prediction of Reading for Individual Children

The percentage of subjects who were poor readers in an earlier study of the community (Badian 1984) was taken as the base rate to determine the number of subjects at risk for poor reading. Although, overall, the cutoff on the HSB correctly identified 92% of the subjects as good or poor readers at grade 6, 58% of the poor readers were not identified. Furthermore, two-thirds of the children who scored below the HSB cutoff score were good readers.

Because of concern about mispredictions for individual children, in spite of a fairly high multiple correlation (.65) of the screening test (HSB) variables with third grade reading, Badian (1986) examined all the data available for the 189 boys who scored above the HSB cutoff score. In a stepwise regression no biographical variable made a contribution, but visual inspection of both biographical data and screening test scores led to four sets of criteria for poor readers, and correct classification of all but two subjects as good or poor readers.

As a preliminary part of the current study, cluster analyses were computed, with the screening scores and biographical data of the boys, as variables. Although meaningful clusters were formed, the clustering technique did not improve accuracy of prediction of reading. Hence, the visual inspection method was applied to the data available for all subjects. In the earlier study (Badian 1986) subjects who scored below the HSB cutoff were investigated separately, and in a different manner, from those who scored above the cutoff. The four sets of predictive criteria from the study of third grade boys were the starting points in the current study, although there was no strong expectation that the sets of criteria for grade 6 subjects would be identical with those applicable at grade 3. Three of the five sets of criteria to identify grade 6 boys, who were poor readers, were very similar to those established for grade 3 boys. The fourth set of criteria applied only to boys who scored below the HSB cutoff, and who would not have been included in the third-grade visual inspection. The fifth set had no precedent in the earlier study, and the sixth set applied only to girls, who had not been studied previously in this way.

The percentage of boys who met a set of criteria to identify poor readers was 9.5 (including three good readers), and the percentage of girls was 2.2. In a tentative validation of the sets of criteria, the records of the 342 boys and 346 girls, born in the years immediately following the birth-years of the subjects in this study (1976–1980), were examined. Screening test scores and parent questionnaires were available for these 688 children. Approximately 12% of the boys and 3% of the girls met a set of criteria (with two boys meeting two sets). A substantial proportion of these 688 children will not be available for follow-up at grade 6, and some have already moved out of the community. How many of the children will be poor readers by late sixth grade remains to be seen. However, a high proportion of these younger children meeting criteria for poor readers are known to be dyslexic or are slow learners.

By classifying the 444 subjects of this study according to their screening test scores and background characteristics, it was possible retrospectively to identify 96% of poor readers, compared with only 42%, when the HSB cutoff score was the criterion. Identification of good readers increased from 95% to 99%.

For three of the five groups of male poor readers, inability to name most capital letters at age 4 was one of the most salient predictive characteristics. These boys could name no more than 3 or 4 letters out of 13, compared with an average of 8 to 9 for preschool children in the community. The three groups differed in other ways, however. The first group of boys, all of whom were dyslexic, had a positive family history of learning disability. They displayed a relative strength in fine motor tasks, as preschoolers, were not noted to have attention problems (ADD), and they tended to be later-born children of large birth-weight. Most of these boys were higher in performance than verbal IQ, when older. Boys in another of these three groups (Group 4) were poor in naming colors and/or shapes, as well as in letter-naming. As preschoolers they were low on both verbal and fine motor tasks, but were relatively strong in gross motor skills. They also had a positive family history of learning disability and were of lower SES. Although the boys of group 4 obtained low HSB total scores, their mean verbal and performance IQs at follow-up were similar to those of group 1, and three of the four were classified as dyslexic. Group 5 boys, by contrast, although poor in letter-naming, were at least average on verbal tasks, but had a history of birth and neonatal problems, serious illness, and ear infections. The two boys in this group, and also the severely dyslexic boy who had moved away, all had above average verbal IQ, when first evaluated at 4 to 6 years, with significantly lower performance IQ.

Among the other two groups of boys, group 2 subjects showed both verbal and nonverbal weaknesses at age 4, but no serious deficit in naming letters, colors, etc. They tended to be first- or second-born children, who had no family history of learning disability, but had had difficult births, and displayed ADD characteristics as preschoolers. The last group of boys (group 3) has much in common with the "articulatory and graphomotor dyscoordination" dyslexic subgroup described by Mattis (1978). These boys, who had family history of learning disabilities, were of normal birth weight, and had no prenatal or birth problems, presented with a history of a speech delay, poor spoken language skills, a poor pencil grasp, and relatively low pencil and paper copying skills. These boys, for the most part, showed no difference between verbal and performance IQ, when older. All were classified as dyslexic in this follow-up. A number of boys who became good readers displayed most of the group 3 characteristics, at age 4. For those with no family history of learning disability, the long-term prognosis was good, although there tended to be reading difficulties in the early grades.

Most of the girls who were poor readers were slow learners at follow-up. As preschoolers they had low scores on most verbal tasks. They were also poor at drawing a person, and showed a severe deficit on gross motor tasks. There were signs of ADD at age 4, they had a family history of learning disability, and tended to be of below average SES. The most remarkable finding about the small number of female poor readers was that verbal intelligence was usually average (>90) at the time of the first evaluation at age 5. However, later verbal IQ was significantly lower, and below 90 in every case. The male poor readers did not show such a change.

Comparatively little research has focused on dyslexic females or on female poor readers. In this study of virtually all of the children in a community entering school over a 5-year period, a minimal number of girls (less than 3%) were poor readers. However, results suggest that, when a girl is a poor reader at age 11 or 12, low full scale IQ, and, in particular, low verbal IQ is usual, and there is likely to be a family history of learning disability. The male poor readers showed much more variability in their characteristics than did the females, and in only three of the five boys' groups of poor readers was a positive family history a necessary criterion. Gualtieri and Hicks (1985) stressed that neurodevelopmental disorders of childhood, such as dyslexia, are largely mediated by the genotype in females, and by a genotype with environmental interaction in males.

In this study most male poor readers were classified as dyslexic, but most of the females as slow learners because, in the girls, neither verbal nor performance IQ was average. Among the boys studied by Satz (Satz and Morris 1981), the dyslexic poor readers could not be distinguished from the nondyslexic along any of several dimensions. Satz concluded that his results raised serious doubts as to the clinical or research value of the diagnosis of dyslexia, at least as applied to the general population of white male school children. Although Yule and Rutter (1976) argued that specific reading retardation and general reading backwardness are associated with different rates of educational progress and different characteristics, the two groups overlapped considerably, with no fewer than 76 children in common. Among the boys of this study the two classified as slow learners were similar in their reading problems, and in most other respects, to the majority, who were classified as dyslexic.

False Positives

The 20 children in this population, who appeared to be at risk as preschoolers, because of low HSB scores, but who were satisfactory readers later (false positives), tended to have a history of low birth weight, convulsions, high fever, and surgery. At age four they showed signs of ADD, but they were no more likely than other good readers to have a family history of learning disability. It is probable that low birth weight and illness in infancy and early childhood may have delayed the progress of the false positives, so that they scored low on the preschool screening test. However, with special help in school, and no strong genetic predisposition to dyslexia, they were much more successful at learning to read than the valid positives, most of whom had a family history of reading disability. The genetic contribution of dyslexia has been well attested (DeFries 1985; Smith and Goldgar 1986). Although the false positives scored low on the total HSB as preschoolers, only one of them met a set of the predictive criteria used to identify poor readers. Hence, with application of the group criteria only one of the 20 would still be classified as a false positive.

Evaluation of the false positives following screening revealed some serious underlying conditions, including a hearing loss, a petit mal seizure disorder not previously diagnosed, a severe cogenital heart deficit, and muscular dystrophy. In spite of these and other problems, reading was acquired with relatively little difficulty by most false positives. Many other children in this population scored well on the HSB and were average or superior readers later, in spite of such conditions as cerebral palsy, hearing loss (associated with maternal rubella), juvenile diabetes, cystic fibrosis, serious birth defects, histories of serious illness, and pregnancy and birth complications.

The general impression received from the study of this population is that most children acquire reading skills with little or no difficulty, in spite of adverse histories. A history of birth trauma, chronic illness, etc. appears to be associated with delays in development and difficulties in school only in a minority of cases. The small proportion of children who do have serious difficulty in acquiring reading skills have, with very few exceptions, a family history of learning disability, although a substantial proportion of slow learners also has a history of prenatal and birth problems.

Special Help Received by Poor Readers and High-Risk Children

Most children scoring below the HSB cutoff (valid and false positives) began to receive special help at, or soon after, kindergarten entry, and a minority had been in a special preschool class. A higher proportion of false negatives than valid positives had received special preschool help. This early intervention may have increased their scores on the screening test and made it appear that they were in need of little, or no, further help. Because they appeared to be more capable, false negatives were less than half as likely as the false and valid positives to be in a special early childhood class in the first two years of school. However, the majority of them (about 80%) did receive some type of special help beginning no later than first grade. The amount and type of special help received by valid and false positives in the first two years of school was very similar. Therefore, the significantly better progress in reading skills of the false positives cannot be accounted for by any difference in instruction.

The poor readers of this study progressed slowly in reading, in spite of well designed early childhood programs stressing language and other skills thought to underlie reading, and in spite of continuing special help for the majority. Similar findings with regard to progress in reading were reported in a study of all children in this community born in 1970 (Badian 1988). The literature abounds with studies indicating that the academic outlook for children with early reading problems is poor. (For a review see Schonhaut and Satz 1983). The children for whom early intervention appears to be most effective are those who, like the false positives in this study, are delayed as preschoolers because of birth trauma, illness, etc., but who do not have a family history of learning disability or dyslexia.

Conclusions

The current study was undertaken because, although most screening tests can accurately predict which children will become good readers (e.g. Feshbach et al. 1974; Satz et al. 1978), they are much less accurate in identifying future poor readers. The prognosis for many children with reading problems is not good, but we can assume that, without special intervention, the reading skills of dyslexic children would be even more impaired. Schonhaut and Satz (1983) concluded that exposure to an intensive reading method, such as the Orton-Gillingham program, is a factor in better academic outcome. If future dyslexic children can be differentiated from other children appearing to be at risk, at an early age, they can be taught more intensively and by methods demonstrated to be more effective for dyslexic children.

An attempt was made to determine which children will be persistent poor readers by scrutinizing screening test scores and other information known about each child for sets of characteristics shown by dyslexic children and other poor readers as preschoolers, but not by most good readers. If, in the future, a young child meets the predictive criteria for one of the groups of poor readers, it is this child who should receive the most intensive early help available, and the advantage of special reading techniques. Other children appearing at risk are likely to improve with more limited special help of a general remedial type.

As the findings are based on a local screening battery with its own norms, it is not known whether similar results would be obtained with other screening batteries or with other populations. The findings reported here may lead other researchers to look for similar ways of prospectively identifying individual poor readers, using biographical information and available screening tests. Meanwhile, the findings must be validated on further groups of children in the same community.

REFERENCES

Badian, N. A. 1982. The prediction of good and poor reading before kindergarten entry: A 4-year follow-up. *Journal of Special Education* 16:309–318.
Badian, N. A. 1984. Reading disability in an epidemiological context: Incidence and environmental correlates. *Journal of Learning Disabilities* 17:129–136.
Badian, N. A. 1986. Improving the prediction of reading for the individual child: A four-year follow-up. *Journal of Learning Disabilities* 19:262–269.
Badian, N. A. (1988). The prediction of good and poor reading before kindergarten entry: A nine-year follow-up. *Journal of Learning Disabilities* 21:98–103.
Colligan, R. C., and Bajuniemi, L. E. 1984. Multiple definitions of reading disability: Implications for preschool screening. *Perceptual and Motor Skills* 59:467–475.
DeFries, J. C. 1985. Colorado Reading Project. In D. B. Gray and J. F. Kavanagh (eds.). *Biobehavioral Measures of Dyslexia*. Parkton, MD: York Press.
Eisenberg, L. 1978. Definitions of dyslexia: Their consequences for research and policy. In A. L. Benton and D. Pearl (eds.). *Dyslexia: An Appraisal of Current Knowledge*. New York: Oxford University Press.
Feschbach, S., Adelman, H., and Fuller, W. W. 1974. Early identification of children with high risk of reading failure. *Journal of Learning Disabilities* 7:639–644.
Finucci, J. M. 1978. Genetic considerations in dyslexia. In H. R. Myklebust (ed.). *Progress in Learning Disabilities*, Vol. IV. New York: Grune and Stratton.
Fletcher, J. M., and Satz, P. 1984. Test-based versus teacher-based predictions of academic achievement: A three-year longitudinal follow-up. *Journal of Pediatric Psychology* 9:193–203.
Geschwind, M. 1983. Biological associations of left-handedness. *Annals of Dyslexia* 33:29–40.
Gibney, F. J. 1984. *Holbrook*. Boston, MA: Massachusetts Department of Commerce.
Gualtieri, T., and Hicks, R. E. 1985. An immunoreactive theory of selective male affliction. *Behavioral and Brain Sciences* 8:427–441.
Horn, W. F., and O'Donnell, J. P. 1984. Early identification of learning disabilities: A comparison of two methods. *Journal of Educational Pscyhology* 76:1106–1118.
Jansky, J. J. 1978. A critical review of "Some developmental and predictive precursors of reading disabilities". In A. L. Benton and D. Pearl (eds.) *Dyslexia: An Appraisal of Current Knowledge*. New York: Oxford University Press.
Jansky, J., and de Hirsch, K. 1972. *Preventing Reading Failure*. New York: Harper and Row.
Jorm, A. F., Share, D. L. MacLean, R., and Matthews, R. 1986. Cognitive factors of school-entry predictive of specific reading retardation and general reading backwardness: A research note. *Journal of Child Psychology and Psychiatry and Allied Disciplines* 27:45–54.
Koppitz, E. M. 1968. *Psychological Evaluation of Children's Human Figure Drawings*. New York: Grune and Stratton.
Lindquist, G. T. 1982. Preschool screening as a means of predicting later reading achievement. *Journal of Learning Disabilities* 15:331–332.
Lindsay, G. A., and Wedell, K. 1982. The early identification of educationally "at risk" children revisited. *Journal of Learning Disabilities* 15:212–217.
Mann, V. A., and Liberman, I. Y. 1984. Phonological awareness and verbal short-term memory. *Journal of Learning Disabilities* 17:592–599.

Mattis, S. 1978. Dyslexia syndromes: A working hypothesis that works. *In* A. L. Benton and D. Pearl (eds.). *Dyslexia: An Appraisal of Current Knowledge*. New York: Oxford University Press.

McCarthy, J. 1970. *McCarthy Scales of Children's Abilities*. New York: Psychological Corporation.

McKinney, J. D. 1984. The search for subtypes of specific learning disability. *Journal of Learning Disabilities* 17:43–50.

Meehl, P. E., and Rosen, A. 1955. Antecedent probability and the efficiency of psychometric signs, patterns or cutting scores. *Psychological Bulletin* 52:194–216.

Rubin. R. A., Balow, B., Dorle, J., and Rosen, M. 1978. Preschool prediction of low achievement in basic school skills. *Journal of Learning Disabilities* 11:664–667.

Rutter, M. 1978. Prevalence and types of dyslexia. *In* A. L. Benton and D. Pearl (eds.). *Dyslexia: An Appraisal of Current Knowledge*. New York: Oxford University Press.

Satz, P., and Fletcher, J. M. 1979. Early screening tests: Some uses and abuses. *Journal of Learning Disabilities* 12:56–60.

Satz, P., and Morris, R. 1981. Learning disability subtypes: A review. *In* F. J. Pirozzolo and M. C. Wittrock (eds.). *Neuropsychological and Cognitive Processes in Reading*. New York: Academic Press.

Satz, P., Taylor, H. G., Friel, J., and Fletcher, J. 1978. Some developmental and predictive precursors of reading disabilities: A six year follow-up. *In* A. L. Benton and D. Pearl (eds.). *Dyslexia: An Appraisal of Current Knowledge* New York: Oxford University Press.

Schaer, H. F., and Crump, W. D. 1976. Teacher involvement and early identification of children with learning disabilities. *Journal of Learning Disabilities* 9:91–95.

Schonhaut, S., and Satz, P. 1983. Prognosis for children with learning disabilities: A review of follow-up studies. *In* M. Rutter (ed.). *Developmental Neuropsychiatry*. New York: Guilford Press.

Silva, P. A., McGee, R., and Williams, S. 1985. Some characteristics of 9-year-old boys with general reading backwardness or specific reading retardation. *Journal of Child Psychology and Psychiatry and Allied Disciplines* 26:407–421.

Silver, A. A. 1978. Prevention. *In* A. L. Benton and D. Pearl (eds.). *Dyslexia: An Appraisal of Current Knowledge*. New York: Oxford University Press.

Silver, A. A., and Hagin, R. A. 1976. *Search*. New York: Walker Educational Book Corp.

Smith, S. D., and Goldgar, D. E. 1986. Single gene analyses and their application to learning disabilities. *In* S. D. Smith (ed.). *Genetics and Learning Disabilities*. San Diego: College-Hill Press.

Vellutino, F. R. 1979. *Dyslexia: Theory and Research*. Cambridge, MA: M. I. T. Press.

Wechsler, D. 1967. *The Wechsler Preschool and Primary Scale of Intelligence*. Cleveland: Psychological Corporation.

Wechsler, D. 1974. *Wechsler Intelligence Scale for Children-Revised*. New York: Psychological Corporation.

Wilson, B. J., and Reichmuth, M. 1985. Early-screening programs: When is predictive accuracy sufficient? *Learning Disability Quarterly* 8:182–188.

Wolf, M. 1984. Naming, reading, and the dyslexias: A longitudinal overview. *Annals of Dyslexia* 34:87–115.

Yule, W., and Rutter, M. 1976. Epidemiology and social implications of specific reading retardation. *In* R. M. Knights and D. J. Bakker (eds.). *The Neuropsychology of Learning Disorders*. Baltimore: University Park Press.

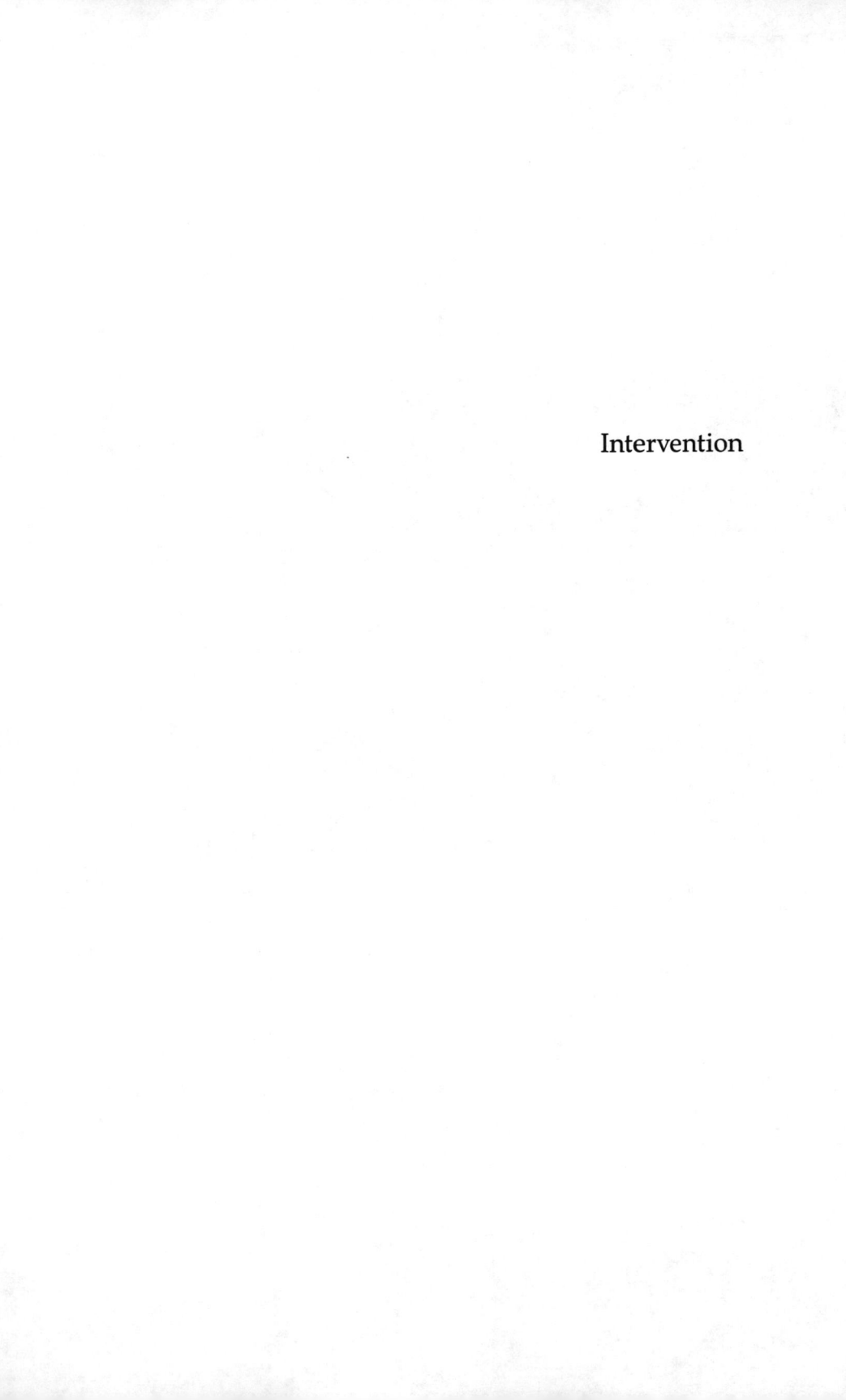

Intervention

5

Slingerland Screening and Instructional Approaches for Children At-Risk for School

Barbara K. Keogh, Sue Sears, and Nancy Royal

There is increasing support for the idea that school failure can be prevented or at least minimized through sensitive and powerful early screening for potential problems. An emphasis on prevention rather than remediation has both intuitive and practical appeal. In human terms the stress and unhappiness associated with failure can be minimized; in economic terms the costs of remediation and special services can be reduced. Thus, there is little argument about the importance of early identification of potential problems, yet there are controversies and differences of opinion about how to accomplish the goal. Several aspects of early identification deserve discussion; both conceptual and methodological, they involve questions of what should be assessed and how and when assessment should take place.

On a conceptual level screening for early identification necessarily involves decisions about the nature of development, the rel-

This study was conducted with support from the Fisher Foundation of Tucson, Arizona, and by Grant HD 11944 from the National Institute of Child Health and Human Development to the Sociobehavioral Research Group of the Mental Retardation Center at UCLA.

evance of particular developmental or child-based domains for learning, and the influences of context or situation on a child's competence in school. On an operational level central issues relate to the technical adequacy of measurement and to the feasibility and practicality of implementation. Both conceptual and operational issues are influenced by the level of identification sought: that is, whether the goal is screening or diagnosis. As emphasized by Cross and Goins (1977) and by Keogh and Daley (1983), screening is an important step in early identification as it serves as a "red flag" or first level indicator. The goal in traditional screening approaches is to identify individuals or subgroups who require further study. In-depth assessment is viewed as the function of diagnosis, and is usually individual and comprehensive. In contrast to diagnosis, many screening procedures do not provide differentiated information on which to base individualized intervention or remediation as they assess a relatively few variables. In some instances, however, screening is more broadly based, and the content is closely tied to instructional programs; in such cases, screening information may be of use in instructional planning. The issue of instructional relevance is important for both screening and diagnosis in schools, yet is often overlooked or untested. This criterion must be included in assessing the utility of screening procedures.

In sum, to be useful, screening techniques must meet certain criteria: they must be appropriately applied with large numbers of children, feasible to administer in terms of time and level of complexity of administration, simple to score, and directly interpretable. In addition, and of obvious importance, the content of the screening measures must have instructional relevance and predictive validity.

The research reported here focussed on the Slingerland Revised PreReading Procedures (Slingerland 1977) as a screening technique for identification of problem learners. School based work with the Slingerland PreReading Procedures demonstrates that they can be given to groups of young children and can be administered and scored by classroom teachers (Royal 1986). In earlier work based on a larger sample of children, Keogh et al. (1987) described the factor structure of the Procedures and identified significant associations between kindergarten screening scores and achievement in the first two grades of school. The procedures, thus, have demonstrated feasibility for screening. However, the predictive validity of the procedures for subsequent achievement of at-risk children and the possible influence of specialized instruction on risk status are uncertain. The present study was carried out (1) to test the power of the Slingerland PreReading Procedures for identifying young school age children as at-risk for achievement, and (2) to begin assessment of the impact of Slingerland instruction on the performance of at-risk children.

Plan of Study

The study was conducted in a large school district in southern California. Kindergarten pupils were screened with the Revised Slingerland PreReading Procedures (Slingerland 1977). The screening scores, combined with recommendations from the teachers, were used to identify pupils as at-risk or non-risk. Approximately half of the at-risk pupils were placed in Slingerland instructional programs, the remaining pupils in conventional classrooms. At the end of grades 1, 2, and 3 all pupils remaining in these schools were tested with the Stanford Achievement test as part of the district testing program. Results reported here are focussed on comparisons among three groups of pupils: at-risk in Slingerland programs, at-risk in conventional programs, and non-risk in conventional programs.

METHODS

Subjects

The Initial kindergarten sample consisted of 433 children (233 boys, 200 girls) enrolled in five schools in a large urban school district. Schools varied from low to middle-high in socioeconomic level and in representation of language/cultural groups. The proportion of Hispanic pupils in schools ranged from 68% in School A to 31% in School E. Only English-speaking children were included in the study. Chronological age mean and standard deviation were 72.56 months, and 4.66 months for the group as a whole. There were no significant age differences between boys and girls. At the end of the kindergarten year children were identified as at-risk or non-risk according to classroom teachers' recommendations and scores on the Slingerland PreReading Procedures (see procedures section). One-hundred and fifty-one, or approximately 35%, of the sample were identified as at-risk and recommended for Slingerland or other special programs. Of the at-risk sample, 59% were boys and 41% were girls. At the end of grade one 97 of the at-risk children were still in District schools. One-third of the at-risk children (N = 33) were in Slingerland classes, 26 were in alternative programs, and 38 were assigned to conventional classes. Placement was in part a function of availability of space in the Slingerland program and parents' wishes. Placement was carried out entirely by district personnel, not the research team. The analyses reported are based on three groups: at-risk Slingerland placed, at-risk conventional placed, and non-risk conventional placed. Follow-up data were not available for children in special education programs. Slingerland kindergarten screening scores for the two at-risk groups and the non-risk group are found in table I.

Complete first grade follow-up data were available for 270 of the original kindergarten sample. The grade one Slingerland samples included 71 children previously identified as at-risk. At the end of second grade, achievement scores were gathered for 165 children, 49 of whom had been identified as at-risk at kindergarten. The third grade sample consisted of 140 children, 47 of whom were in the at-risk category at kindergarten.

TABLE I
Slingerland Factors and Total Scores and
DAP Derived Scores for First Grade Placement Groups

Test	N	M	SD	Range
Factor A				
At-risk/Slingerland	33	10.52	5.22	2 to 22
At-risk/Conventional	38	10.26	4.24	1 to 21
Non-risk/Conventional	85	16.55	4.52	5 to 25
Factor B				
At-risk/Slingerland	33	23.15	5.00	9 to 31
At-risk/Conventional	38	24.97	5.17	12 to 31
Non-risk/Conventional	88	28.61	3.05	13 to 32
Factor C				
At-risk/Slingerland	32	7.97	3.00	3 to 14
At-risk/Conventional	38	9.53	2.81	4 to 15
Non-risk/Conventional	86	13.57	1.78	10 to 16
Factor D				
At-risk/Slingerland	33	11.24	2.67	4 to 16
At-risk/Conventional	37	11.08	2.53	3 to 16
Non-risk/Conventional	86	12.19	2.30	3 to 16
Slingerland Total				
At-risk/Slingerland	32	63.25	8.37	46 to 80
At-risk/Conventional	30	67.06	7.79	48 to 80
Non-risk/Conventional	85	83.97	7.65	66 to 101
DAP Derived IQ				
At-risk/Slingerland	19	105.26	15.82	87 to 150
At-risk/Conventional	30	100.20	19.12	73 to 144
Non-risk/Conventional	73	110.82	18.48	67 to 172

Procedures

The Slingerland PreReading Procedures consist of 12 subtests or dimensions tapping a range of visual, auditory, memorial, and associational domains. As shown in earlier work (Keogh et al. 1987) the 12 dimensions are grouped into 4 clear and distinct factors; Factor A, Visual-Motor Processing; Factor B, Auditory Processing; Factor C, Visual Processing; and Factor D, Language Processing. Two subtests (3 and 10) were found to be independent. The Procedures yield scores for dimensions, factors, and total. In earlier analyses of the PreReading Procedures, Keogh et al. found consistent and strong relationships between kindergarten Slingerland PreReading scores and reading and arithmetic performance at grades 1 and 2. These analyses were carried out using data from the large sample of approximately 433 children, and the findings were based on the group as a whole. Analyses reported here were focussed on particular subgroups of children in an effort to identify more specific child and background correlates of risk.

All testing with the Slingerland PreReading Procedures was done in small groups in the children's classroom by their classroom teachers. Tests were scored by teachers according to the manual of instructions, then reviewed by the Director of the Slingerland program. Follow-up achievement testing with the Stanford Achievement Test was carried out by school district personnel in the spring of the children's first, second, and third grades. Testing was done in the classrooms by the classroom teachers. Achievement test scores were converted to stanines. Results are reported for total reading and total arithmetic scores.

RESULTS

Table II contains summary scores for achievement in reading and arithmetic at grades 1, 2, and 3 for children who were identified in kindergarten as risk or non-risk, and who remained in Slingerland or conventional programs for three consecutive years.

Although the sample sizes for the risk groups are small, the scores allow some comparisons of relative achievement over time. Two points deserve emphasis. First, non-risk children, as a group, consistently ranked higher than their at-risk peers in achievement in reading and arithmetic, these differences were statistically significant at grade 1. At second and third grades only the differences between at-risk Slingerland placed children and the non-risk group

TABLE II
Means and Standard Deviations of Achievement Scores
for At-Risk and Non-Risk Children in Slingerland or
Conventional Instructional Programs for All Three Years*

	Kindergarten At-Risk		Kindergarten Non-Risk
Achievement	Slingerland	Conventional	Conventional
Grade One	N = 33	N = 38	N = 89
Reading Total	3.79 (1.19)	4.66 (1.76)	5.79 (1.77)
Math Total	4.58 (1.06)	4.95 (1.27)	6.25 (1.76)
Grade Two	N = 12	N = 18	N = 57
Reading Total	3.75 (1.77)	4.50 (1.51)	5.46 (1.75)
Math Total	4.25 (1.06)	4.50 (1.47)	5.51 (1.71)
Grade Three	N = 13	N = 13	N = 40
Reading Total	3.92 (1.61)	4.54 (1.51)	5.35 (1.69)
Math Total	3.85 (1.52)	4.92 (1.66)	6.13 (1.82)

*All scores are reported in stanines.

were statistically significant for both reading and arithmetic. Second, in general, at-risk children placed in Slingerland programs scored lower than their conventionally placed at-risk peers, although at all three grade levels the differences were not large enough to be significant statistically. The differences do raise the possibility, however, that more seriously at-risk children were placed in Slingerland programs.

The associations between the kindergarten Slingerland screening scores and subsequent achievement for the three groups of pupils are show in table III.

It should be remembered that for this group as a whole (initial kindergarten N = 433) the correlations between kindergarten Slingerland total scores and reading were .55 and .62 for grades one and two, respectively; comparable values of r for arithmetic were .58 and .61 (Keogh et al. 1987). The values of r shown in table III are substantially lower than those for the group as a whole and vary according to instructional placement group. Despite limitations on interpretation because of the small sample sizes in the at-risk groups at grades 2 and 3, it appears that prediction is more reliable for the non-risk sample. In order to increase the sample size and to make more direct comparisons of the strength of relationships, the at-risk groups were combined. Pearson r for kindergarten screening and achievement scores at grades 1, 2, and 3 for this combined at-risk group were .247, .417 (p = .05), and .253 for reading total scores. Compar-

TABLE III
Correlations of Slingerland Screening Scores
and Achievement at Grades 1, 2, and 3 for
At-Risk and Conventional Instructional Groups

| Achievement | Kindergarten At-Risk Program | | Kindergarten Non-Risk Program |
	Slingerland	Conventional	Conventional
Grade One	N = 32	N = 36	N = 85
Reading Total	.362*	.094	.517**
Arith. Total	.269	−.096	.441**
Grade Two	N = 12	N = 17	N = 55
Reading Total	.384	.347	.492*
Arith. Total	.495	.176	.543**
Grade Three	N = 13	N = 13	N = 39
Reading Total	.296	.111	.412*
Arith. Total	.657*	.082	.507**

*p = .05
**p = .01

able relationships with arithmetic total scores were .103, .289, and .418 (p = .05), respectively. The magnitude of relationships is lower than that for the non-risk sample.

In an effort to identify possible differential relationships between Slingerland factor scores and achievement, Pearson r were computed for the three subgroups using factor means. These findings are reported in table IV. As expected, in general, relationships were higher for the non-risk children than for the at-risk children. However, there was some variability of strength of relationships according to factors. Factor B, an auditory perception factor, had the most consistent relationships with achievement outcomes across groups. When the three placement groups were combined, the relationships between factors and achievement were substantially increased. These results are shown in table V.

DISCUSSION

Results of these analyses must be interpreted cautiously as the sample sizes of the at-risk groups are small, especially at grades 2 and 3. It should be emphasized that the comparisons reported here were focussed specifically on the at-risk pupils in Slingerland

TABLE IV
Relationships Between Slingerland Factor Scores and DAP
to Achievement in Grades 1, 2, and 3 for Instructional Groups

Kindergarten Screening Variables	At-Risk				Non-Risk	
	Slingerland Program N = 32		Conventional Program N = 36		Conventional Program N = 85	
	Reading	Arithmetic	Reading	Arithmetic	Reading	Arithmetic
Grade One						
Factor A	.083	.340*	−.013	−.068	.237*	.134
Factor B	.409*	.189	.174	.004	.47**	.397**
Factor C	.051	−.034	.109	.053	.248*	.179
Factor D	.225	.053	.186	−.070	.300**	.378**
Total	.362*	.269	.094	−.096	.517**	.441**
DAP IQ	−.143	−.163	.143	−.138	.086	−.013
Grade Two	N = 12		N = 18		N = 55	
Factor A	.084	.351	−.232	.061	.157	.055
Factor B	.376	.324	.418	−.012	.492**	.604**
Factor C	.000	.135	.471*	.374	.180	.230
Factor D	.153	.015	.163	.028	.409*	.462**
Total	.384	.495	.347	.176	.492**	.543**
DAP IQ	−.162	−.153	.328	−.114	.081	−.078
Grade Three	N = 13		N = 13		N = 39	
Factor A	.511	.680*	−.493	−.178	.143	.046
Factor B	.176	.261	.195	−.027	.455**	.608**
Factor C	−.201	.033	.338	−.036	.050	.061
Factor D	−.245	.027	−.025	.219	.193	.333*
Total	.296	.657*	.111	.082	.412**	.507**
DAP IQ	−.015	.002	.385	.273	.184	.093

*p = .05
**p = .01

and coventional programs, not on the kindergarten sample as a whole. Earlier analyses (Keogh et al. 1987) of the larger data set revealed statistically significant and meaningful associations between kindergarten screening scores and subsequent achievement. These correlations were replicated in the non-risk group reported here. However, the associations between screening scores and primary grade achievement scores were substantially lower for both at-risk groups, especially the at-risk conventional program sample (see table III). Differences in the magnitude of these associations underscore the somewhat tenuous status of risk as identified early on. Possible reasons for children's poor performance on screening mea-

TABLE V
Relationships Between Slingerland Factors Scores and DAP
to Achievement in Grades 1, 2, and 3: Risk and Non-Risk Groups Combined

Kindergarten Screening Variables	Reading	Arithmetic
Grade One	N = 153	N = 153
Factor A	.358**	.345**
Factor B	.498**	.397**
Factor C	.412**	.375**
Factor D	.303**	.283**
Total	.574**	.517**
DAP IQ	.147	.042
Grade Two	N = 84	N = 84
Factor A	.257*	.250*
Factor B	.504**	.467**
Factor C	.381**	.391**
Factor D	.352**	.338**
Total	.539**	.541**
DAP IQ	.104	−.048
Grade Three	N = 65	N = 65
Factor A	.279*	.353**
Factor B	.400**	.465**
Factor C	.273*	.372**
Factor D	.142	.341**
Total	.448**	.604**
DAP IQ	.206	.143

*p = .05
**p = .01

sures are many, and include cognitive, affective, motivational, linguistic, and cultural/experiential factors. Any one or all of these might reduce performance on a given day, thus, a low test score may be an inaccurate index of potential performance. In contrast, good performance on screening measures is a reasonably good indicator that a child is ready for instruction. Said directly, the predictive power of screening measures may be more reliable for higher scoring pupils than for those who score low.

In addition to possible differences in the reliability of test scores at different performance levels, it may well be that interactions of instructional programs and children's performances vary for different levels or kinds of risk. Examination of stanine mean values suggests that there was a trend for the differences in reading achievement among groups to be somewhat smaller over time. Stanine mean scores increased slightly between first and third grades for the Slingerland placed group, but decreased slightly for the conventionally placed samples. It is not possible to infer from the present data whether this trend was related to the Slingerland instructional program or to other influences, including sample characteristics or measurement limitations. However, from the summary scores reported in table II, it is clear that overall, at-risk children as a group did not achieve as well as their non-risk peers; at all three grades the at-risk groups' achievement scores were lower than those for the non-risk sample. Thus, the Slingerland Procedures at kindergarten did have predictive validity for identifying children at risk for achievement.

It should be noted, too, that the Slingerland factor scores differed in strength of association with achievement scores according to groups. Factor B, an auditory perception factor with major language demands, was the best predictor of subsequent achievement in both reading and arithmetic for the non-risk conventional program sample. Factor B was also the best predictor of reading for the at-risk Slingerland placed group for the first two grades. However, at grade 3, Factor A, a visual perception factor, was more strongly associated with achievement. No pattern of factor associations with achievement was discernible for the at-risk conventional program group.

One interpretation of the inconsistent correlations of screening scores and achievement scores for the at-risk groups is that pupil-program interactions may vary according to the nature of risk. That is, risk children may be differentially vulnerable to the content and methods of instruction. At grade one the at-risk Slingerland group performed better in arithmetic than in reading. The Slingerland program is directed specifically at reading, and by grade three the reading scores had improved slightly, although the gains were not large enough to reach statistical significance; at the same time, the arithmetic scores decreased slightly. For the conventionally placed at-risk group the reading score decreased somewhat and the arithmetic score was stable. Given the limits of this study it is not possible to test directly the possible interactions between pupils and instructional methods. However, the notion of differential risk clearly deserves further study.

Finally, examination of our data by schools suggested that factors other than children's abilities were important in school success. To illustrate, 34% of the children identified as at-risk at kindergarten remained in the school district at the end of the third grade; the comparable figure for the non-risk group was 40%. Examination of the total sample in terms of socioeconomic status (SES) of the schools revealed that there was a higher attrition rate in the lower SES than in the higher SES schools. In the highest SES schools the percent of kindergarten children still in school at grade 3 was 46%. In the lowest SES schools the comparable figure was 22%. If consistency of instruction has an impact on achievement in school, than a large number of children in this sample were at-risk whatever their individual attributes or abilities.

GENERALIZATIONS AND IMPLICATIONS

We can draw only tentative generalizations from the results of this study as the number of children in the samples was small and the educational status of the children at the end of elementary school is not known. Overall, our findings are consistent with a growing research literature which argues for the complexity of early identification and which infers the need for careful and long-term studies of risk (see Garmezy and Rutter 1983; and Werner and Smith 1982 for discussion of major longitudinal research on this topic). The present report was based on work with Slingerland approaches to screening and early identification. Yet, our findings, along with results of other investigators (e.g., Hinshaw et al. 1986; Silver and Hagin 1980; Satz et al. 1978), identify some important implications for future work on this topic.

First, we wish to emphasize that risk for achievement is not simple to conceptualize or to assess. Risk is clearly not captured by a single test or set of screening procedures. Risk is a multivariate construct that includes child characteristics and a range of social, economic, and instructional factors. In addition to child attributes, a whole set of familial and social influences may contribute to risk or non-risk status. These personal, social/environmental, and instructional influences may work separately or in tandem to enhance or dimish school performance. Thus, it is clear that we must broaden our notion of risk and assess many factors or conditions that contribute to risk or non-risk status. The traditional model for early screening and identification has been to focus specifically, often exclusively, on the children themselves. Further, most screening measures assess a relatively narrow range of children's abilities. Central to the present discussion is the issue of what should be included as screening data. We suggest that early identification procedures must take into account children's social-behavioral as well as cognitive, perceptual, and motor abilities, and that situational or contextual as well as child characteristics must be considered in early identification decisions.

Considering first child characteristics, there is considerable evidence to suggest that children's temperament influences their school experiences (Keogh 1982; Keogh and Burstein 1988). Classroom behaviors such as staying in one's seat, following the teacher's directions, and getting along with other children have also been shown to be important contributors to success or failure in school (Forness, Guthrie, and Hall 1976). These behavioral competencies are different from the more cognitive or perceptual tasks of copying a circle or square or repeating words or numbers from memory. The latter provide important but limited snapshots of children's readiness for school. We propose that, at the very least, behavioral and cognitive domains are important sources of early identification information, and that both should be represented in screening approaches.

Second, from a somewhat different but related perspective we emphasize that the findings in this study demonstrate that socioeconomic variables are strongly associated with children's school experiences, even to the continuity of their schooling. This is not a new finding but underscores the question of the predictive value of traditional screening approaches for children from particular economic, social, or cultural backgrounds. It is clear that school districts, schools, and classrooms differ in curricula, in instructional approaches and emphases, and in the competencies and philosophies of their instructional staffs. These differences may affect the nature of the school program for individual children. Given these differences, it should not surprise us that early identification data are not 100% accurate. Early test or screening data are only one part of a multivariate picture of children's readiness for school. Thus, accurate assessment of children's readiness for school must include a range of data that tap both child and situational factors.

Third, the implications of identification as at-risk need careful consideration. Using the traditional child-focussed model of risk, it is possible to classify accurately approximately two thirds to three fourths of kindergarten age children as risk or non-risk. However, using this screening model, a substantial number of children are misclassified or misidentified, especially in the at-risk groups. The implications or possible negative consequences of misclassification as at-risk have not been well documented, but we must raise questions of possible expectancy effects on teachers' and parents' perceptions of children when at-risk identification occurs. We must also consider possible effects of children's self-perceptions on their attitudes and motivations in school.

Finally, the findings from this study, like many other reports of early screening, are limited by the relatively short time to followup. From our work we know how the study children achieved through the third grade only. Werner and Smith's (1982) longitudinal study of a cohort of "at-risk" children documented that some of the children grew stronger over time and that risk status was in part related to age and social-situational demands. In addition to differences in situational demands, there are real changes in the demands inherent in school tasks. In this regard, Satz et al. (1978) found that perceptual skills were strongly associated with early reading skill, but that language competence became more important at higher grades. In a sense, these findings infer that our approach to early identification must involve the documentation of discontinuities as well as continuities of development and achievement. The search for understandable and predictable discontinuities is a formidable task, yet will likely lead to more accurate and more powerful approaches to early screening. Statistics documenting the number of children who achieve below grade level in basic school tasks and/or who develop specific learning problems are sobering, and identification and intervention are important steps in reducing later school failure for many children. Screening approaches such as the Slingerland can provide important information about children's readiness for formal instruction in school. The findings in this study suggest that the Slingerland Procedures do, with reasonable accuracy, identify children at-risk for school. The Procedures are useful and feasible as one component of screening. Yet, it is clear that there are many complexities and potential problems in the development of effective and equitable early screening techniques. The difficulties of the task should not deter our efforts, however, as the educational futures of many children are closely tied to our ability to identify and provide appropriate instructional support.

REFERENCES

Cross, L., and Goin, K. W. 1977. *Identifying Handicapped Children: A Guide to Case Finding, Screening, Diagnosis, Assessment, and Evaluation.* New York: Walker & Co.

Forness, S., Guthrie, D., and Hall, R. 1976. Followup of high risk children identified in kindergarten through direct classroom observation. *Psychology in the Schools* 13(1):45–49.

Garmezy, N., and Rutter, M. (eds.) 1983. *Stress, Coping, and Development in Children.* New York: McGraw-Hill.

Hinshaw, S., Morrison, D., Carte, C., and Cornsweet, C. 1986. Factor composition of the SEARCH scanning instrument in kindergarten. *Journal of Psychoeducational Assessment* 4(2):95–101.

Keogh, B. K. 1982. Children's temperament and teachers' decisions. *In* R. Porter and G. M. Collins (eds.) *Temperament Differences in Infants and Young Children*. London: Pitman.

Keogh, B. K., and Burstein, N. D. 1988. The relationship of temperament to preschool children's interactions with peers and teachers. *Exceptional Children* 54(5):456–461.

Keogh, B. K., and Daley, S. 1983. Early identification: One component of comprehensive services for at-risk children. *Topics in Early Childhood Special Education* 3(3):7–16.

Keogh, B. K., Royal, N., Sears, S., Daley, S., and Pelland, M. 1987. The factor structure and predictive power of the Slingerland PreReading Screening Procedures. (Technical Report). Los Angeles, CA: University of California.

Royal, N. 1986. *The Long Term Consequences of Specific Language Disabilities: The Secondary Years*. Doctoral dissertation, University of San Diego.

Satz, P., Taylor G., Friel, J., and Fletcher, J. 1978. Some developmental and predictive presursors of reading disabilities: A six year followup. *In* A. L. Benton and D. Pearl (eds.) *Dyslexia: An Appraisal of Current Knowledge*. New York: Oxford University Press.

Silver, A., and Hagin, R. 1980. An interdisciplinary model for the prevention of learning disabilities. *In* R. M. Knights and D. J. Bakker (eds.) *Treatment of Hyperactive and Learning Disabled Children: Current Research*. Baltimore: University Park Press.

Slingerland, B. H. 1977. *Revised PreReading Screening Procedures*. Cambridge, Mass.: Educators Publishing Service.

Werner E. E., and Smith, R. 1982. *Vulnerable but Invincible: A Longitudinal Study of Resilient Children and Youth*. New York: McGraw-Hill.

6

Studies of the Effects of Teaching Auditory Segmenting Skills Within the Reading Program

Diane J. Sawyer

The relationship between auditory segmentation of phonemic units and reading acquisition is well established. Children who are poor phonemic segmenters when introduced to reading instruction, tend to be less skilled word readers at some later time (see Downing and Valtin 1984; Yaden and Templeton 1986 for reviews). Further, low literate adults appear to be quite limited in the ability to segment phonemes (Read and Ruyter 1985; Morais, Cary, Allegria and Bertelson 1979; Dougherty 1981) as are dyslexics (Russell 1982; Torneus 1984) and the reading-disabled population (Fox and Routh 1983; Beech and Harding 1984; Kamhi and Catts 1986; Ellis and Large 1987). Increasingly, researchers are recommending inclusion of tests of phonological segmentation to identify children who may be "at risk" for success in reading (Blachman 1983, Mann 1984; Share, Jorm, MacLean, and Matthews 1984; Stanovich, Cunningham, and Cramer 1984). Further, many researchers over the years have suggested that if phonological awareness is not established when reading instruction begins, reading programs should provide for direct teaching of segmenting (Liberman 1974; Rosner 1974; Wallach and

Wallach 1976; Williams 1979: Fox and Routh 1984; Juel, Griffith, and Gough 1986; Byrne 1984). Some also suggest that the instructional method used to introduce reading be selected so that children who have not developed phonological awareness are taught using a whole word or whole language approach while those who have established phonological awareness are introduced to reading via a phonics approach (Bryant and Impey 1986; Mann 1984; Huba 1984; Ehri 1978; Henderson 1980; Rowe and Cunningham 1983; Yopp 1985). To date, I have found no studies that have attempted to test the validity of those various recommendations with large samples in school settings. However, the data generated by a series of three longitudinal studies designed to validate a test of auditory segmentation (Sawyer 1987) might serve such a purpose. Children in these studies were given tests of auditory segmentation of words and syllables or phonemes at various times in their kindergarten and/or first grade years. Training in auditory segmentation at each level not yet mastered was provided in kindergarten and/or first grade. Further, in conjunction with the third study, the established instructional program was changed for those who were segmenting at the word or phrase level. A predominantly sound-symbol program was replaced with the language experience approach with emphasis on whole language and on learning personally important words as whole units.

The questions addressed in this report involve a retrospective examination of data gathered in conjunction with this series of longitudinal studies. This examination of the data seeks to clarify the relationships between early segmenting performance and subsequent reading achievement when training in segmenting is provided and when the beginning reading approach is more compatible with individual levels of attainment in segmenting. Specifically, this retrospective investigation addresses the following questions: (1) Is later reading achievement among poor segmenters in kindergarten or first grade distinguishable from that of average or superior segmenters when their beginning reading program is supplemented with training in segmentation? (2) Do poor achievers within such a program demonstrate patterns of performance on measures of auditory segmentation, or other available readiness measures, that might assist in the early identification of "at risk" individuals? (3) What insights might be gained regarding reading failure through examination of the tests records and personal files of the poorest readers in the three cohorts?

METHOD

Subjects

The subjects were enrolled in a suburban school system in central New York State. The district serves a varied population including village, suburban, and rural residents. The socio-economic base is broad with family incomes ranging from below $5,000 to above $75,000. Parent education ranges from less than eight grades of schooling to the completion of doctoral degrees.

Data were collected on 565 children in three cohorts. The first cohort consists of all children enrolled in first grade in the school system (N = 265 at onset). The second and third cohorts consist of only those children entering kindergarten in that school system who had participated in the kindergarten screening in July prior to school entrance (N = 129 and 171 respectively at onset). The average I.Q. within each cohort was 105, 108, and 108 respectively with individual scores ranging from 65 to 140, 72 to 134, and 77 to 143 respectively.

Reading Program

This school system is committed to beginning formal reading instruction in kindergarten for those children considered "ready" for the demands of the published materials in use. The Houghton-Mifflin basal reading series (Dunn, Pescosolido, and Hayward 1978) constitutes the core of the program. However, children believed to be "at risk," based on kindergarten screening, a reading readiness test, and teacher report, were assigned to *Distar* (Englemann and Bruner 1974) as an entre to reading in either kindergarten or grade 1. *Distar* involves a sound-symbol approach to beginning reading. *Distar* was replaced with the language experience approach (LEA), a vehicle for whole language instruction, when the third cohort entered kindergarten.

A "Supplementary Language Program," which I designed at the onset of the longitudinal studies was incorporated into the reading program for all kindergarten and grade 1 students. This supplement was intended to help children become aware of increasingly smaller elements of the spoken language. Several studies have indicated a developmental progression in awareness of language units from words to syllables to sounds. Individual administrations of a test of auditory segmentation indicated the size unit each child could segment (word, syllable, sound). Based on their segmenting performance, children were provided supplementary (to the reading program) experiences for 5 to 10 minutes daily in their classrooms. These activities were designed to promote word or syllable or phoneme awareness. These activities (detailed in Sawyer et al. 1985) included having children locate separate words in a familiar phrase or sentence that is written on the board and "read" in unison by the teacher and reading group (e.g., "Who's been sitting in my chair?"). Children in the word awareness group also "slotted" words in incomplete sentences (e.g., "An apple is _____."), taking turns supplying a word that made sense and "rereading" each new sentence.

Similar beginning activities for the word-part awareness group called attention to inflectional endings added to words when the verb was changed ("I can run." "I am run _____.") thus making the original word look and sound longer. More sophisticated levels of syllable awareness and most phoneme awareness activities were drawn from lessons in the Auditory Motor Program (Rosner 1973).

In the second year of the longitudinal studies, when the third cohort entered school, the language experience approach replaced Distar reading for all "at risk" kindergarten and first-grade children. Word awareness activities were then typically developed within the context of the dictated stories.

Data Sources

Children in the first cohort were administered a test of word and phoneme segmentation in October and again in June of first grade. Results of school administered standardized reading achievement tests were collected in May of their first, second, and third grade years.

Children in the second cohort were administered the same tests of word and phoneme segmentation. Data were collected in October and June of both kindergarten and first grade. In addition, test results were collected from kindergarten screening conducted in July prior to school entrance, and from the annual administration of standardized reading tests at the end of each grade, one through three.

The third cohort was tested for auditory segmenting ability on three occasions during their kindergarten year. First, an abbreviated test of word segmentation and a test of syllable segmentation were administered as part of the kindergarten screening battery in July prior to school entrance. Next, a test of word, syllable, and phoneme segmentation was administered in January. Finally, the same test of word and phoneme segmentation adminstered to the two previous cohorts, was administered in June. Again, results of the kindergarten screening and end-of-year reading achievement tests for grades 1, 2, and 3 were collected. Results of a group intelligence test adminstered routinely in the spring of first grade were also collected for all three cohorts.

The specific tests considered useful for the present retrospective analysis are listed below along with brief descriptions of tasks, where needed.

Test of Auditory Segmentation. (Experimental version of the *Test of Awareness of Language Segments* [Sawyer 1987].) Examiner reads aloud a sentence or word. The child is asked to use small wooden blocks to show the component words or syllables or sounds, depending on the subtest. As each block is drawn from the pile available, the child is asked to name it—give the word it stands for in a sentence or the syllable or sound it represents in a word. Children in the first two cohorts were asked to respond to 18 sentences that increased in length from two to ten words, and 18 one syllable words made up of from two to four phonemes. Children in the third cohort responded to 10 sentences (2 to 6 words) and 20 words containing 1–3 syllables, during the July testing. In January, they were asked to respond to 10 sentences and 16 words—10 were to be segmented into 2 or 3 syllables and 6 into phonemes. In June this group took the same 36 item test administered to the first two cohorts.

Iowa Tests of Basic Skills (Hieronymous, Lindquist, and Hoover 1978). Scores on two subtests, Vocabulary and Reading, were of particular interest for this retrospective study. The Vocabulary subtest requires reading words and selecting one that describes a picture or has meaning similar to another. The Reading subtest requires reading sentences and/or stories at succeeding grade levels and answering questions. This test was administered in the spring of each year.

Gates-MacGinitie Reading Tests—Readiness Skills (Gates and MacGinitie 1966). Administered in October of kindergarten to aid in the establishment of instructional groups. Consists of seven subtests: Listening Comprehension, Auditory Discrimination, Visual Discrimination, Following Directions, Letter Recognition, Visual Motor Coordination, Auditory Blending. Yields a weighted score which was converted to a percentile score.

Cognitive Abilities Test (Thorndike, Hagen, and Large 1971). A group test of verbal intelligence administered in the spring of grade one.

Peabody Picture Vocabulary Test (Dunn and Dunn 1981). An

individual test of receptive vocabulary administered in July prior to kindergarten. Yields a mental age and intelligence quotient.

Test of Auditory Comprehension of Language (Carrow 1973). An individual test of comprehension of words and various syntactic structures. Administered in July prior to kindergarten, it yields a percentile rank for age.

Anton Brenner Developmental Gestalt Test (Brenner 1964). An individual test of perceptual and conceptual differentiation, considered to be a measure of general social readiness. It was developed to be predictive of reading and number readiness. Administered in July prior to kindergarten, it yields a raw score that may be compared to typical scores obtained by the norming population. These are presented as score ranges obtained by the first through the fourth quartiles.

Letter Names. Upper and lower case letters, printed one per card, are presented individually during the kindergarten screening in July. Raw score is total correctly named of 52 presented.

Procedure

Six years after the initiation of the longitudinal studies, and one year after completion of data collection for the third cohort, achievement profiles were examined in an attempt to discern the relative impact of segmentation training on reading achievement over the span of the studies. To address this question, cut-off points were established within the range of scores obtained on the *Test of Awareness of Language Segments* (TALS). Children in the first and second cohort combined, who were tested in October of grade 1 and who obtained scores of 0–18 (primarily able to segment sentences into words) were considered poor segmenters. Those with scores of 19–23 (some emergent ability to segment phonemes) were considered moderately skilled segmenters. Children with scores of 24–36 (gaining control over phoneme segmentation) were considered highly skilled segmenters. Reading achievement on the *Iowa Tests of Basic Skills* (ITBS) was noted for each of these groups across the primary grades (1–3). T-tests of differences between the means of these three groups were calculated for each year.

Similarly, score cuts established for beginning kindergartners on the TALS were employed to derive groupings of poorly skilled, moderately skilled, and highly skilled segmenters within the third cohort. Score groups of 0–11, 12–17, and 18–30 were imposed. Low performers were establishing control over segmenting words in sentences while the moderately skilled had a beginning knowledge of syllable segmentation. Children in the highly skilled segmenting group had greater facility with syllable segmentation, some were at or near mastery of this unit. Again, reading achievement scores on the ITBS for children in these score groups were averaged for each grade level, first through third. T-tests of the differences between the means were calculated.

To examine the possibility that the performance of the very poorest phonemic segmenters at the end of first grade might reveal useful patterns for identifying children "at risk" in reading, individual achievement was tabulated for grades 1–3 across the first two cohorts.

Similarly, I examined the potential that selected readiness measures and I.Q. might have for predicting reading achievement among the poorest achievers at each grade level. Children in each cohort whose Reading subtest scores placed them below the 36th percentile were identified. This cut-off for the ITBS serves to identify students whose achievement is six or more months below grade placement in first through third grades. Correlations were calculated for intelligence and selected readiness measures with Reading subtest scores for these students at each grade within each cohort. The largest correlations obtained at each grade were squared to estimate the percent of variance a particular variable might explain. SAS™ procedures were applied for all statistical analyses reported in this paper.

Finally, five students were identified whose ITBS Reading subtest scores were consistently below the 36th percentile for grades 1–3, despite reading support services over extended periods. Individual pupil personnel files, containing details of all testing and documentation of all support services offered, were examined. Patterns of strengths and weakness were considered.

RESULTS

Reading Achievement for Three Levels of Segmenting Ability

Table I shows the level of reading achievement attained each year, on the average, by children considered to be poorly skilled, moderately skilled, or highly skilled segmenters at the beginning of first grade. Approximately one-third of these children had received direct instruction in auditory segmentation during their kindergarten year. All received such training in first grade.

On the average, poorly skilled segmenters scored at grade level on standardized achievement tests throughout the primary grades. Moderately skilled segmenters consistently scored some-

TABLE I
Reading Achievement Among Children in Three Different Score Groupings
on the TALS in October of First Grade (Cohorts 1 and 2 combined)

Iowa Subtests Grades 1–3 (N = 380–323)	0–18 (N = 57–78) Low		19–23 (N = 59–66) Mid.		24–36 (N = 207–236) High	
	X̄(Percentile)	S.D.	X̄(Percentile)	S.D.	X̄(Percentile)	S.D.
Vocabulary –1	47.6*	16.5	62.4*	15.6	73.6*	16.3
Reading –1	49.1*	14.8	63.1*	16.1	74.3*	15.8
Vocabulary –2	50.3*	23.0	71.8	16.7	79.8	15.6
Reading –2	49.1*	21.7	67.9*	17.8	76.1*	17.4
Vocabulary –3	56.3*	25.4	67.6*	19.6	79.4*	17.3
Reading –3	43.0*	22.0	60.1*	22.4	71.7*	22.6

*Significantly different from all other means at $P < .05$

what above grade level, and skilled segmenters consistently performed at a level approximately six to nine months above grade placement (based on conversion tables provided in the ITBS manual).

T-tests of differences between the means show that the reading achievement of each segmenting score group is significantly different ($P < .05$) from that of all others for all but one comparison. Achievement on the vocabulary subtest in second grade was not significantly different when highly skilled segmenters were compared with those in the mid range. This same pattern was noted when achievement patterns of the first cohort (all children enrolled at the grade level) was examined independent of that of the second cohort (approximately one-half of the students enrolled at the grade level).

An evaluation of student achievement within the school system over a five year period was completed when the second cohort entered second grade. That report showed first grade reading achievement for the first two years of these longitudinal studies to be considerably improved over previous years. On the average, achievement all along the continuum had risen (the poorest achievers were obtaining higher scores as were the middle and high achieving students). During that period, average intelligence and district demographic variables remained about the same.

The pattern of achievement noted suggests that, on the average, direct instruction in auditory segmentation in kindergarten and/or first grade may increase both segmenting ability and reading achievement. Relatively speaking, however, the poorest segmenters at the beginning of first grade, those who have some skill in segmenting words in sentences but virtually no skill in phoneme segmentation, will continue to lag behind their classmates in reading attainment throughout the primary grades.

Somewhat different patterns were noted, however, for the third cohort. Table II shows the level of reading achievement attained each year, on the average, by children considered to be poorly, moderately, or highly skilled segmenters, at the word and syllable level, at the beginning of kindergarten. As for the first two cohorts, children who had not yet mastered auditory segmentation received direct instruction in kindergarten and in first grade until mastery of phonemic segmenting was established.

On the average, poorly skilled segmenters at the beginning of kindergarten (those who had some skill in word segmentation but virtually no skill in syllable segmentation) scored somewhat above grade level on the ITBS throughout the primary grades. Moderately skilled segmenters (some ability at the syllable level) consistently

TABLE II
Reading Achievement Among Children in Three Score Groupings
on the TALS Administered in July prior to Kindergarten Entrance (Cohort 3)

Iowa Subtests Grade 1 –3 (N = 155–119)	TALS Scores					
	0–11 (N = 10–21) Low		12–17 (N = 36–54) Mid.		18–30 (N = 73–98) High	
	X̄(Percentile)	S.D.	X̄(Percentile)	S.D.	X̄(Percentile)	S.D.
Vocabulary –1	60.5*	22.3	72.9*	19.7	81.4*	14.7
Reading –1	67.9	19.7	74.3	17.8	84.7*	13.5
Vocabulary –2	68.6	22.0	63.7	24.9	78.7*	15.6
Reading –2	67.7	19.3	70.1	26.0	84.1*	15.7
Vocabulary –3	64.1	22.0	67.4	22.8	78.5*	15.1
Reading –3	64.3	15.9	67.6	26.6	73.8	18.2

*Significantly different from all other means at $P < .05$

achieved at a level approximately one-half to one year above grade placement, while those who were highly skilled syllable segmenters at the beginning of kindergarten achieved at a level approximately one to two years above grade placement.

T-tests of differences between the means show that a significant difference ($P < .05$) among groups occurred only for performance on the Vocabulary subtest at the end of grade 1 (word reading). For four comparisons (Vocabulary in grades 2 and 3 and Reading for grades 1 and 2) performance by the poorly skilled and moderately skilled segmenters is not statistically different. On the third grade reading subtest, no group is significantly different from the others.

The pattern of reading achievement noted for highly, moderately, and poorly skilled word and syllable segmenters at entrance to kindergarten suggests a clear advantage for the highly skilled segmenters on word reading (Vocabulary) and on sentence and paragraph comprehension (Reading) through grades 1 and 2. However, poorly skilled and moderately skilled classmates, on the average, demonstrated above average reading achievement throughout the primary grades.

Taken together, these analyses of reading achievement across the three cohorts suggest the following: (1) direct instruction in auditory segmentation, as part of the reading program in kindergarten and grade 1, may have a generally facilitative effect on reading for students who have not mastered phoneme segmenting by the beginning of first grade. (2) When joined to the language experience approach (LEA) to beginning reading, training in auditory segmenting for those who have not mastered word and/or syllable segmentation tends to blur distinctions in reading achievement typically found between low and more skilled segmenters. The reading achievement of poorly skilled and moderately skilled segmenters in the third cohort, when such a strategy for beginning reading instruction was employed, appears superior to that attained by the first two cohorts when the *Distar* program was used with such children. Achievement differences may be due to the fact that LEA initially emphasizes the whole word approach to reading, an emphasis on units more readily identified by poorly skilled segmenters than are the phonemic units emphasized in the letter/sound instruction of *Distar*.

Reading Achievement Among the Poorest Phonemic Segmenters

Most of the research on auditory segmentation identifies phonemic segmenting ability as a principal predictor of subsequent reading achievement. Poor phonemic segmenters at the end of kindergarten or during first grade are generally found among the poorest readers at some later time. However, few studies have included training in phonemic segmenting.

In an attempt to discern whether very low phonemic segmenting scores obtained subsequent to segmentation training might be useful in identifying children "at risk" for reading, individual achievement scores for those who passed less than one-third of the 18 items on the phoneme segmenting subtest in June of first grade were tabulated for each of the first two cohorts. Table III shows that the number of students obtaining these significantly low scores is quite small. Further, despite their segmenting performance, reading achievement varies greatly.

It appears that very low phoneme segmenting scores following one or two years of training is not a wholly reliable index of future difficulties in reading. Inspection of table III suggests that, at best, such scores may signal potential for reading difficulty in the future. Only those three children with well above average intelligence consistently scored above average on the ITBS subtests. Of the remaining 10, all encountered difficulty on the ITBS on one or more occasions during the primary grades (scores below the 40th percentile). However, only two of the seven showing scores for all three grades obtained consistently poor ITBS scores. Among the children in these two cohorts, very poor phonemic segmenting skills at the end of grade 1 was not a generally reliable indicator of future achievement.

This conclusion gained further support from examination of records indicating those children who had received special support services in reading over their entire elementary school careers (K-5 or 6 for the first two cohorts). Of those who had scored less than 50% on the phoneme segmentation test at the end of first grade and were still in the school system, only 10 of the 32 in the first cohort had received special services while only 2 of the 6 in the second cohort were so helped. Thus, even when we consider the possibility that some children may perform better on timed group-achievement tests than they might perform on a daily basis in the classroom, and thus be referred for special supportive services despite relatively adequate test scores, low phoneme segmenting scores at the end of grade 1, in and of themselves, tell us little about future levels of reading achievement among children in these studies.

TABLE III
Scores for Intelligence and Percentile Ranks for ITBS Subtests in Grades 1–3
Among Very Weak Phoneme Segmenters in June of Grade One—Cohorts 1 and 2

	I.Q.	1—Voc	1—Read	2—Voc	2—Read	3—Voc	3—Read
Cohort 1							
Phone Seg 0–5	137	99	99	99	98	89	94
	92	35	39	18	4	7	4
	74	20	70	•	•	•	•
	90	25	34	18	19	20	21
	88	40	37	67	54	48	48
	102	35	20	•	•	29	32
	99	61	42	54	51	42	39
	81	46	44	14	34	37	24
	85	53	39	10	12	•	•
Cohort 2							
Phone Seg 0–5	96	12	51	35	66	57	34
	100	39	55	29	9	40	29
	114	96	99	87	89	•	•
	122	80	95	78	92	84	69

•Indicates missing data

Other Correlates of Poor Reading Performance

Since very poor phoneme level segmenting at the end of grade 1 proved to be a poor index of consistently low reading achievement during the primary years, it was decided to examine the relative strength of other available indexes to identify potentially "at risk" children. Table IV shows the largest correlations obtained between reading achievement, intelligence, various readiness variables (PPVT, GMRST, TACL, Anton Brenner, letter names) for cohorts two and three, and subtest scores for segmenting at different times for those who scored below the 36th percentile on the Reading subtest of the ITBS for any given grade, 1–3. In most cases the sample size is quite small and the correlations obtained with ITBS Reading, though moderate to strong in some instances, did not reach significance. Many significant correlations were obtained, however, for segmenting and other readiness variables with the Vocabulary subtest (word reading).

Table IV shows that segmenting scores yielded among the highest correlations obtained across three cohorts. Results obtained for the third cohort are particularly interesting since the correlations noted for the prekindergarten administration are quite strong despite very small sample sizes (Reading grades 1 and 3). Similarly, segmenting scores for January of kindergarten appear to be strongly associated with the Vocabulary subtest for grades 1 and 2. For these poor readers in all three cohorts, mean Vocabulary performance (word reading) exceeded that obtained for Reading (comprehension) at each grade level.

The magnitude of the correlations obtained for different levels of segmenting ability at different times appears to suggest that the most consistent indicators of low achievement in word recognition and comprehension in the primary grades may be early measures of word and syllable segmenting. Syllable segmenting tasks, as presented to the third cohort, yielded a strong correlation with Reading and/or Vocabulary at each grade level. However, word segmenting tasks yield among the strongest correlations obtained for ITBS Vocabulary and/or Reading among the poorest readers in all three cohorts. Negative correlations noted for word and phoneme segmenting among the poorest readers in cohort two may serve to underscore the earlier reported finding that the poorest segmenters at the end of first grade were not necessarily the lowest achievers in every case.

TABLE IV
Principal Correlates of Performance on Word Reading and Comprehension Measures of the ITBS Among Students in Three Cohorts

Cohort 1								
May Grade 1 (N = 13)			May Grade 2 (N = 15)			May Grade 3 (N = 26)		
Reading Subtest <36th Percentile								
	r	R²			r	R²		r	R²
Phone Seg Oct 1	.30	.09	Total Seg Oct 1	.33	.11	Cog IQ May 1	.35+	.12
Phone Seg June 1	.26	.07	Word Seg Oct 1	.30	.09	Word Seg June 1	.20	.04
Total Seg Oct 1	.21	.04	Phone Seg Oct 1	.29	.08	Phone Seg Oct 1	.14	.02
Cog I.Q. May 1	− .48		Cog I.Q. May 1	.08	.01			
Vocabulary Subtest								
Word Seg June 1	.51+	.26	Total Seg June 1	.50+	.25	Word Seg June 1	.59**	.35
Total Seg June 1	.41	.16	Total Seg Oct 1	.46	.21	Total Seg June 1	.55**	.30
Word Seg Oct 1	.38	.14	Word Seg Oct 1	.45	.20	Word Seg Oct 1	.52**	.27
Cog I.Q. May 1	.16	.03	Phone Seg June 1	.44	.19	Total Seg Oct 1	.47**	.22
			Cog I.Q. May 1	.39	.15	Phone Seg June 1	.38+	.14
						Phone Seg Oct 1	.35	.12
						Cog. I.Q. May 1	.30	.09

Table IV continued on next page.

TABLE IV *continued*

Cohort 2

	May Grade 1 (N = 8)			May Grade 2 (N = 6)			May Grade 3 (N = 18)	
Reading Subtest <36th Percentile								
	r	R^2		r	R^2		r	R^2
Phone Seg Oct K	.40	.16	Word Seg June 1	.79	.62	Cog I.Q. May 1	.17	.03
TACL Pre-K	.35	.12	Phone Seg Oct 1	.61	.37	Phone Seg Oct 1	.17	.03
Letter Names Pre-K	.22	.05	GMRST Oct 1	.33	.11	Word June 1	.10	.01
Cog I.Q. May 1	−.20		Letter Names Pre-K	.30	.09			
			Cog I.Q. May 1	−.11				
Vocabulary Subtest								
TACL Pre-K	.57	.33	GMRST Oct 1	.42	.18	Letter Names Pre-K	.56**	.31
Cog I.Q. May 1	.24	.06	Cog I.Q. May 1	.39	.15	Word Seg June K	.39+	.15
Word Seg Oct 1	−.79		TACL Pre-K	.38	.14	Anton Brenner Pre-K	.39+	.15
Phone Seg Oct 1	−.64		PPVT Pre-K	−.62		Phone Seg June K	.35	.12
						Cog I.Q. May 1	.30	.09

TABLE IV *continued*

Cohort 3

May Grade 1 (N = 4)			May Grade 2 (N = 9)			May Grade 3 (N = 8)		
Reading Subtest <36th Percentile								
	r	R^2		r	R^2		r	R^2
Word Seg Pre-K	.82	.67	TACL Pre-K	.52	.27	Syllable Seg Pre-K	.69+	.48
Anton Brenner Pre-K	.80	.64	Word Seg Jan K	.48	.23	TACL Pre-K	.68+	.46
Syllable Seg Pre-K	.78	.61	Word Seg June K	.45	.20	GMRST Oct K	.66+	.44
Total Seg Pre-K	.76	.58	GMPCT Oct K	.44	.19	Word Seg Jan K	.64	.44
Letter Names Pre-K	.69	.48	Syllable Seg Jan K	.26	.07	Phone Seg Jan K	.61	.37
Cog I.Q. May 1	.55	.30	Cog I.Q. May 1	.12	.01	Cog I.Q. May 1	.53	.28
Vocabulary Subtest								
Word Seg Jan K	.97*	.94	Syl Seg Jan K	.47	.22	GMRST Oct K	.87**	.76
Syllable Seg Jan K	.90+	.81	Syl Seg Pre-K	.36	.13	Total Seg Pre-K	.85**	.72
Word Seg June K	.88+	.77	Word Seg Pre-K	.33	.11	TACL Pre-K	.81*	.66
TACL Pre-K	.88+	.77	Cog I.Q. May 1	.08	.01	Anton Brenner Pre-K	.67	.45
PPVT Pre-K	.85	.72				Total Seg June K	.63	.40
Total Seg June K	.76	.58				Cog I.Q. May 1	.62	.38
Phone Seg June K	.71	.50				Phone Seg June K	.60	.36
Cog I.Q. May 1	.63	.40				Word Seg June K	.55	.30

+approaching Significance
*Significant at P < .05
**Significant at P < .01

Profiles of the Five Most Disabled Readers

In an attempt to discover whether the most disabled readers in this study shared any common characteristics that might serve our future identification of reading disability, five chidren, who were still in the school system, were identified as having consistently low achievement on the ITBS throughout the primary grades. All had scores below the 36th percentile on Reading across the grades and only two scored above that on Vocabulary on one occasion (53rd and 47th percentiles). Three were members of the first cohort while one was found in each of the other cohorts.

Information collected on these children over the course of the longitudinal studies reveals a mixed pattern. Three were near mastery (15 of 18 items is considered mastery level attainment for both words and phones) on phoneme segmentation at the end of first grade (scores of 13 and 14) while one was not (score of 10). The one individual from cohort three, who was last tested for segmenting ability at the end of kindergarten, showed promise of achieving mastery at both levels by the end of grade 1 (scores of 13 on words and 9 on phones). I.Q.s for all five fell within the normal range (87, 90, 94, 102, 102) as did the receptive language measures for the two from cohorts two and three where such information was available (TACL 50 and 63rd percentile; PPTV, 101 and 112). For these same two, GMRST scores were low to average (34th and 50th percentiles) as were letter recognition scores (1 and 25 of 52). Anton Brenner readiness scores for these two were within the average range (scores consistent with those in the third and fourth quartile of the norming group).

Examination of pupil personnel records showed that three continued to have difficulty in reading beyond the primary grades while two attained scores in the low average range (40–50th percentile). All five had long histories of special help in reading beyond the classroom. One was "suspected" of having an early visual difficulty, one had been treated for an emotional handicap, two had been treated for serious speech/language difficulties and one was simply labeled "a hardworker who continues to lag about one year behind in reading." *Cognitive Abilities Tests* given in third grade showed nonverbal intelligence to be significantly superior for the two with documented language difficulties. Four of the five had been labeled learning disabled at some point in their elementary school careers. All five were boys.

It appears that among the most disabled readers in the three cohorts, a variety of factors might be contributing to low achievement. This finding is consistent with a host of studies conducted since the 1940s. While auditory segmenting ability is well documented as a significant contributor to reading acquisition, it is clear that segmenting ability alone cannot explain reading failure across the range of children in the primary grades.

DISCUSSION

Results of this retrospective study suggest that performance on a measure of auditory segmentation at the beginning of kindergarten or first grade is a good predictor of general levels of reading achievement throughout the primary years. This finding extends those of a host of earlier studies that considered end of grade 1 or grade 2 achievement only. This finding is somewhat surpising, however, since instruction successfully increased and extended segmenting competencies over a one or two year period. Given the predictive power apparent in this study, a measure of auditory segmentation may be a highly useful addition to readiness screening batteries.

It appears, however, that an even greater value may accrue to a measure of auditory segmentation if levels of performance are used both to focus training and to select beginning reading experiences. Comparison of achievement data across the three cohorts suggests that among chidren who have not yet mastered word segmentation when formal reading instruction begins, a whole language approach (LEA) with initial focus on whole words may yield greater long-term gain than a highly structured sound-symbol program (*Distar*). These findings are consistent with those of Dougherty (1982) who found that word awareness and language experience story activities, as a supplement to *Distar* reading, yielded greater gains in word reading over an eight week period than did additional time in the *Distar* program. Children may make greater gains in reading if the demands of the initial instructional materials are consistent with their level of segmenting competence *and* if training is provided to promote growth in segmenting across the levels—word, syllable, and phoneme.

An unexpected finding of this retrospective study is that very poor phonemic segmenters subsequent to training are not necessarily destined to be poor readers. Similarly, all poor readers in this study were not among the poorest phoneme segmenters at the end of kindergarten or grade 1. It appears that while poor phonemic segmenting ability places a child at risk for reading acquisition, relative proficiency at this level is not sufficient to guarantee success in reading.

Finally, among children in these longitudinal studies, word and syllable segmenting scores, as well as phoneme segmenting scores, were among the strongest correlates of poor achievement on both of the ITBS subtests for grades 1–3. Despite very few cases, these correlations often reached significance for vocabulary achievement (word reading) and occasionally approached significance for reading achievement (comprehension). These patterns may be interpreted to suggest (1) that early identification of potentially disabled readers is enhanced by inclusion of a test of auditory segmentation in the screening or readiness batteries of kindergarten or first grade and (2) that measures of segmenting performance may be most effective if tests of awareness of all three types or levels of language units—words, syllables, and phonemes—are included.

This retrospective study indicates that among those who are "at risk" in reading may be children who lag behind age mates in acquiring the earlier maturing word and syllable awareness. It seems reasonable that evidence of a developmental lag or of a phonological processing disorder among poor readers may first appear as slower than typical progress toward mastery of word and syllable segmentation. This might serve to explain the lack of agreement, in this study, between very poor phoneme segmentation at the end of kindergarten or first grade and subsequent achievement. It may be that some of these students were generally slow in acquiring segmenting competence at each level but did eventually acquire competence at all levels. However, others might have had phonological processing disorders that were first evident in difficulties at the level of syllable segmentation. Conceivably, these children may have continued to have difficulty with phoneme segmentation throughout the primary grades and perhaps beyond. Future research directed toward the illumination of this hypothesis seems critical to our understanding of the linkage between rudimentary language processing capabilities and reading acquisition.

REFERENCES

Beech, J. R., and Harding, L. M. 1984. Phonemic processing and the poor reader from a developmental lag viewpoint. *Reading Research Quarterly* 19(3):357–366.
Blachman, B. 1983. Are we assessing the linguistic factors critical in early reading? *Annals of Dyslexia* 33:91–109.
Brenner, A. 1964. *Anton Brenner Developmental Gestalt Test of School Readiness*. Los Angeles: Western Psychological Services.

Bryant, P., and Impey, L. 1986. The similarities between normal readers and developmental and acquired dyslexics. *Cognition* 24:121–137.

Byrne, B. 1984. On teaching articulatory phonetics via an orthography. *Memory and Cognition* 12(2):181–189.

Carrow, E. 1973. *Test of Auditory Comprehension of Language*. New York: Teaching Resources Corporation.

Dougherty, C. 1981. Segmenting ability as a predictor of adult mentally handicapped learner's reading performance. Unpublished manuscript, Syracuse University, Syracuse, N.Y.

Dougherty, C. 1982. First graders' segmenting ability, method of instruction, and beginning reading performance: A readiness perspective. Doctoral dissertation. Syracuse, N.Y.: Syracuse University.

Downing, J., and Valtin, R. (eds.). 1984. *Language Awareness and Learning to Read*. New York: Springer-Verlag.

Dunn, L., and Dunn, L. 1981. *Peabody Picture Vocabulary Test-Revised*. Circle Pines, MN: American Guidance Service.

Durr, W. K., Pescosolido, J., and Hayward, G. A. 1978. *The Houghton Mifflin Basal Reading Series*. Boston: Houghton Mifflin.

Ehri, L. C. 1978. Beginning reading from a psycholinguistic perspective: Amalgamation of word identities. *In* F. B. Murray (eds.). *The Development of the Reading Process*. (International Reading Association Monograph No. 3). Newark DE: International Reading Association.

Ellis, N., and Large, B. 1987. The development of reading: As you seek so shall you find. *British Journal of Psychology* 78:1–28.

Englemann, S., and Bruner, E. C. 1974. *Distar Reading*. Chicago, IL: Science Research Associates.

Fox, B., and Routh, D. K. 1984. Phonemic analysis and synthesis as word attack skills: Revisited. *Journal of Educational Psychology* 76(6):1059–1064.

Fox, B., and Routh, D. K. 1983. Reading disability, phonemic analysis and dysphonetic spelling: A follow-up study. *Journal of Clinical Child Psychology* 12(1):28–32.

Gates, A., and MacGinitie, W. 1966. *Gates-MacGinitie Reading Tests: Reading Skills*. New York: Teachers College Press and Boston: Houghton Mifflin Co.

Henderson, E. H. 1980. Developmental concepts of word. *In* E. H. Henderson and J. W. Beers (eds.). *Developmental and Cognitive Aspects of Learning to Spell: A Reflection of Word Knowledge*. Newark, DE: International Reading Association.

Hieronymous, A. N., Lindquist, E. F., and Hoover, H. D. 1978. *Iowa Tests of Basic Skills*. Boston: Houghton Mifflin Co.

Huba, M. E. 1984. The relationship between linguistic awareness in prereaders and two types of experimental instruction. *Reading World* May:347–363.

Juel, C., Griffith, P. L., and Gough, P. B. 1986. Acquisition of literacy: A longitudinal study of children in first and second grade. *Journal of Educational Psychology*, 78(4):243–255.

Kamhi, A. G., and Catts, H. W. 1986. Toward an understanding of developmental language and reading disorders. *Journal of Speech and Hearing Disorders* 51:337–347.

Liberman, I. 1974. Segmentation of the spoken word and reading acquisition. *Bulletin of The Orton Dyslexia Society* 23:65–77.

Mann, V. A. 1984. Longitudinal prediction and prevention of early reading difficulty. *Annals of Dyslexia* 34:117–136.

Morais, J., Carey, L., Allegria, J., and Bertelson, P. 1979. Does awareness of speech as a sequence of phones arise spontaneously? *Cognition* 1:323–331.

Read, C., and Ruyter, L. 1985. Reading and spelling skills in adults of low literacy. *Remedial and Special Education* (RASE) 6(6):43–52.

Rosner, J. 1974. Auditory analysis training with prereaders. *The Reading Teacher* 27(4):379–384.

Rowe, D. W., and Cunningham, P. M. 1983. The effect of two instructional strategies on kindergarteners' concept of word. *In* J. Niles and L. A. Harris (eds.). *Searches for*

Meaning in Reading/Language Processing and Instruction. Thirty-second Year Book. Rochester, N.Y.: National Reading Conference, Inc.

Russell, G. 1982. Impairment of phonetic reading in dyslexia and its persistence beyond childhood-Research note. *Journal of Child Psychology and Psychiatry and Related Disciplines* 23(4):459–475.

Sawyer, D. J. 1987. *Test of Awareness of Language Segments.* Rockville, MD: Aspen Publishing Co.

Sawyer, D. J., Dougherty, C., Shelly, M., and Spaanenburg, L. 1985. Auditory segmenting performance and reading acquisition. *In* Charlann Simon (ed.). *Communication Skills and Classroom Success: Assessment of Language-Learning Disabled Students.* San Diego: College-Hill Press.

Share, D. L., Jorn, A. F., MacLean, R., and Matthews, R. 1984. Sources of individual differences in reading acquisition. *Journal of Educational Psychology* 76(6):1309–1324.

Stanovich, K. E., Cunningham, A. E., and Cramer, B. B. 1984. Assessing phonological awareness in kindergarten children: Issues of task comparability. *Journal of Experimental Child Psychology* 38:175–190.

Thorndike, R. L., Hagin, E., and Large, I. 1971. *Cognitive Abilities Test.* Boston: Houghton Mifflin Co.

Torneus, M. 1984. Phonological awareness and reading: A chicken and egg problem? *Journal of Educational Psychology* 76(6):1346–1358.

Wallach, M. A., and Wallach, L. 1976. *Teaching All Children to Read.* Chicago: University of Chicago Press.

Williams, J. P. 1979. The ABD's of reading: A program for the learning disabled. *In* L. B. Resnick and P. A. Weaver (eds.). *Theory and Practice of Early Reading* (Vol. 3). Hillsdale, N.J.: Lawrence Erlbaum Associates.

Yaden, D. B., and Templeton, S. (eds.). 1986. *Metalinguistic Awareness and Beginning Literacy.* Portsmouth, N.H.: Heinemann.

Yopp, H. K. 1985. Phoneme segmentation ability: A prerequisite for phonics and sight word achievement in beginning reading? *In* Niles, J., and Lalik, R. (eds.). *Issues in Literacy: A Research Perspective.* Thirty-fourth Yearbook. Rochester, N.Y.: National Reading Conference, Inc.

7

Rhyme Recognition and Reading and Spelling in Young Children

Lynette Bradley

RHYMING: A PRE-SCHOOL SKILL

Most young children enjoy using words and before they are bound by adult conventions they use language in enchanting and original ways. We hear them experimenting with language when they are playing. They may describe what they are doing even though no-one else is there, or talk to their toys, but often they simply seem to be practicing using words, exploring the sounds in them, enjoying and listening to the sounds, and even making up new words using those sounds. Children whose development is normal indulge in this word play at a very early age. They are aware of the sounds in words long before they go to school, and it has been suggested that they begin to organize words on the basis of the sound similarities in them as soon as they begin to talk. Vihman (1981) described the child's strategy of using one word to represent

---

The research reported in this paper has been supported by the E.S.R.C.

two or more words that share some phonological characteristics; a child of 15 months settled on "bi" for "bird," and then also for "book," "bread," and "banana." Categorizing words by their first sound in this way occurs in the first year, but it is more usual for preschool children to group words together when they rhyme with each other.

The Russian writer Chukovsky (1963) described the young child's fascination with rhymes in great detail. He believed that children respond to the phonological features of words from the time they begin to speak. His book about the preschool child's language is full of examples of the spontaneous rhymes that young children from different countries produce when they are playing with words. Chukovsky tells us that rhyming begins in the cradle, and that, although children delight in this rhythmic, melodic play, even to the extent of getting drunk on rhymes, it is difficult to think of a more rational system of practice in phonetics than such frequent repetition of all possible sound variations.

We have recently reported empirical data that support Chukovsky's claims. We have been following a group of 66 young children in a longitudinal study since they were 3 years old. We hoped to discover whether the young child's skill with familiar linguistic routines, like nursery rhymes, affected the development of phonological awareness. At the beginning of the study, when the average age of the children was 3 years 4 months, we took measures of their knowledge of nursery rhymes. We also tested their phonological skills at regular intervals over the next 15 months. We found that these three-year-old children were more likely to respond to our tests of phonological skill, the detection and production of rhyme and alliteration, than to other measures of phonological awareness. We also assessed other skills and intelligence, and parental social class and educational levels. We found a strong and highly specific relationship between the young child's knowledge of nursery rhymes and success on tasks of phonological awareness which remained significant when differences in intelligence and social background were controlled. Measures of nursery rhymes and of the detection and production of rhyme and alliteration were related to early reading (at mean age 4 years 5 months) but not to early arithmetic skills (Maclean, Bryant, and Bradley 1987). It has already been established through many studies that phonological awareness is important in learning to read (Wagner and Torgeson 1987). These data suggest that the origins of phonological skill lie in the child's early word play.

READING PROBLEMS AND RHYMING

Although preschool children are enthralled by rhymes, many children with reading and spelling problems find them extremely difficult. When I was assessing children referred to a clinic because of their learning problems I was surprised to find that many of the learning-disabled children could not recognize rhymes. The learning-disabled population is a heterogeneous one and I did not expect so many of the children to have the same difficulty.

As rhyming is such a natural part of early language development it seemed possible that there was a link between the children's learning problems and their lack of rhyming skill. A clinic population is not a representative sample by any means; so to investigate the extent of this problem in children with learning problems I tested 62 children who attended normal schools but had been referred to the Psychological Services because of their educational failure (56 boys and 6 girls). The children chosen were of average or above average intelligence so that their retardation in written language skills could not be attributed to any general intellectual deficit; nor was their retardation, after psychological investigation, thought to be the result of known primary emotional distrubance or known organic etiology. The children's ages ranged from 8 years 4 months to 13 years 5 months, but their reading levels ranged from below 6 years to 9 years 4 months. In other words they were reading two to three years below the level expected for children of their age and intelligence. Further details of this group of learning-disabled children are given in table I.

I saw the children individually, and spoke to each child about nursery rhymes and about words that sound similar to each other. I encouraged them to discover these sound connections through word play. Then I gave each child three simple rhyming tasks.

The Rhyme Tasks

In the first task I asked each child to listen and to tell me which was the odd word out of four words I said to them. I gave them 6 trials in each of three conditions. In the first two series three of the words I said rhymed while the fourth did not (for example, weed, *peel*, need, deed; *nod*, red, fed, bed), and in the third series three of the words began with the same sound but the fourth did not (for example, pen, pig, *hat*, pup). Two of the boys could not remember four words, so I excluded them from the trials.

TABLE I
Details of the Reading Age Match Groups

	N	Age	Reading Age	Spelling	IQ (WISCR/R)
			Mean		
Backward readers	60	10yr 4mth	7yr 7mth	6yr 10mth	108.7
Normal readers	30	6yr 10mth	7yr 6mth	7yr 2mth	107.9

In the second task I asked each child to produce rhymes to each of ten words that I said to them.

The third task was similar to the first rhyming task, but instead of saying rhyming words to the children the words for the six trials in each condition were written on cards. Each child was shown a card on which were listed four words, and asked to point to the word which was the odd one out. The children did not have to read the words.

Control Group

I also needed to know how children with no reading problems would fare on these rhyming tasks. If I compared the backward readers to children of the same age who were reading normally and who could manage the rhyming tasks well (the traditional comparison at this time) I would not find out whether learning to read had helped the good readers' rhyming skills, or whether being good at rhymes had helped them learn to read. I decided to compare the backward readers with younger children who were learning to read normally and were at the same level as the backward readers. My reason for making this comparison was to try to distinguish between cause and effect. If the young children were better at rhyming than the older backward readers this would suggest that appreciating the sounds in words had helped the younger children learn to read. The learning-disabled children's reading problems could have been caused by their difficulty with rhymes. I tested more than 100 young children who were reading normally for their age and intelligence and found 30 children who were reading at the same level on the same tests as the backward readers, and who also matched them in intelligence as measured by the Weschler Intelligence Scale for Children—Revised (WISC–R). The details of this group of young normal readers are given in table I together with details of the older backward readers.

I gave these young normal readers the same rhyming tasks that I had given to the older backward readers. Many of these little children could not remember four words in the rhyme judgement task, but I did not exclude them, as they could invariably tell me which word did not rhyme with the other three.

When I looked at the results of the rhyming tests I found that there was a startling difference between the two groups in both of the rhyming tasks where they had to listen to the sounds in words (tasks 1 and 2). The difference between the groups of both tasks was significant. The young normal readers were far superior to the backward readers at categorizing sounds and detecting rhymes in spoken words, even though the backward readers were on average $3^{1}/_{2}$ years older and of superior intellectual ability.

On the rhyme judgement task (task 1) the results were simply scored on the number of errors each child made out of the six trials in each of the three series. Putting the series together, 91.7% of the 60 backward readers made errors and 85% made more than one error. Only 53.3% of the young normal readers made errors and only 27.7% made more than one. A clear developmental trend was found among the normal readers but not among the backward readers although the 9 backward readers who only made one or no errors had a significantly higher spelling age than the rest, suggesting that difficulties in categorizing words by their sounds may have particularly harmful effects on spelling among learning-disabled children.

On the third rhyme task where the presentation was a visual one there was a marked contrast. No errors at all were made by 92.3% of the young readers and by 86.6% of the backward readers and this difference between the groups was not a significant one.

These data (Bradley 1979, 1984) suggested that one cause of the learning-disabled child's reading and spelling problems could be *difficulty in recognizing and appreciating rhymes* and sound similarities in spoken words, a skill that develops in early childhood. Indeed there is now abundant evidence that many backward readers have difficulty on phonological tasks (Bradley and Bryant 1978; Snowling, Stackhouse, and Rack 1986). But why does an appreciation of rhymes seem to have such a powerful effect on reading and spelling skill?

RHYMING, READING, AND SPELLING

The answer is really a very simple one. An appreciation of rhyme helps children learn to read and to spell for three reasons. Let us consider them one at a time. The first is that rhyme helps children develop phonological awareness. The young child knows that "hen" and "pen" are different words; if he can hear that these different monosyllabic words sound alike he is analyzing the words into h/en and p/en segments and recognising that the spoken syllable can be made up of more than one unit. When children repeat strings of rhyming words, and make up words to achieve rhyme—and this is a natural part of the word play of pre-school children (for example, jelly, belly, melly, telly)—they are analyzing the words within the syllabic unit, at phonemic level.

The second and third reasons go beyond phonemic awareness. When we come to learn to read and to spell it is useful if we can learn to read and write all the words that are in our vocabulary. If each of these words was unique we would never be able to accomplish such a daunting task. There would be thousands and thousands of words that we had to recognize and to remember individually. This would be impossible. But fortunately we have several ways of categorizing words so that we can reduce this learning load. Some of these ways depend on being able to read and to recognize words, but we can also learn to group words together through spoken language. We do not have to wait until we go to school or until we begin to learn to read or to spell. For, as Vihman and Chukovsky have pointed out, babies are categorizing spoken words in their early word play; it seems to be a natural part of the young child's language development.

Chukovsky gives us the first clue about the connection between rhyming and categorizing words when he tells us that rhyming word play offers frequent repetition of all possible sound variations. Rhyming is the most natural way to learn to group words by their sounds, for rhyming words have more sounds in common than any other words except for identical words. Rhyming words are identical from the stressed vowel onward. This makes the sound connection an easy one for most children to hear. So rhyming is also the most natural way to learn to categorize words, and this is one way to cut down on the number of words we have to learn. If the child can hear the connection between "round," "pound," "found," "sound," "mound," "bound," "hound," and "ground," *AND* if he *understands* the significance of this connection, he only needs to learn one of these words. He has moved beyond the c.a.t.–b.a.g. level of thinking; he is still dealing with a smaller unit than the syllable, but is dealing with larger segments within the syllabic unit, which is an efficient way to work in this and similar situations.

Our third reason involves an appreciation of the rhyme connection between words that sound alike, and then the connection between those sound categories and the alphabetic code. When children understand the implications of rhyme in this way they have made a further connection, between the rhyming connections that they hear, and the patterns of letter strings that represent these similar sound patterns. As competent readers we do this all the time. We often use our knowledge of the way one word looks to help us read or write a word we are not sure about, for example of "taught" to read or spell "caught." We might use our knowledge about the word "long" to help us read or spell "kalong," even if we do not know that a kalong is a Mexican flying bat. Again, this does not involve generalization at the level of the grapheme or phoneme, but much larger units. Our knowledge about sound categories and their connection with orthographic patterns becomes reciprocal: we go from one to the other as necessity dictates.

To sum up, an appreciation of rhyme gives children a powerful advantage when they come to learn to read and to spell. Through their rhyming games children learn to analyze words within the syllabic unit at the level of the phoneme, and this is essential if we are to learn to use the alphabetic code. Hearing rhyming connections also gives children a way of categorizing words and so reduces the number of words they have to learn when they come to read and spell. Children who then make the connection between these rhyming categories and the letter string patterns that these words also share can generalize from one word to another when they try to read or to spell new words.

It is obvious that children who learn to talk very late or whose linguistic experience is limited may miss out on a great deal of practice in sound categorization. Without rhyme appreciation children may learn to read and spell using a whole word strategy, but eventually they could reach a plateau in their reading. They will have a problem trying to read new words, especially when they have no contextual cues to help them. Older children studying new subjects such as chemistry, where the vocabulary is not familiar to them, often experience difficulty at this stage. Spelling will continue to cause difficulty.

Many backward readers receive remedial teaching and are taught about word groups. They have 'word group' books, and write lists of words that share common sound and orthographic patterns. But in my experience many of these children do not *understand* the *CONCEPT* that we are trying to teach. They may repeat the sound rule parrot fashion, but they do not really understand the connections and cannot use the principle in their general reading and writing.

A new longitudinal study (Bradley 1988) followed young children who had just begun to read and spell to see how skill with rhymes helped them to make these connections between sound and orthographic categories.

MAKING CONNECTIONS BETWEEN SOUND CATEGORIES AND ORTHOGRAPHIC PATTERNS

One hundred seventy-seven five- and six-year-old children were tested on a number of measures including reading (Neale 1958; Schonell 1971) and spelling (Schonell 1950; Bradley 1988) to find 60 children who could read only a few words. The average age of these 60 children was 6 years 5 months old, their average IQ was 107.6 (WISC–R), and the average number of words each child read on the tests was 5.

We wanted to measure the children's skill with rhymes, and also their ability to remember words by their appearance, and to see if these skills affected each other as they developed. To find a measure of each child's memory for letter strings we saw the children individually and showed them written words one at a time. The words were high frequency words with irregular spelling patterns: ask, how, also, high, laugh, voice, color, answer, thousand, and believe. Each word was presented for five seconds and then removed, and the child immediately wrote the word. The average number of words that each child remembered was 2.4 words.

We also gave each child the sound categorization test that we have used on previous occasions (Bradley 1984); we said four words one at a time and the child's task was to spot the odd word out. The two rhyme conditions in this test involve making judgements about congruent rhymes: the words we say to them sound and look alike (for example, wag, rag, bag, *leg; men*, red, bed, fed). The children managed this task perfectly well; chance level on this test is 2.5 (out of 8 trials) correct, and the average score was 5.3. We also introduced a new *incongruent* rhyme judgement task in which the odd word had a similar pattern to the other words but sounded different (for example, beak, *steak*, freak, leak), or where words sounded alike but looked different (for example, saw,* for, *were*, more). The children listened to these words too and were even better at this rhyme judgement task; chance level was again 2.5 correct and the average score was 5.5.

The children were followed in school over the next three

---

* British pronunciation rhymes with for and more.

years, and tested when they were 7 and 9 years old. A series of fixed order multiple regression analyses showed that skill at making judgements about congruent rhymes (words that both sound and look alike) made a significant contribution to the children's memory for letter strings at age 7, and to spelling at age 9 (with intelligence, age, and reading, spelling and memory for letter strings at pre-test controlled). The children's skill at remembering letter strings at age 7 also contributed to success in spelling at age 9 (with spelling at age 7, age and intelligence and sound categorization controlled). Although scores on the incongruent rhyme task were related to later reading skill there was no relationship between skill on the incongruent rhyme task (words that rhyme but look different) and memory for letter strings or with spelling. (See figure 1a, b, and c.)

These surprising results show that the relationship between rhyming and spelling is a very specific one. Once the young child

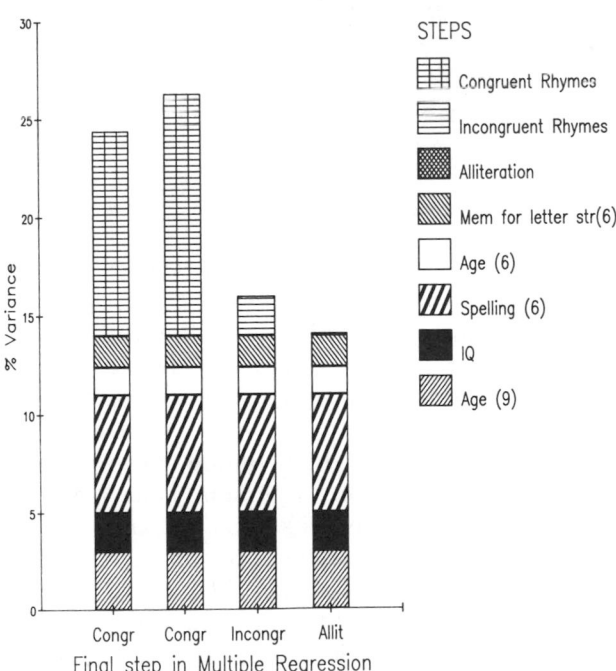

Figure 1a.

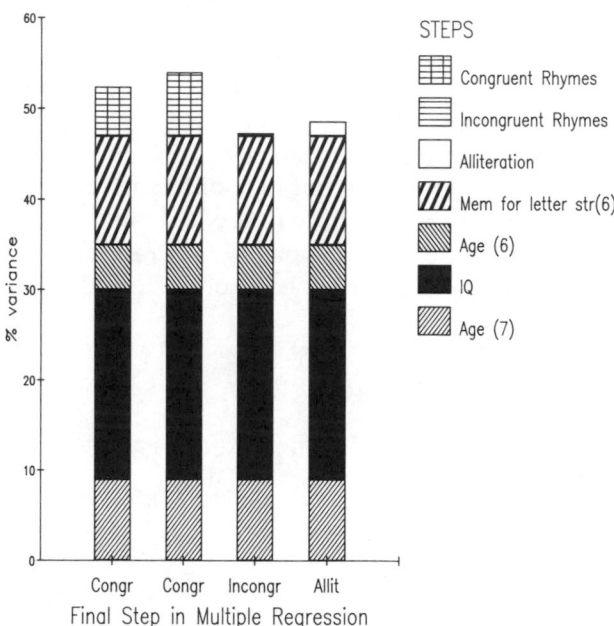

Figure 1b.

has learned to categorize words that rhyme, and then *learns that this means that these words will (usually) have similar letter patterns*, he has made an important discovery which has a direct influence on spelling skill. But why should the young child's skill at making rhyme judgements about words that sound alike affect his memory for the way words look?

I believe that the young child coming to learn to read and to spell is faced with something of a dilemma. How is he going to remember what all the words look like that he wants to read and to spell? It is very helpful to develop phonemic awareness, and to be able to work words out from the way they sound. But that is not enough by itself. It will not help with words that must be remembered as letter strings: words like "people" and "friend," or homonyms such as "so," "sow," "sew," or "there," and "their." If how-

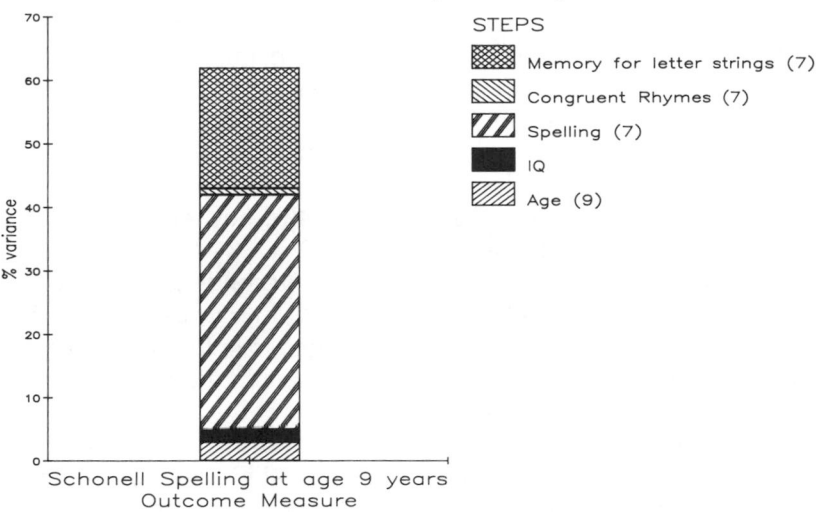

Figure 1c.

ever, young children have learned to make the rhyming connection and then ALSO realize that these words that sound alike have similar letter patterns, they have immediately cut down the number of word patterns that they need to remember. In fact, if we think of just some of the word groups that can be categorized like this we can see that once the child has his memory store organized in this way he can tackle the task much more efficiently. As he no longer has to remember each and every word individually he has more memory available to cope with words that MUST be remembered as letter strings.

This does not mean that only homonyms or irregular words will be committed to memory as letter strings. As children see more and more printed words and become proficient and experienced in reading and spelling they will remember more and more words orthographically. The congruent rhyme connection, however, does suggest one way in which the beginning reader comes to grips with an initially overwhelming task.

I now turn to a study which shows that children who recognize rhymes when they come to school make better progress in reading and in spelling than children who do not recognize rhymes.

LONGITUDINAL EVIDENCE FROM PRE-READERS

These longitudinal data come from a large scale project that was carried out in Oxford over a four year period (Bradley and Bryant 1983; 1985). Our hypothesis was that the experience that a child has with rhyme before he goes to school might have a considerable effect on his success in learning to read and write once he gets there. Our study combined a longitudinal design with a training study. We used both methods because we felt that the strengths and weaknesses of the two designs were complementary, and that together they would help us to establish whether any relationship that we found was a causal one.

Initially we tested 403 4- and 5-year-old children on categorizing sounds (Bradley 1984) as well as on other measures. None of the children could read when the study began. We found that these young non-readers could detect the sound similarities in words perfectly well (see table II).

We followed the children in school over the next three years and then administered tests of reading, spelling, and arithmetic. There were high correlations between the initial sound categorization scores and the children's reading and spelling over 3 years later when the children were 8 to 9 years old. Fixed order multiple regression analyses showed that these relationships remained strong even when the influence of intellectual level at the time of the initial and final tests and of differences in memory were removed. These data showed that a definite relationship exists between the child's skill at categorizing sounds before he learns to read and later success in reading and spelling.

TABLE II
Examples of Words Given to Pre-readers and
Their Scores on the Sound Categorization Tests

	4-yr Group		5-yr Group	
	Words Given to Children	Mean Correct (out of 10)	Words Given to Children	Mean Correct (out of 10)
Sounds in common				
First sound	*tap* hat ham cup cut *fun*	5.69	bus bud bun *rug* pip pin *hill* pig	5.36
Middle sound	pin tin *man* *mug* log dog	7.53	*hug* dig pig wig red *lid* fed bed	6.89
End sound	bun gun *hut* *pal* map cap	7.42	bun gun *hut* sun *pal* map cap gap	6.67

But simply to show this connection did not prove that the relationship was a causal one, as both skills could have been determined by some unknown third factor. The design of our project included a training study as a check that any relationship was a causal one.

Training Children with Difficulty in Sound Categorization

Sixty five children with low scores on the original sound categorization tasks (two standard deviations below the mean) were selected from our original group of 403 children. These 65 children were carefully matched for age, verbal intelligence, sex, and scores on the sound categorization test across two experimental and two control groups. The training began in the second year of the project and involved 40 ten minute training sessions, which were spread over a two year period, for each child.

The two experimental groups (Groups 1 and 2) were taught to categorize words by their sounds. With the help of colored pictures of familiar objects these children were taught that the same word shares common beginning (hen, hat), middle (hen, bed) and end (hen, man) sounds with other words. Thus these children, who had not yet learned to read, learned that the one syllable word "hen"— one speech unit—has three different sounds in it, as the word hen has been categorized in three different ways. Although we had intended to begin training the children using the rhyme connection, we had to alter our plans and introduce groups of words that began with the same sound first. This was because these young children did not understand terms like "word," "sound," and "end of word," whereas the terms "first," "start," and "begin" were familiar to them.

We began with sound categories that had many instances of words beginning with the same first sound so that the children learned the concept we were trying to train, and not just to associate a particular sound with a particular set of words that were always the same words. Once the children had had some experience with first sound sets (for example, bed, bus, book; bell, bat, box, bag) and use of the terms "word" and "sound," we moved to training, using the rhyme connection. These children had their attention drawn to the different sounds in words through the medium of rhyme, for rhyme is the easiest sound connection to hear, since rhyming words have so many sounds in common. We only used rhyming words that both sound and look alike. The children would name the pictures for a particular sound group, for example hen, men, and pen, and be asked what they could hear about these words that sounded the same. They would be encouraged to discover that the words sounded the same at the end. Then a different word would be introduced, for example hen, men, and leg, and the children asked which word did not rhyme with the other two. They would be encouraged to discover that "leg" did not rhyme because it sounded different at the end. Later in the training, the same process would be followed to introduce children to the mid sound in the words. They would be asked to say why "man" did not rhyme with "hen" and "pen." By a process of elimination they discovered that the words were all different at the beginning, and that they were all the same at the end, so the difference had to be somewhere else.

Group 1 received this training only, but in the second year of training study, children in the second experimental group received training that had proved successful for children referred to the clinic for children with learning problems. This enabled us to test the efficacy of this teaching method experimentally. For a part of each session the children in Group 2 were encouraged to use plastic alphabetic letters to make the words they had already categorized by sound. Initially these children would make the first word, for example "hen," and then discard these letters when they went to make the word "pen." But they soon learned that they needed the same letters to represent the sounds that the word group had in common. So these children were trained to appreciate all facets of rhyme: analysis, categorization, and generalization.

Groups 3 and 4 were control groups. Group 3 received the same number of training sessions as Groups 1 and 2, and were taught to categorize using exactly the same words and the same picture cards. But here the categories were conceptual ones; the children were taught that the same word could be classified in different ways (for example, hen, man: living things; hen, bat: animals; hen, pig: farm animals). The progress of the training followed the same pattern as the sound categorization training in every way, except that these children learned to categorize the same words by meaning. Group 4 were tested but not trained.

In the fourth year of the project when the children were 8 to 9 years old they were tested on standardized tests of reading, spelling and mathematics. The main test results are detailed in table III.

The training had had a considerable effect that was specific to reading and spelling. The children trained on sound categorization alone (Group 1) were ahead of the control group trained on conceptual categorization only (Group 3) by 3–4 months on all standardized tests of reading and spelling. This result supported our causal hypothesis. Group 2, trained on sound categorization and also

TABLE III
Training Study: Details of Groups and Mean Final Reading and Spelling Levels

		Mean Scores			
		Experimental Groups		Control Groups	
Groups		1	2	3	4
N		13	13	26	13
Initial EPVT		103.00	103.00	102.34	102.69
Final IQ (WISC/R)		97.15	101.23	102.96	100.15
Final educational tests					
Schonell: reading age (months)		92.23	96.96	88.48	84.46
Neale: reading age (months)		93.47	99.77	89.09	85.70
Schonell: spelling age (months)		85.97	98.81	81.76	75.15

Reading and spelling mean scores are adjusted for two covariates: age and I.Q.

shown how these sound categories are represented by similar letter strings succeeded even better than Group 1. The members of Group 2 were 8 and 10 months ahead of the trained control group on the respective reading tests, and 17 months ahead in spelling. This confirms our hypothesis that children are more successful in spelling when they make this further connection between sound categories (rhymes) and letter string patterns.

Put together, our longitudinal and training results provided powerful support for our hypothesis that the awareness of rhyme and alliteration which develops long before children go to school has a striking influence on their eventual success in learning to read and to spell. But as the differences in reading and spelling between Group 1 (trained in sound categorization alone) and Group 3 (trained in semantic categorization) were not significant, the question of causality was not completely resolved.

THE IDENTIFICATION AND
PREVENTION OF LEARNING DIFFICULTY

Our training study also showed that we can identify children who have difficulty recognizing rhymes in spoken words before they learn to read. Moreover our results showed that intervention can be remarkably effective. The children who had been trained to recognize the connection between rhyming words and orthographic patterns made excellent progress; and by the end of the project, when they were 8 to 9 years old, they had a higher spelling level

than the 300 or so children who had no sound categorization difficulty initially. On the other hand the children in the control group
were making little progress.

More than four years after this project finished I was able to
have 63 of these 65 children tested again. Post-testing some time after a training study has finished is a stringent test of any intervention, but a gap of this magnitude is probably unique. The psychologist who tested the children had not met any of them before, had no
previous connection with the study, or any idea which groups any of
the children had been in.

The children were now almost 13 years old (average age 12
years 11 months). The children were given the original Schonell tests
of reading and spelling and Neale reading, but because these reading tests have a ceiling of 11 years 6 months and are extrapolated
after that level up to 12 year 6 months the children were also given
the Boder reading test. This reading test is a word reading test similar to the Schonell but it continues to adult level.

In the four years since our training study ended most of the
children from the control groups had attended remedial reading
classes (46% of the children in Group 3 and 54% in Group 5, as
against only 23% of Group 1 and 7% of Group 2). Many children
from the control groups are still receiving help. This specialized
training for the control group children might be expected to redress
the differences that existed between the experimental and control
groups when our training ended. In fact this did not happen.

The results of the tests showed that the advantages gained by
the experimental groups as a result of less than 10 hours training
when they were 6 and 7 years old had been maintained more than
four years later (Bradley 1987). The members of the experimental
group trained in sound categorization only were ahead of the
trained control group (Group 3) on all four reading and spelling
tests. The Group 1 advantage over Group 3 did not reach significance because of ceiling effects on the tests and because of the varia-
tion within the groups, but the consistent superiority on every test
except mathematics, where the position was reversed, provided
conclusive support for our causal hypothesis. (See figure 2.)

Children taught the connection between sound categories
and letter strings at the age of 6 and 7 (Group 2) were still ahead of
the trained control group by 9 months in reading and 14 months in
spelling on the original tests. As 46% of the children were at ceiling
on the reading test and 25% at ceiling on the spelling test these differences are an understimate of the true differences between the
groups, and further support our causal hypothesis. Even with ceil-

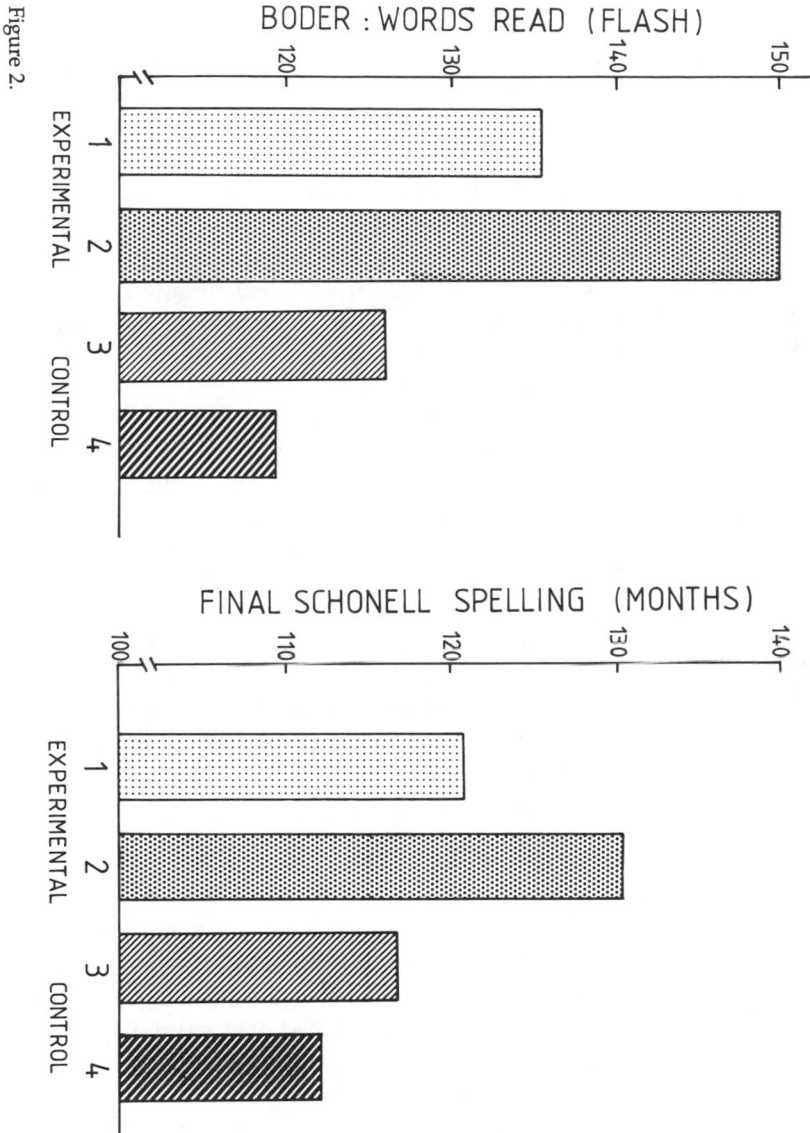

Figure 2.

BODER : WORDS READ (FLASH)

FINAL SCHONELL SPELLING (MONTHS)

159

ing effects, the differences between the groups were significant on the Boder test: the children in Group 2 made better progress than all other groups, and this difference was significant at post-test between Group 2 and Group 4.

These results are particularly powerful. It is quite remarkable that time has not changed the order of the progress made by the different groups in reading and spelling at all. The training we gave to control Group 3 in categorization was obviously better than no training at all; those children who received no help in those early school years are now years behind their peers in reading and in spelling. The help that was given to the children in the control groups by the remedial services after the project finished had an effect; these children have made progress since we last saw them. But neither control group have been able to make up the ground they lost in those early years in school.

The type of intervention that is given is definitely important. All the children had severe problems with sound categorization at the beginning of the project; that is why they were included in the training study. Teaching the children about sound categories obviously had an effect. And even though these children initially had extreme difficulty with sound categories, this effect was a lasting one. Nevertheless teaching to their weakness might not be the most effective way to train them. Certainly the children who were taught about sound categories, and also taught how these sound categories are represented by similar letter strings, made the most impressive progess. The earlier studies have given us sound theoretical reasons why this training is so successful.

CONCLUSIONS

On the whole our results are encouraging. Young children obviously enjoy the songs and rhymes and linguistic routines which seem to be so beneficial as informal practice in sound categorization from the time they begin to learn to talk. Word play, singing games, and nursery rhymes need to be a part of the everyday experience of our preschool children. We need to encourage children who are slow to talk, or who are reluctant to take part in nursery activities to join in these routines.

There are many studies that show that learning disabled children have difficulty with phonological tasks. Our data show that the relationship between early phonological awareness and success in reading and spelling is a causal one. We can test children's skill at sound categorization at an early age, before they begin to read. We cannot be sure that all children who have difficulty with sound categorization at 4 and 5 will have problems with reading and spelling later on. The test of sound categorization is not a certain predictor of reading difficulty by any means; reading is a complex skill, and there are many reasons children fail (Bradley 1987; Bradley and Bryant 1985; Bryant and Bradley 1985). But we know that children who are proficient at sound categorization make better progress in reading and spelling, and that all children will benefit from practice in this skill. It would be preferable to identify a five-year-old child who needed some help, who may in fact pick up these skills quite quickly, than to miss a child who might have continuing difficulty and subsequently fail.

The outlook for children with this problem if they do not receive help at an early stage is particularly gloomy. The children in our longitudinal study who were not trained were backward in reading and spelling by the time they were 8 years old, and they did not catch up. On the other hand our results were particularly encouraging, for we also showed convincingly that intervention can be effective IF the intervention occurs early enough, before the child fails, and IF the intervention is appropriate.

One of the most delightful ways of introducing children to rhymes is by fostering a return to those highly enjoyable interactions between mothers and young children through the formation of mother and toddler nursery rhyme groups. These groups often exist for other reasons. In England groups were started by Margaret Shephard to introduce young children to music, but it soon became apparent that the easiest medium was nursery rhymes and singing games rather than musical instruments. Eventually, groups were started with mothers and new babies at a doctor's surgery as support groups for the mothers. In both cases it soon became apparent that even reluctant participants gained in many ways from these groups. For the most part this came about because the infants enjoyed the rhyming games so much. Even babies a few months old were anticipating what was coming next, especially in the action rhymes. There was a carry over from rhyming in the groups to other times of the day (Shephard and Meinhard 1985). This would be a marvellous and simple way to re-introduce our young mothers and babies to the shared enjoyment of an activity that would have many lasting benefits. The only requirements are the participants themselves.

REFERENCES

Bradley, L. 1979. *Perceptual and Cognitive Difficulties Experienced by Able Backward Readers*. Doctoral thesis. University of Reading.

Bradley, L. 1981. *Sound Pictures*. Basingstoke and London: Macmillan Education

Bradley, L. 1984. *Assessing Reading Difficulties: A Diagnostic and Remedial Approach*. Second Edition. Basingstoke and London: Macmillan Education.

Bradley, L. 1988. Making connections in learning to read and to spell. *Applied Cognitive Psychology* 2:3–18.

Bradley, L., and Bryant, P. E. 1978. Difficulties in auditory organisation as a possible cause of reading backwardness. *Nature* 271:746–747.

Bradley, L., and Bryant, P. 1983. Categorising sounds and learning to read: A causal connection. *Nature* 301:419–421.

Bradley, L., and Bryant, P. 1985. Rhyme and reason in reading and spelling. *International Academy for Research in Learning Disabilities Series*. Michigan: University of Michigan Press.

Bryant, P. E., and Bradley, L. 1985. *Children's Reading Problems: Psychology and Education*. Oxford: Basil Blackwell Ltd.

Chukovsky, K. 1963. *From Two to Five*. Berkeley and Los Angeles: University of California Press.

Maclean, M., Bryant, P., and Bradley, L. 1987. Rhymes, nursery rhymes and reading in early childhood. *Merrill-Palmer Quarterly* 33(3):255–282.

Neale, M. 1958. *Neale Analysis of Reading Ability*. London: Macmillan Education.

Schonell, F. 1950. *Diagnostic and Attainment Testing in Teaching*. London: Oliver and Boyd.

Schonell, F., and Goodacre, E. 1971. *The Psychology and Teaching of Reading*. London: Oliver and Boyd.

Shephard, M., and Meinhard, E. 1985. *In Tune with Each Other*. Documentary film: Milton Keynes: Pace Productions.

Snowling, M., Stackhouse, J., and Rack, J. 1986. Phonological dyslexia and dysgraphia: A developmental analysis. *Cognitive Neuropsychology* 3:309–339.

Vihman, M. 1981. Phonology and the development of the lexicon: Evidence from children's errors. *Journal of Child Language* 8:239–264.

Wagner, R., and Torgesen, J. 1987. The nature of phonological processing and its causal role in the acquisition of reading skills. *Psychological Bulletin* 101(2):192–212.

8

Preschool Prevention of Reading Failure: Does Training In Phonological Awareness Work?

Ingvar Lundberg

Suppose we had a very strong correlate to success or failure in early reading acquisition. Suppose further that we could assess the child's level of this correlate well before school start. A reasonable educational implication then would be to develop a preventive strategy by identifying a group of children at risk and attempt to raise their level by appropriate training at the kindergarten stage.

Over the past decade it has become increasingly clear that language processing disabilities lie at the core of most children's reading problems. Thus, early language development is one of the strongest predictors of later reading acquisition. More specifically, the language problems of reading disabled children center on phonological processing abilities (for recent reviews, see Morais, Alegria and Content 1987; Wagner and Torgesen 1987), which is a relatively specific deficit not attributable to general intelligence. So we might actually have a key factor for preventive intervention. We can screen children for phonological skills in the preschool period and start our preventive actions.

However, there may be difficulties with this approach. At least, some underlying assumptions have to be tested. First, so far we have no conclusive evidence that the relevant phonological skills are trainable at the preschool level. And we do not know if these skills are easily transferred to reading acquisition.

Secondly, even though there might be a strong correlation between phonological development, especially segmentation skills, and later reading achievement (e.g. Lundberg, Olofsson, and Wall 1980), there are still cases of false alarms and misses. Some children with poor phonological awareness in the preschool period will not develop reading disability in school, while some children with normal phonological skills will turn out to have serious reading difficulties. Or seen retrospectively, we will find, among a large group of reading disabled children, some children with no history of phonological delay. A risk-group-identification approach will thus not necessarily be effective in identifying a significant proportion of later reading problems.

Thirdly, our hypothetical prevention strategy presupposes a causal relationship between phonological awareness and reading. Finally, it should be emphasized that, even if successful treatment of phonological difficulties were available, there may still be continuing environmental influences acting on both early language delay and reading.

With all these precautions in mind, I will here present a series of investigations which, taken together, may clarify the relationship between phonological awareness and reading to the extent that educational implications can be drawn. Thus, I will present evidence for a causal interpretation. I will also report data demonstrating that children can be trained in phonological awareness in kindergarten outside the context of formal reading instruction. More specifically, I will attempt to show what is actually learned in such training. Our most recent studies indicate that early training in phonological awareness has a very specific impact on reading and spelling acquisition and does not entail just a general kind of cognitive arousal.

STUDY 1: Comparison of Poor and Normal Readers in Grade 2–6

A great number of studies have demonstrated the relationship between capacity for analyzing speech in submorphemic segments and reading ability (e.g., Leong 1986; Liberman 1982). A typical result can be illustrated from Lundberg (1982), where poor readers and age-matched normal readers of equal intelligence were compared in tasks requiring explicit segmental analysis and manipulation. The child was asked what was left when a part of a word, syllable, or phoneme, was subtracted (e.g. /lo/ from "melody" or /s/ from "school"). The difficulty of the task for some children is illustrated in the following case: An 8-year-old dyslexic boy reacted violently when he was told that /dile/ had been deleted from the word "crocodile." Instead of analyzing the word, he answered with resentment: "You have cut off his tail." Apparently he could not shift his attention from content to linguistic form. No wonder he had trouble learning to read.

From each of the grades 2, 3, 4, 5, and 6 we selected 10 poor and 10 normal readers. Figure 1 presents the results. In grade 2 the difference between the two groups was quite remarkable. In fact, the overlap between the groups was almost none. From grade 3 and on, however, the difference was far less, although consistent and still significant.

The marked improvement from grade 2 to grade 3 for the poor readers is open to alternative interpretations. An obvious possibility is that the technical decoding aspects of reading, especially grapheme-phoneme translation, play a less important role after the first school years. Being a poor reader in grade 2 probably means something else in grade 3 and beyond. Higher linguistic functions and the handling of high-order orthographic structures (mor-

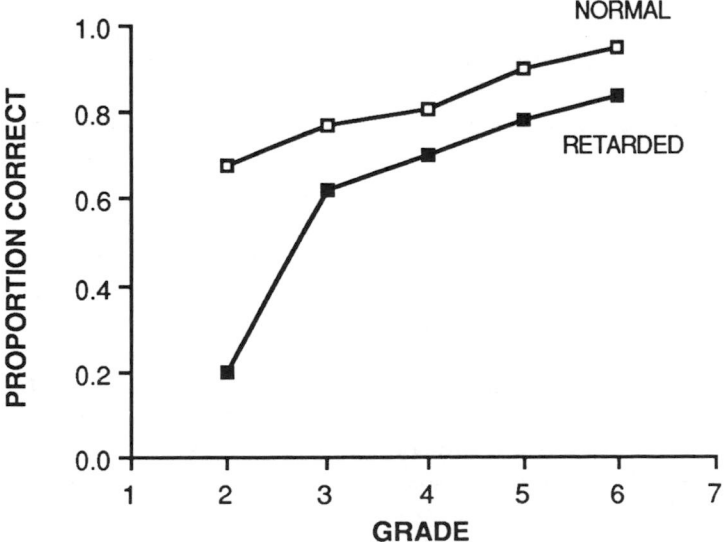

Figure 1. The mean proportion correct responses on the subtraction test as a function of school grade for normal and poor readers respectively.

phemes, spelling patterns) might be more critical for successful reading in the later stages. The change might also reflect the positive effects of remedial teaching with strong emphasis on decoding skills, normally offered to poor readers in grade 2.

Although the results apparently invite intriguing interpretations, the correlational nature of the findings is obvious. And as monotonously repeated, correlation does not prove causation. We cannot rule out the possibility that segmentation skill is the result of reading skill rather than being a prerequisite for reading acquisition.

STUDY 2: Longitudinal Prediction

Our first study was cross-sectional, i.e., different children were assessed at the different grade levels. A next natural step was to follow a group of children from the preschool period when they cannot read through the first school years. If it turns out that children with low phonological awareness at a prereading stage are likely to become poor readers later in school, we have at least come closer to a causal interpretation. What develops later can hardly be the cause of something preceding it. However, there is nothing to ensure that the established relationship is a causal one. The two variables, phonological awareness and reading skill, could both be affected by some unknown factor. Thus, we have to attempt to rule out the influence of such factors by including measures of, for example, general intellectual abilities or the ability to shift attention from content to form in non-linguistic tasks. Without such controls we cannot rule out the possibility that the observed correlation between phonological awareness and reading is spurious and reflects nothing but a common factor of cognitive maturity.

In our study (Lundberg, Olofsson, and Wall 1980) 200 children were followed from kindergarten to grade 2. A broad set of metalinguistic tests were given in kindergarten. The testing program also included non-linguistic decentration tests (visual analysis) and Raven. Reading and spelling were assessed in grades 1 and 2. A detailed multivariate analysis based on causal modeling (path analyses) was reported in the paper. Here we will only summarize the findings. A very generalized index of basic skills in reading and spelling (based on six measures) expressed the performance level in school. More than half the variance (54%) of this index could be accounted for by preschool measures of phonological awareness.

A more precise way of expressing the predictive power is to calculate the expected scores on the criterion variable and compare these with the scores actually obtained. The expected scores on the generalized index of reading and spelling were determined from the multiple regression equation implied by the trimmed path model. The predicted score for each child was then compared with the score actually obtained in school. Table I summarizes the predictive success when we restrict our concern to the extreme categories. From a preventive perspective the lowest quartile is of course of main interest.

Most of the children predicted to fall in the lowest reading and spelling quartile in school in fact had scores in that category. Only a few achieved at an average level, and none appeared in the top quartile. Likewise, the prediction of success in school was quite powerful. Only one child was misclassified.

Although this investigation has taken us a step further and might carry specific implications for preventive actions, we actually need to have more direct evidence of the trainability of phonemic awareness and its causal relationship to reading acquisition. Not even in a well controlled longitudinal study can one be sure that there is no unknown factor at work.

STUDY 3: The Effect of Training

Testing the validity of the causal hypothesis requires an experimental approach, where phonological awareness skills are manipulated via training. An important requirement in training studies is that they include adequate control groups to check for general

TABLE I
Predictive Classification of Children in Different
Achievement Groups According to the Multiple Regression Equation

		Observed achievement level (basics) in school			
		Lower quartile	Average	Upper quartile	
	Upper quartile	1	8	21	30
Predicted Category	Average 25–75 pct	7	42	9	58
	Lower quartile	24	8	0	32
					120

effects that have nothing to do with the hypothesis per se, such as increased motivation or confidence due to the extra attention given to a treatment group. In the study to be summarized a control group was thus included in which a training program was given that was structurally similar to the experimental program except for the fact that it only included non-linguistic sounds.

Another requirement is that confounding between phonological awareness training and reading instruction should be avoided. If phonemic awareness is taught while the children are learning to read, it will be difficult to determine the effectiveness of the phonological awareness training, since it interacts in an unknown way with procedures in the very teaching of reading.

In the present study (Olofsson and Lundberg 1983, 1985) 95 preschool children were divided into three experimental groups and two control groups. They were all given a pretest in kindergarten to assess the level of phonological awareness. Then followed an 8-week training period, where the experimental children had daily exercises and games related to metalinguistics (puns, rhyming, comparing words, initial sound deletion, syllable segmentation, phoneme analysis, etc). The three experiment groups had different degrees of structure of systematicity of the training program. As already mentioned, one of the control groups had non-verbal auditory training, while the second control group followed the ordinary Swedish preschool curriculum which does not include any formal or informal reading instruction. After the 8-week period a post-test of phonemic awareness was given. The training program, especially if it was given under systematic and highly structured conditions, significantly increased the level of phonemic awareness among the preschoolers (see figure 2).

We could thus conclude that it is possible to develop metaphonological skills by training, even among illiterate preschoolers outside the context of formal reading instruction. Preoccupation with letters does not seem to be of critical importance to get conscious access to the phonemic level of language.

The crucial question is, does this training effect transfer to the acquisition of reading and spelling in school? Do children who have enjoyed the benefit of a preschool training program in phonological awareness meet the written-language demands more easily than other children? Unfortunately, the results were not very encouraging. Great variance, ceiling effects, and group heterogeneity created many difficulties in the evaluation of the long-term effects. However, some indications of a positive impact are worth mentioning.

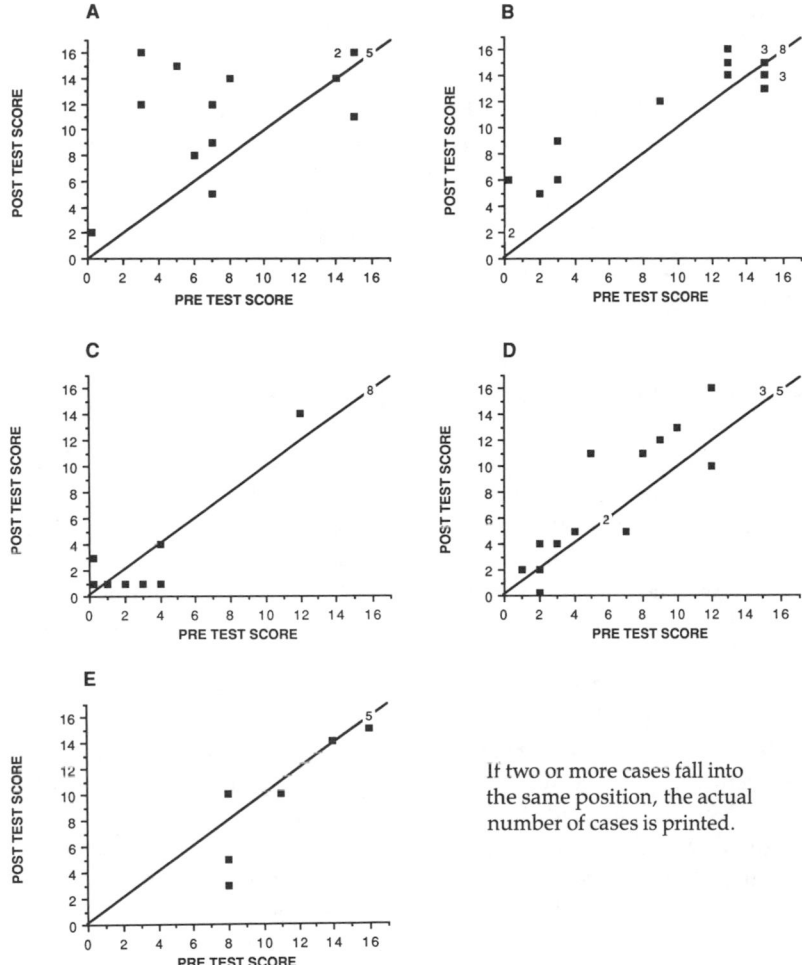

Figure 2. Total post-test score (synthesis + analysis) plotted against total pre-test score. Group a) structured training in phonemic awareness b) structured but less supervised training in phonemic awareness c) spontaneous training in phonemic awareness d) nonverbal auditory perception training e) ordinary preschool program

For the experimental groups, practically all children with medium to high scores on the preschool tests scored high on the reading test in school, while similar children in the control groups were distributed over the whole range of reading scores. This asymmetry may be interpreted as follows: Explicit phonemic awareness training is a sufficient condition for preventing reading failure if it is given to children with high or medium initial level of phonemic awareness. It seems as if the training program helps some children take better advantage of their preschool phonemic awareness when starting reading acquisition at school. Or otherwise expressed, the training substantially reduced the number of children who would have failed in reading despite a reasonably well developed level of phonemic awareness at the preschool stage. Thus, we have not obtained strong support for a risk-identification strategy.

The short training period, the relatively small size of the groups and the ceiling effects call for a new, more extensive investigation.

STUDY 4: The Effects of an Extensive Program

The general design of the present study was similar to study 3. In addition to a broad set of metaphonological tests, the assessment program now also included language comprehension, vocabulary, letter knowledge, and pre-reading ability. General intellectual ability was measured by Raven. Mathematics was included in the school assessment to permit the evaluation of the specificity of the preschool training effect.

As is often the case in field studies, it was not possible or feasible to assign subjects to treatment groups randomly. Instead, various measures were taken to minimize pre-existing differences in relevant variables between the participating groups. We also had to consider the risk of diffusion of treatment. For example, well developed communication between teachers in the experimental group and teachers in the control group might entail exchange of ideas and material related to the treatment program.

The experimental group consisted of 235 children attending 12 different preschool classes on the island of Bornholm, Denmark. The control group consisted of 155 children from the most western part of the country, i.e., a maximum of geographical distance separated the groups. Great care was taken to select control children from socio-economic strata highly equivalent to those of the experimental children, i.e., lower middle class and working class from rural and semi-rural areas without large industries or institutions for higher education. Regular national assessments had demonstrated a slight advantage for the control group areas in school achievement. From a conservative point of view, this was not considered as a disadvantage.

The experimental children had an extensive period of metaphonological training in kindergarten (daily sessions for 8 months according to a highly structured plan). The level of phonological awareness as well as some other variables (see above) were assessed before (pretest) and after the 8 month-period (post-test) for the two groups. (Further details are given in Lundberg, Frost, and Petersen 1988).

Figure 3 shows the change in total scores on the set of metaphonological tests from pretest to post-test for the two groups. We have here a nice, significant cross-over interaction and can thus safely conclude that there is a substantial treatment effect. So, once again we have an affirmative answer to the question of whether or not phonological awareness can be taught in kindergarten.

Let us now approach the question of "what is actually learned during the training?" When the experimental groups and the control group were compared on the other variables—language comprehension and letter knowledge—no differences whatsoever could be observed. The two groups had exactly the same average development from pretest to post-test. Thus, we can conclude that the training effect was specific to the metaphonological domain.

The metaphonological tests represented a broad spectrum of tasks with various demand characteristics. There were reasons to suspect heterogeneity in the underlying structure of the domain (Lundberg 1978; Backman 1983; Stanovich, Cunningham, and

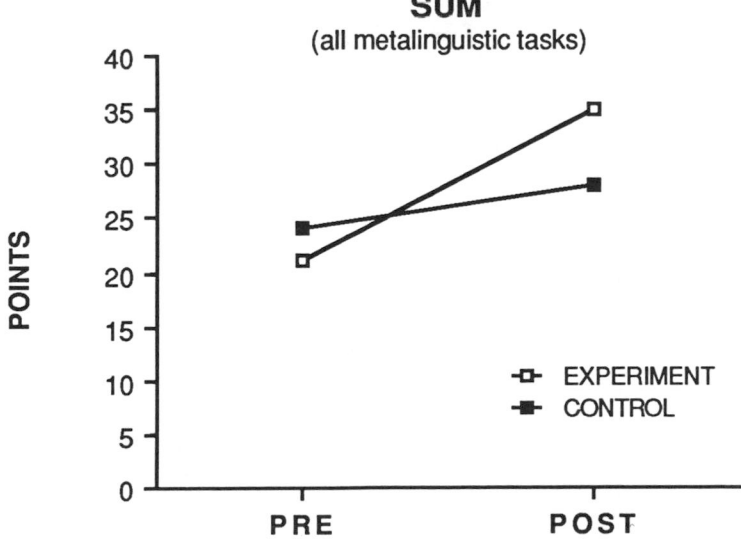

Figure 3.   The change in total scores on metaphonological tasks from pretest to post-test for the two groups.

Cramer 1984). Thus, we performed a confirmatory factor analysis (LISREL) which strongly supported a model where a basic distinction is made between a latent factor for phonemic awareness and another for syllable and word units as the basis for phonological awareness. Rhyming was considered somewhat in the periphery of the metaphonological space.

Armed with these distinctions we could now make a more detailed analysis of our data to localize the training effect more specifically. Rhyming as well as word/syllable manipulation showed very modest, although significant, differential effects. On the phonemic factor, however, the training effect was quite dramatic as is seen in figure 4.

Rhyming and the manipulation of superphonemic segments seem to develop more or less spontaneously in all children attending kindergarten, although some benefit might result from a well planned program of games and exercises. The real winner, however, in such a program is phonemic awareness.

The evidence presented so far suggests that phonological awareness can precede reading ability and develop independently. As we have seen, however, phonemic segmentation ability does not tend to develop spontaneously. Morais et al. (1987) have emphasized the crucial role of letters as the proper medium for developing phonemic awareness. Apparently, an external representation system,

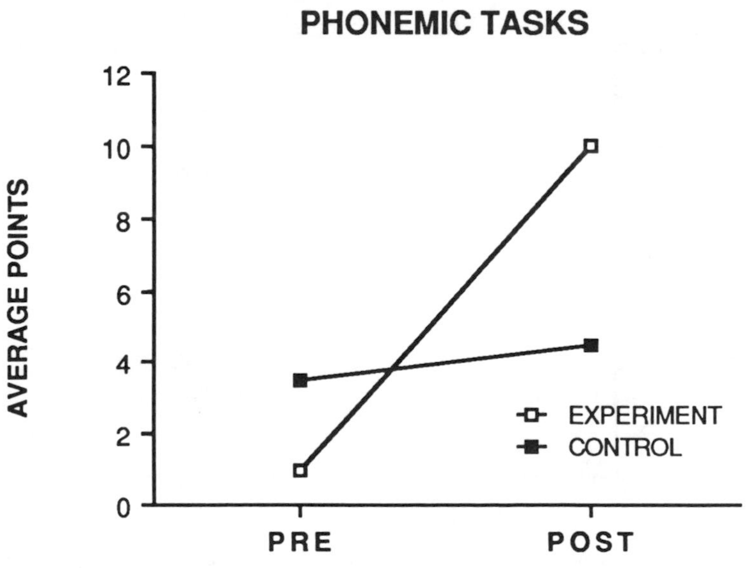

PHONEMIC TASKS

Figure 4. The change in scores on phonemic tasks.

like the letters of the alphabet, is not necessary for learning how to segment words into phonemes. The crucial factor seems rather to be explicit instruction. And, of course, normal reading instruction often entails a sufficient degree of explicitness. Perhaps, the issue of the causal direction of the relationship between phonological awareness and reading (the chicken-and egg-problem) has its solution here.

Now the crucial question still remains. Does the preschool training facilitate reading and spelling acquisition in school? A simple test of reading words was given after seven months in grade 1. The test was repeated eight months later in grade 2. The task was to read a list of words silently, and for each word mark the corresponding picture (out of four alternatives). The achievement measure was the number of correctly read words over a 10 minute period. Spelling ability was assessed by a dictation test with highly frequent words. This test was given in grade 1 as well as in grade 2. The results are presented in figures 5 and 6.

In both reading and spelling, there is a significant difference between the experiment group and the control group. For reading there is also a significant interaction between group and grade.

In a multiple regression analysis the relationship between the preschool tests and the performance in grade 2 was studied. As far as reading was concerned only two independent variables entered the equation. At the first step phonemic skills yielded an R = .58. The second step included language comprehension, and now R =

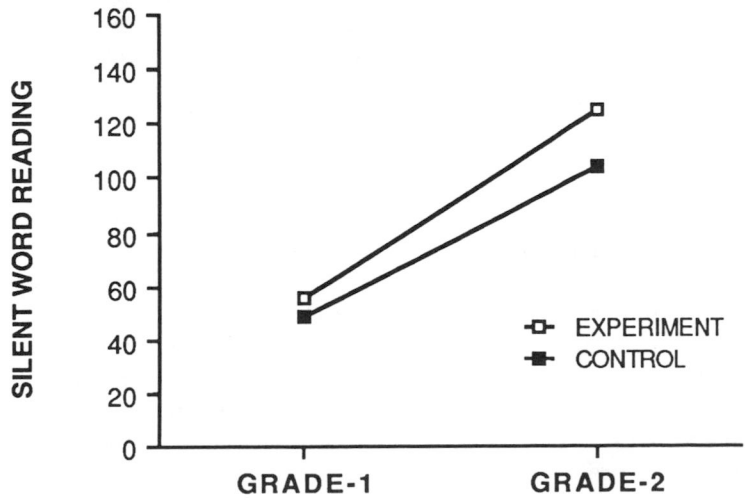

Figure 5.   Reading performance in grade 1 and grade 2 for the two groups.

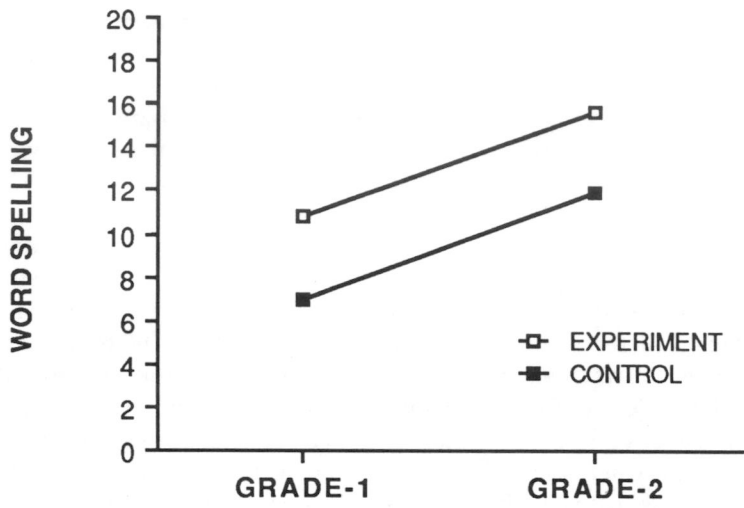

Figure 6.   Spelling performance in grade 1 and grade 2 for the two groups.

.60. For spelling in grade 2 only phonemic skills entered the equation, and R = .61. All remaining independent variables were insignificant. Once again, we have confirmed the strong predictive power of phonemic awareness in preschool.

As pointed out by Bryant and Bradley (1985) it is not enough to assess literacy skills in school. The theory concerns a specific connection between phoneme segmentation in kindergarten and later reading and spelling. We should not expect a relationship with other educational skills like mathematics. Some eight months from the school start a mathematics test was given. The control group actually significantly outperformed the experiment group. The difference in this direction justifies the conclusion that the preschool training is specifically related to literacy.

Who profits from the preschool training? From a preventive point of view, where high-risk children are the focus, it would be an advantage if the results could demonstrate that children with low scores on the preschool assessment made the largest advances. Unfortunately, this was not the case. Instead, the Mathew-effect tended to operate here as well as in many other educational contexts. Thus, the difference between the experiment group and the control group in reading and spelling (the treatment effect) was smaller for children in the lowest quartile of metaphonological scores at the pretest in kindergarten as compared to children from the highest quartile, where the treatment effect was substantial.

CONCLUSIONS

We have now answered most of our questions. The significant relationship between phonological awareness and reading disability found in the first study has, in the light of the following studies, been interpreted as a causal relationship. Although we have not studied it here, we should recognize the possibility of a reciprocal causation, where reading acquisition has a positive effect on phonological awareness.

The single most powerful predictor of reading and spelling skills in the first school years is the level of phonological awareness, especially phonemic segmentation.

We have also demonstrated that phonological awareness can be developed among illiterate children without confronting them with written language. It seems as if explicit training is a prerequisite for the development of phonemic segmentation skills.

Preschool training of phonological awareness facilitates the acquisition of reading and spelling. Although most children profit from this training, it seems as if those with high initial level profit most.

Although no radical cure for preventing reading failure seems to exist, the findings presented here and by other researchers provide an optimistic direction for intervening measures in early education.

REFERENCES

Backman, J. 1983. The role of psycholinguistic skills in reading acquisition: A look at early readers. *Reading Research Quarterly* 18:466–479.

Bryant, P., and Bradley, L. 1985. *Children's Reading Problems*. Oxford: Basil Blackwell.

Leong, C. K. 1986. The role of language awareness in reading proficiency. *In* G. Th. Pavlidis and D. F. Fisher (eds.). *Dyslexia: Its Neuropsychology and Treatment* (pp. 131–148).

Liberman, I. Y. 1982. A language-oriented view of reading and its disabilities. *In* H. Myklebust (ed.). *Progress in Learning Disabilities* (Vol. 5, pp. 81–101). New York: Grune and Stratton.

Lundberg, I. 1978. Aspects of linguistic awareness related to reading. *In* A. Sinclair, R. J. Jarvella, and W. J. M. Levelt (eds.). *The Child's Conception of Language* (pp. 83–96). Berlin: Springer-Verlag.

Lundberg, I. 1982. Linguistic awareness as related to dyslexia. *In* Y. Zotterman (ed.). *Dyslexia: Neuronal, Cognitive and Linguistic Aspects* (pp. 141–153) New York: Pergamon Press.

Lundberg, I., Frost, J., and Petersen, O. P. 1988. Effects of an extensive program for stimulating phonological awareness in preschool children. *Reading Research Quarterly* 23.

Lundberg, I., Olofsson, Å., and Wall, S. 1980. Reading and spelling skills in the first school years predicted from phonemic awareness skills in kindergarten. *Scandinavian Journal of Psychology* 21:159–173.

Morais, J., Alegria, J., and Content, A. 1987. The relationship between segmental analysis and alphabetic literacy: An interactive view. *Cahiers de Psychologie Cognitive* 7:415–430.

Olofsson Å., and Lundberg, I. 1983. Can phonemic awareness be trained in kindergarten? *Scandinavian Journal of Psychology,* 24:35–44.

Olofsson, Å., and Lundberg, I. 1985. Evaluation of long-term effects of phonemic awareness training in kindergarten: Illustrations of some methodological problems in evaluation research. *Scandinavian Journal of Psychology* 26:21–34

Stanovich, K. E., Cunningham, A., and Cramer, B. 1984. Assessing phonological awareness in kindergarten children: Issues of task comparability. *Journal of Experimental Child Psychology* 38:175–190.

Wagner, R. K., and Torgesen, J. K. 1987. The nature of phonological processing and its causal role in the acquisition of reading skills. *Psychological Bulletin* 101:192–212.

9

Invoking Precursors Of Deficient Reading

Dirk J. Bakker

PRECURSORS OF POOR READING: AN EXPERIMENT

Fifty-three boys and girls participated in a recent longitudinal study (Licht et al. 1986; Licht et al. 1988) which covered an age range of 5 (second year of kindergarten) to 8 years (third grade of primary school). Reading (words/sentences) and dichotic listening (digits; free recall) tests were administered each year and word-elicited brain potentials were recorded as well. The stimuli that were used to evoke the brain potentials were normal and degraded words (parts of the letters sifted out), flashed at the center of a screen. The words had to be read aloud and voice-onset times (VOT) were recorded by a voice key. Recording of the word-elicited potentials (WEP) was at left and right temporal (T3, T4) and parietal (P3, P4) locations on the scalp. Peak, latency, and principal component analyses were applied to the WEP data (for more details one is referred to Licht et al. 1986 and Licht et al. 1988).

In third grade, some of the children ended up as good readers and some as poor readers. Of current interest is the question of whether any parameter of dichotic listening, WEP or VOT, recorded during kindergarten, would differentiate between good and

177

poor readers in third grade. In order to answer this question, the five best reading boys and the five best reading girls were selected in third grade, as well as the five worst reading boys and five worst reading girls (Ten Ham 1987). The original data were analyzed by means of analyses of variance, with Group (good *vs* poor reading), Condition (normal *vs* degraded words), Sex (boys *vs* girls), Year (1 *vs* 2 *vs* 3 *vs* 4), Hemisphere (left *vs* right), and Location (temporal *vs* parietal) as independent variables and with dichotic listening scores, voice-onset times, peak latencies, and wave-form component scores as dependent variables. Of present interest are the Year × Group interaction effects.

Significant results were as follows. Good, as opposed to poor, third grade readers at the kindergarten age showed: (1) longer voice-onset times to degraded than to normal words; (2) longer N400 latencies in the left than in the right hemisphere, especially in the temporal area; and (3) robust parietal slow-wave positivity. The parietal slow wave, according to Licht et al. (1986, 1988), is most sensitive to perceptual complexities, whereas the N400, according to them, may be related to first evaluation of the presented word. Kindergarten children who are candidates for efficient reading seem to invest vigorously in the perceptual analysis of script, as is suggested by the robust parietal slow wave they show and by their relatively long voice-onset times to perceptually degraded words. Children in kindergarten who are candidates for poor reading, on the other hand, do not seem to be very impressed by the perceptual features of script and appear to be hurried in their decision as to what the presented word looks like (low N400 latencies, especially in the left temporal area).

In view of these outcomes, it is tempting to speculate that most of the third grade poor readers showed an L-type bias, according to our classifcation of dyslexia (Bakker 1979, 1983, in press; Bakker and Vinke 1985). However, it is not possible to check this speculation with the criteria set for dyslexia subtyping since these criteria were not used in the longitudinal study. This is unfortunate in view of the growing evidence that the reading-disabled population is heterogeneous and that different disability subtypes exist (Rourke 1984). Thus, it might be fruitful to search after the precursors of subtypes, rather than addressing reading disability as a homogeneous anomaly. To that purpose we have begun an investigation into the predetermination and prevention of L- and P-type dyslexia. Before discussing the design of this project a few words will be devoted to the L/P typology.

L- AND P-TYPE DYSLEXIA

Initial Versus Advanced Reading

For decennia it has been believed that the mechanisms underlying reading and reading disability are to be found in the left cerebral hemisphere. However, evidence is available to show that initial reading is primarily mediated by the right hemisphere and that the cerebral mediation of reading shifts to the left hemisphere at some point during the learning-to-read process. The initial right hemispheric bias is thought to be due to the prevalence of perceptual feature analysis during reading. Advanced reading requires the use of semantic and syntactic strategies that are primarily generated by the left hemisphere (Bakker 1979, 1983). The 'hemispheric shift' referred to is evidenced by the results of the longitudinal study mentioned earlier (Licht et al. 1986, 1988). It was found that reading performance is predominantly associated with right hemispheric WEP-component scores during kindergarten and grade 1 and with left hemispheric WEP-component scores during grades 2 and 3. Thus, the initial and advanced stages of the learning-to-read process seem to be primarily subserved by the right and left hemisphere respectively, the shift of the 'hemispheric balance' occurring at 7–8 years of age.

L- Versus P-Type Dyslexia

One could imagine that some children, while starting the learning-to-read process appropriately with the predominant generation of right hemispheric strategies, subsequently get stuck when they fail to shift to the predominant generation of left hemispheric, i.e., syntactic and semantic, reading strategies. These children, who have been labeled P-type dyslexics, show a preoccupation with the perceptual features of script, such as the shape and visuo-spatial arrangement of the graphemes. They tend to read slowly and in a fragmented fashion without, however, making many substantive errors. One could also imagine that some other children, who have been called L-type dyslexics, start off learning to read inappropriately by the untimely generation of linguistic reading strategies generated by the left hemisphere. These children tend to overlook the perceptual features of script and to generate syntactic and semantic fantasies while reading. They read in a hurried fashion and frequently make substantive errors, such as omissions, additions, and word mutilations (Bakker 1979).

Validity of The L/P Classification

The results of investigations into the external validity of the L/P typology have indicated that L- and P-dyslexic children, as classified on the basis of their reading styles (reading speed and type of reading errors), differ with regard to: (1) the lateral distribution of WEP-response shapes, latencies, and amplitudes (Bakker 1986; Bakker and Licht 1986); (2) the development of these distributions with age (Bakker and Vinke 1985); (3) the effect of neuropsychological treatments, both in terms of modifications in the lateral distribution of WEP-parameters and changes in scholastic achievement (Bakker, Moerland, and Goekoop-Hoefkens 1981; Bakker and Vinke 1985); and (4) the efficacy of noötropic medication (Bakker, Van Leeuwen, and Spyer 1987).

Treatment of L- and P-Type Dyslexics

Left hemispheric reading strategies predominate in L-dyslexics from the very onset of the learning-to-read process. In accordance with the notion that they have more or less skipped the stage of right hemispheric predominance in control of reading, they might profit from specific stimulation of the right hemisphere. P-dyslexics, who supposedly suffer from the inability to make the right to left hemispheric shift in the control of reading, might profit from specific stimulation of the left hemisphere. Stimulation of the right hemisphere in L-dyslexics and of the left hemisphere in P-dyslexics can be accomplished by the presentation of reading material in one of the visual half-fields or by the presentation of this material to the fingers of one of the hands. Hemisphere-specific stimulation (HSS) has been shown to be effective in a number of studies (Bakker in press; Bakker et al. 1981; Bakker and Vinke 1985). In comparison to control treatments, HSS appears to enhance reading accuracy and efficiency most consistently in L-dyslexics. Changes in scholastic achievement scores were found to correlate with modifications in the lateral distribution of WEP-parameters.

Example: Treatment of L-Type Dyslexia

In one study (Bakker and Vinke 1985) L-type dyslexic children were divided into five treatment groups: L1, L2, L3, L4, and L5. All subjects were treated during 22 sessions, one session a week, each session lasting for about 45 minutes. Reading and spelling tests were administered and WEPs recorded prior to and after the treatments. L1-children were treated by presenting all reading material to the right hemisphere, i.e., by flashing words to be read in the left visual field (HSS of the right hemisphere). The L2-subjects received a control treatment in that the same words as used for L1 were now flashed in the central visual field (hemisphere-nonspecific stimulation). No treatment was provided for L5, this group being yet another control group. The L3-treatment was created on proposal of the classroom teachers. They had been inquiring about a treatment that would be more easily transferable to the classroom situation and that might be as effective as HSS of the right hemisphere (L1). It was decided to have the L3-subjects read perceptually complex texts (figure 1). Complexity was accomplished by transforming the words

AcHMed mOEt lAcHeN. "DaT wEET I k AllAnG'

, ZEgT hIJ. "DAt Is TWEe GULdEN. '

'Nee', ZEgt DE JuF, 'dAt iS niet GOed. '

'WeLlEs', zegt AChmed.'IK hEb hEt ZeLf

geZi en. IK wAS op De MaRkt. Daar StOnd:

Figure 1.   An example of perceptually complex text (from Bakker in press).

in the children's reading books into the same words, now printed in a mixture of typefaces. The perceptual complexity that resulted from this was assumed to enhance right hemispheric involvement in the processing of text (hemisphere-alluding stimulation [HAS]). L4 served as a control for L3; the L4-children read the L3-texts, without special emphasis on the perceptual aspects of the text.

It was predicted that the L1- and L3-treatments should bring about better reading and spelling improvement than the control treatments (L2, L4, L5) and that these improvements would be associated with treatment-induced electrophysiological changes in the hemispheres. The main results of this investigation are graphically represented in figure 2, which indicates that the L1-treatment was differentially effective with regard to: (1) reading efficiency (percentage of errors relative to number of words and sentences read); (2) the number of spelling errors; and (3) a verbal index, i.e. a reading/spelling composition score. Reading efficiency also improved in the case of treatment with perceptually complex texts (L3). Selective treatment of the right hemisphere (L1) induced changes in the electrophysiological activity of the hemispheres and the changes appeared to correlate with improvement measures of reading ability

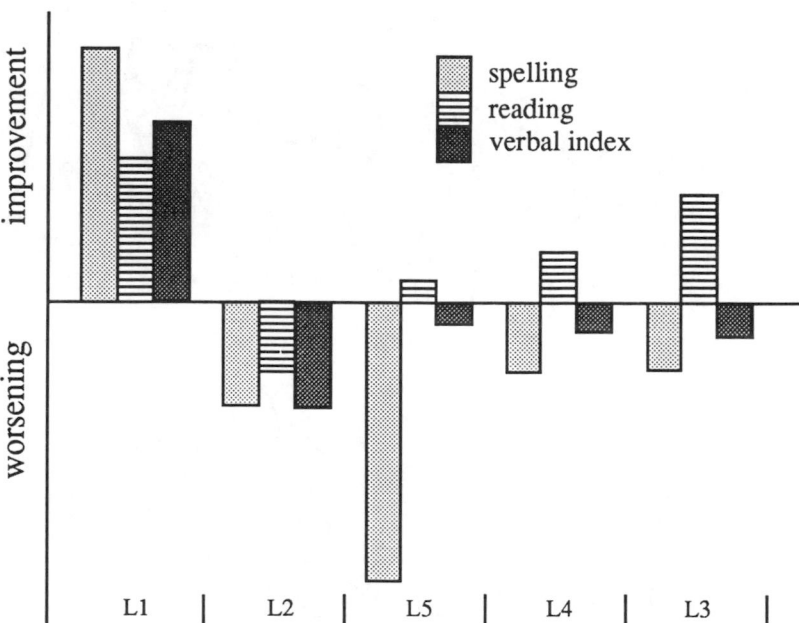

Figure 2.   Effects of hemisphere-specific (L1) and hemisphere-alluding (L3) stimulation versus control treatments (L2, L4, L5) in L-type dyslexia (from Bakker 1987).

(Bakker and Vinke 1985). These findings are in accordance with the predictions and confirm the results of other studies (Bakker et al. 1981; Bakker in press). Neuropsychological treatment of P-type dyslexia has also been shown to be effective, although less consistently so across investigations, than is the case with the treatment of L-type dyslexia (Bakker in press).

PREVENTION OF L- AND P-TYPE DYSLEXIA

A project dealing with the predetermination and prevention of L- and P-type dyslexia was launched in 1986. This project aims at tracing *latent* L- and P-type dyslexia and at preventing the manifestation of these anomalies by appropriate hemispheric stimulation during the preschool years. Initially some 1500 children in their first year of kindergarten participated. The classroom teachers were requested to indicate whether a child was most likely, likely, doubtfully, unlikely, or most unlikely to develop reading/writing/language problems. According to these teachers, approximately 150 children were likely or most likely to develop such problems. These 150 children, as well as approximately 50 children in a norm group, were subsequently administered a Dutch version of the Florida Kindergarten Screening Battery (FKSB) (Satz and Fletcher 1982). Only those subjects who, according to both the teachers and the FKSB results, were designated as being at risk for later reading/writing/ language problems continued participation in the project. A factor analysis of FKSB-scores revealed a language/speed (I) and visuoperceptual (II) factor. A high score on factor I combined with a low score on factor II was considered indicative of the risk of developing an L-type dyslexia, whereas the reverse pattern of factor scores was considered indicative of the risk of developing a P-type dyslexia. Some 80 L- and P-risk children could be identified (± 40) L- and ± 40 P-risks).

The next step in the project will be the external validation of these L-risk and P-risk selections through the administration of type-sensitive tests and the registration of left and right hemispheric brain potentials. The 40 L-risks, as well as the 40 P-risks, will be divided randomly into a number of treatment groups. The experimental and control treatments will basically parallel those used by Bakker and Vinke (1985). Thus, the experimental treatments will include right hemisphere stimulation in latent L-types and left hemisphere stimulation in latent P-types. The children will still be in kindergarten when the treatments start. The project will be completed in 1989. The predictions are that those children who have received a control treatment will, by then, show signs of an L- or P-dyslexia and that the experimentally treated children will not show these signs or will show them to a lesser degree. There is some confidence that precursors of L- and P-dyslexia can be traced during the pre-school years. This optimism is based on a most recent finding of one of our ongoing projects, which indicates that L- versus P-traits of dyslexic children are also present in their biological parents.

REFERENCES

Bakker, D. J. 1979. Hemispheric differences and reading strategies: Two dyslexias? *Bulletin of The Orton Society* 29:84–100.

Bakker, D. J. 1983. Hemispheric specialization and specific reading retardation. *In* M. Rutter (ed.) *Developmental Neuropsychiatry.* (pp. 498–506). New York: Guilford Press.

Bakker, D. J. 1986. Electrophysiological validation of L- and P-type dyslexia. *Journal of Clinical and Experimental Neuropsychology* 8:133.

Bakker, D. J. 1987. Leerstoornissen: Een hoofdstuk uit de neuropsychologie van het kind. *In* J. F. Orlebeke, P. J. D. Drenth, R. H. C. Janssen, and C. Sanders (eds.) *Compendium van de Psychologie, Deel 9* (pp. 109–138). Muiderberg, Netherlands: Coutinho.

Bakker, D. J. in press. *Neuropsychological Treatments of Dyslexia.* New York: Oxford University Press.

Bakker, D. J., and Licht, R. 1986. Learning to read: Changing horses in mid-stream. *In* G. Th. Pavlidis and D. F. Fisher (eds.) *Dyslexia: Neuropsychology and Treatment* (pp. 87–95). London: Wiley.

Bakker, D. J., Moerland, R., and Goekoop-Hoefkens, M. 1981. Effects of hemisphere-specific stimulation on the reading performance of dyslexic boys: A pilot study. *Journal of Clinical Neuropsychology* 3:155–159.

Bakker, D. J., Van Leeuwen, H. M. P., and Spyer, G. 1987. Neuropsychological aspects of dyslexia. *In* D. J. Bakker, C. Wilsher, H. Debruyne, and N. Bertin (eds.) *Developmental Dyslexia and Learning Disorders* (pp. 30–39). Basel: Karger.

Bakker, D. J., and Vinke, J. 1985. Effects of hemisphere-specific stimulation on brain activity and reading in dyslexics. *Journal of Clinical and Experimental Neuropsychology* 7:505–525.

Licht, R., Bakker, D. J., Kok, A., and Bouma, A. 1988. The development of lateral event-related potentials (ERPs) related to word naming: A 4-year longitudinal study. *Neuropsychologia* 26:327–340.

Licht, R., Kok, A., Bakker, D. J., and Bouma, A. 1986. Hemispheric distribution of ERP components and word naming in preschool children. *Brain and Language* 27:101–116.

Rourke, B. P. (ed.) 1984. *Learning Disabilities in Children: Advances in Subtype Analysis.* New York: Guilford Press.

Satz, P., and Fletcher, J. 1982. *Florida Kindergarten Screening Battery.* Odessa, Florida: Psychological Assessment Resources, Inc.

Ten Ham, J. 1987. *Verschillen in Ontwikkeling Tussen Goede en Zwakke Lezers in Hemispherische Asymmetrie.* Drs-thesis, Free University, Amsterdam.

Ongoing Studies

10

The Early Identification of Developmental Language Disorders and the Prediction of the Acquisition of Reading Skills

Barbara C. Wilson and Donald A. Risucci

Developmental language disorders (DLD) have become widely recognized as significant developmental problems. DLD, mild, moderate, or severe, occurs in as many as 8%, or approximately 1 out of every 12, white middle class children (Allen and Bliss 1978). The percentage increases to 14 if a broader spectrum of children is included (Ludlow 1980). These disorders are characterized by difficulties in receiving, processing, and/or in expressing spoken language, and are attributed to atypical central nervous system function (Rapin and Wilson 1978). Since language is believed to be critical to the development of a wide range of cognitive functions, it is important to identify children with DLD at the earliest possible age, and to assess and classify these children in terms of those abilities thought to be predictive of later cognitive development. Theories concerned with the relationships between language and cognitive development have pointed to a number of cognitive and linguistic functions that can be assessed during the preschool years and that provide the clinician with information useful in the identification, description, and classification of children with DLD. Studies designed to predict the development of later reading abilities are of particular importance since reading is probably the most frequent academic area to be adversely affected by DLD.

Most contemporary theories associate reading disorders with linguistic deficits (e.g., Liberman 1983; Vellutino 1979). The basic assumption underlying this position suggests that reading skills are built upon those processes that subserve spoken language comprehension and that reading and oral language share a common knowledge base or lexicon. Developmental deficits in linguistic processing, then, could be seen as contributing to the presence of developmental reading disorders. For example, early difficulties in the processing of spoken phrases or sentences could be related to later deficits in the comprehension of written material; an inadequate lexicon might affect written word recognition; inadequacies in phonologic awareness could be viewed as contributing to a variety of reading problems including deficits in word attack skills. While the processes associated with comprehension of spoken language are considered by many to be among the precursors of adequate reading skills, and indeed form the foundation on which reading is based for most children, there are several other processes involved in reading ability. These include visual-spatial and visual-discrimination skills. Other processes, attention, retrieval and visual memory, for example, are associated with the fact that reading comprehension requires the integration of an extremely complex set of cognitive processes and among many other things, also requires the ability to attend selectively and to relate to stimulus patterns with memory representations (Gibson and Levin 1975).

Empirical studies have generally supported the relationship between deficient language skills and learning disorders. (See Fletcher 1981, for a comprehensive review.) Several retrospective studies have documented language deficits among children with reading disorders (e.g. Mattis, French, and Rapin 1975; Satz et al. 1978; Wiig and Semel 1976). Several prospective studies have shown that a high percentage of children with early identified language disorders go on to develop reading disorders (Wolpaw, Nation, and Aram 1977; Fletcher and Satz 1980; Wilson and Risucci 1986). Few studies have provided longitudinal data that could be used to examine those variables that predict the nature and severity of reading disorders among children identified as DLD during their preschool years. Moreover, the results of previous studies are difficult to interpret because of the heterogeneity among samples of children identified simply as "language disordered." If a neuropsychological approach to the identification of preschoolers with developmental language disorders and the prediction of their later reading abilities is to be relevant, it ought to be able to provide information concerning those processes that underlie language development, reading acquisition, and later reading comprehension. Furthermore, a classification of DLD based on the neuropsychological assessment ought to be useful for the creation of homogeneous groups and differential prediction as to the incidence and type of reading disorder observed during the early school years when reading instruction begins. Evaluation of the classification's predictive validity, on the basis of longitudinal data, would serve to delimit its value for these purposes. Ultimately, this information should be useful for decisions regarding subtype-specific intervention strategies. But first, how do we identify DLD?

SCREENING FOR DLD

If one accepts the definition of DLD as a failure to develop age-appropriate language in the absence of mental retardation, hearing loss, primary emotional disturbance, or frank neurological damage, an appropriate screening must address these exclusionary criteria. The initial requirement prior to the screening of young children suspected of DLD, retardation, or autism should involve the documentation of hearing adequate for the acquisition of speech. We have identified too many children over the years who were referred with a presumptive diagnosis of DLD, retardation, or autism who had not had the benefit of an adequate hearing assessment and who were found to be significantly hearing impaired.

Once adequate hearing has been documented, by auditory evoked cortical response measures if necessary, the language pathologist then should screen for the appropriateness of receptive and expressive language development. In our own setting, structured and unstructured play situations and a brief video tape of a silent "funny story" are provided as vehicles for eliciting indications of vocabulary, retrieval ability, syntax, morphology, comprehension, expression, and pragmatic skills. The language pathologist is asked to make a determination as to the typicality and age-appropriateness of the language development. The cognitive-linguistic aspect of the screening, conducted by a neuropsychologist, is designed to document further the level of linguistic competence and to demonstrate the absence of global deficiences if the diagnosis of DLD is to be supported. Selected items from psychometric tests are administered to address those specific neuropsychological constructs that are carried forward into subsequent detailed neuropsychological assessment.

The model for the early identification of developmental language disorders to which we subscribe stems from our approach to neuropsychological assessment in general, which focuses on processes and functions, and relationships among them, rather than on individual tests and test scores. We begin by thinking in terms of neuropsychological constructs such as Visual and Auditory Cognition, Memory, and Word Retrieval, for example, and selected measures that we think most adequately reflect those functions.

NEUROPSYCHOLOGICAL CONSTRUCTS

The neuropsychological constructs shape the content of the screening, as well as the more detailed assessment, and guide the interpretation of the data. Constructs are selected which are thought to be the most relevant to the description of the processes involved in language function and for which we have standardized measures. These constructs include Auditory Perception, assessed by measures which are inferentially related to pre-semantic processing of the auditory stimulus. Deficits here warrant referral for detailed study. Additional constructs include several levels of Auditory Cognition, which relate to the ability to respond to questions, statements, or directions in an auditory-input/vocal-output paradigm. Different levels reflect increasing complexity of comprehension and expression. Other constructs that are included in the screening include Short Term Auditory Memory for both linguistically organized (sentences) and non-linguistically organized stimuli (digits, unrelated words, nonsense syllables). Semantic Word Retrieval includes the production of words in response to categorical cues such as food or animals, and to pictures or objects.

Constructs that involve the visual modality include Visual Discrimination, which requires match-to-sample responses. Visual Spatial constructs refer to functions requiring the analysis and synthesis of visually presented materials. These may be representational, such as pictures of real objects, and non-representational, such as block designs. We propose several levels of Visual Cognition, analogous to Auditory Cognition, involving tasks that require either a vocal or motor response to visually presented materials. Task demands vary from simple discrimination to higher-order problem solving. Tasks related to the Short Term Visual Memory construct are analogous to those related to Auditory Memory in terms of representational (pictures of real objects) or non-representational ("nonsense" shapes) characteristics of the stimulus. (See Wilson 1987, for a detailed description of the assessment model, the constructs and the tests used to assess them.) In the screening situation, an appraisal is made of the child's abilities in the selected domains, characterized by the constructs described above in addition to others. The patterns of relative function and dysfunction are appraised and viewed in conjunction with the results of the language assessment, and the historical and behavioral data available.

We consider observational data to be vital to the understanding of the child's functioning characteristics, in this instance with particular reference to aspects of expressive language and pragmatic skills. Since there are no standardized measures currently available that adequately capture the relevant aspects of expressive language or pragmatics, we are in the process of establishing norms for a set of observational scales for use in providing such information. The more detailed neuropsychological assessment involves the same model, but permits a more detailed assessment of the child's cognitive-linguistic abilities. Since we select subtests from among the range of standardized tests, each in a different metric, we transform all scores into percentile scores to facilitate inter-disciplinary communication. This also permits us to generate bar graphs to provide a pictorial representation of the child's neuropsychological profile. For example, figure 1 represents the profile of a 3-year 6-month-old child with severe verbal apraxia who was unable to produce intelligible running speech. The profile demonstrates not only his inability to respond to auditory perceptual tasks (AP) that required repetition or closure, but also his average ability to discriminate like-sounding phonemes in quiet and noisy surround conditions (ADq, ADn). He was able to produce only a few intelligible one word responses at the Auditory Cognitive 1 level, and scored nothing beyond that as the response demands increased. On the same basis, as a result of his vocal output deficits, he was unable to repeat the stimuli presented in the memory tasks (AM1, 2, 3), nor could he respond to the semantic retrieval (SR) task demands.

On the other hand, he demonstrated average abilities in Visual Discrimination (VD), Visual Spatial skills (VSp1, 2), and in the Visual Cognitive tasks (VC1, 2, 3), although a drop-off in level of function is noted on the more complex VC3 demands. Visual Memory (VM1, 2) was low average to borderline, and fine and graphomotor skills (FM, GrM) were in the deficient range, not surprisingly since other motor apraxias are frequently seen in conjunction with

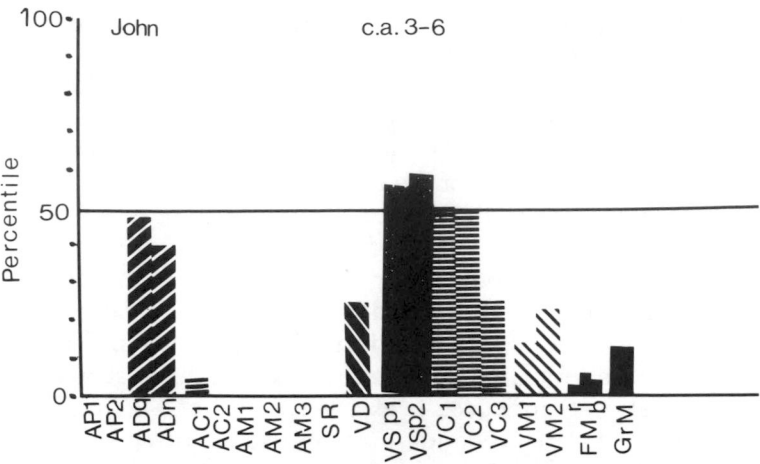

Figure 1.   The neuropsychological profile of a 3-year 6-month-old child with a developmental language disorder, characterized by deficits in the auditory-verbal areas. In this instance, a verbal apraxia, rather than the presence of a primary receptive disorder, accounts for the low scores.

verbal or oral apraxias. What this profile also shows is that without knowing this child or having access to a clinical description, one could not tell from the data alone whether he was demonstrating a severe receptive and/or expressive disorder.

Figure 2 represents the profile of another child, 4 years, 2 months of age, who shows relative inefficiencies in aspects of auditorily mediated functions in contrast to visually mediated functions. AP skills are above average; AC and AM tasks were low average to borderline. (Neither the AD nor SR tasks were completed on this child, who found the task demands extremely frustrating). On the other hand, visually mediated functions were, in general, in the average to high average range with the notable exception of VC2 which requires associational and categorizing skills. His score here is perhaps related to his inability to perform the within-category auditory-vocal semantic retrieval tasks. VM1, requiring the sequencing of pictures of common objects from memory, was also poorly completed. This is typically converted into a verbal task, with children (and adults) spontaneously naming the pictures, and recreating the sequence on the basis of verbal rather than visual recall. It is possible that his retrieval deficit limited his ability to name rapidly and to retrieve the sequence. None of the data related to the motor measures were available. This profile represents the measures of cognitive-linguistic abilities in a child with a functionally significant

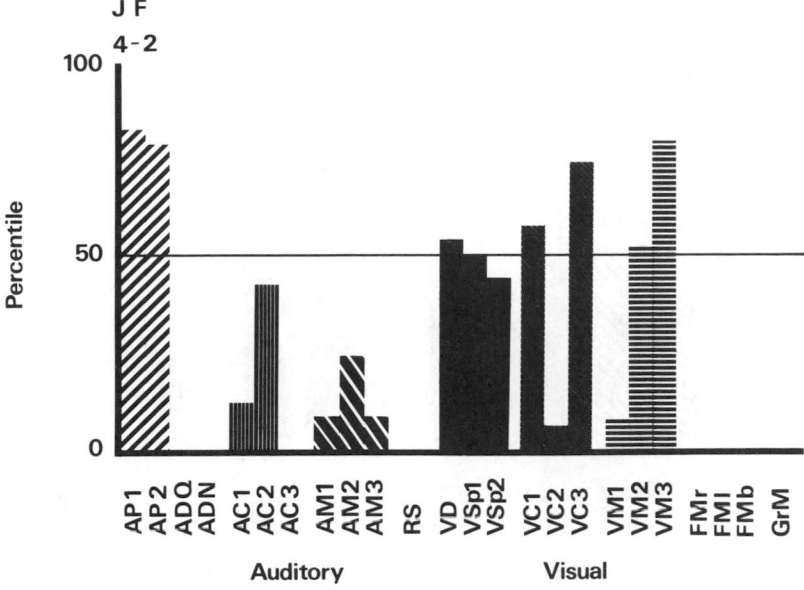

Figure 2. The neuropsychological profile of J. F. at 4 years 2 months of age. His developmental language disability is characterized by relatively inefficient auditory-verbal skills in contrast to visually mediated functions. He was identified as having an auditory-semantic comprehension deficit.

receptive disorder. A follow-up, but truncated evaluation at 8 years, 4 months, presented in figure 3, indicates an increase in auditory-verbal abilities, mirrored by an increase in visually mediated skills, so that the relative discrepancy between the two processing modalities continues to obtain. This child has a significant reading disability and receives special services.

A COGNITIVE-LINGUISTIC CLASSIFICATION OF DLD

After looking at many profiles over the years, it became clear that the clinical observations we make relative to the commonality among groups of children—the "he's just like Johnny Smith" phenomenon—are systematic and seem to be represented by prototypic clinical profiles. We moved then into the development of a cognitive-linguistic typology or classification of DLD. We were interested in producing a clinically useful typology that would be data based, clinically generated, and empirically validated. On the basis of a sorting of psychometric data, which we profiled as demon-

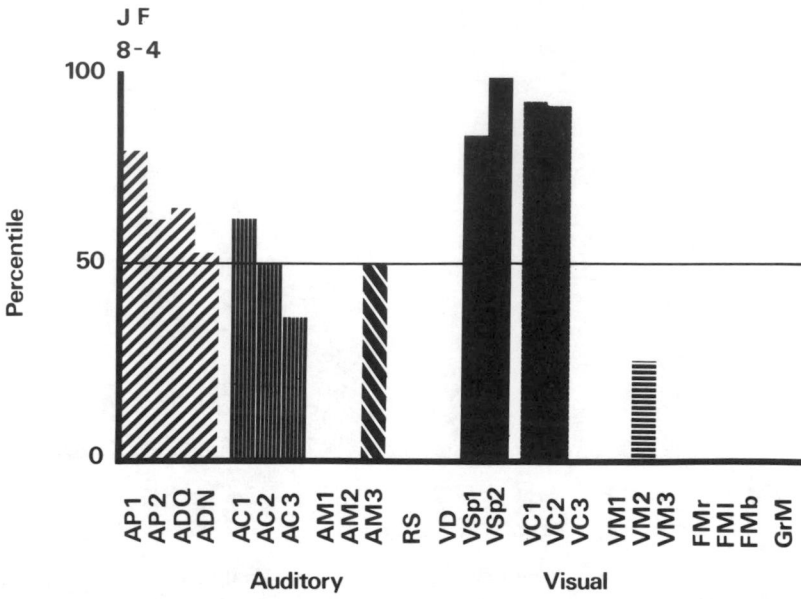

Figure 3.   The neuropsychological profile of John F. at 8 years 4 months of age. Performance in both auditory-verbal and visually mediated areas have improved over his performance at 4 years 2 months of ago so that the relative discrepancy between the two processing modalities is still in evidence.

strated above, eight DLD subtypes were identified. Because of limited numbers we were able to validate empirically only five of the subtypes. Several hypothesized receptive subtypes were collapsed into one because of the small number of subjects and measures available. An expressive-formulation group, a group characterized by short term auditory memory and retrieval deficits, a group with subtle organizational deficits and a group with global language deficits were the others involved in the validiation study. The classification is being refined through continued theory development and empirical validation studies and by the addition of quantified observational data regarding expressive language and pragmatic skills which cannot be captured by standardized tests currently available. (See Wilson and Risucci 1986, for futher information regarding the development of the typology.) The work to date has led us to look for external validation procedures. We have taken a step in this direction by demonstrating abnormal latencies in response to increased frequency of the auditory stimulus, especially among children in the "Receptive" subgroups (Danto, Wilson, and Risucci 1987).

LANGUAGE AND READING

The relationship between language disorders and reading disabilities has been amply documented in the literature (Fletcher 1981). We have further documented this relationship in the current longitudinal study and have developed a model for the classification of DLD related disabilities. We are continuing to refine this classification of neurocognitive patterns found among DLD preschool children (Wilson and Risucci 1986) by adding quantified estimates based on clinical observations to assist in the clarification of tests scores. Because such data are not available for the group involved in the present study, we have used the original "Generation 1" classification including only those subtypes that were empirically validated (Risucci 1984). The neuropsychological constructs, their subtest composition, and the description of the rules for inclusion will be found in tables I and II. Although the original classification was based on over 100 preschool children, several of the receptive and expressive subtypes were collapsed for the original analysis because of low base rates for some of the groups. This has undoubtedly introduced more within-group variance than is desirable. We plan to address this issue as our sample size permits.

A PRELIMINARY PREDICTION STUDY

The current study addresses the following questions: (1) Can ability in decoding and in reading comprehension during the early school years be predicted in DLD children on the basis of neuropsychological assessment data obtained during their preschool years? (2) Does the incidence, nature, and severity of later reading disorders differ with respect to DLD subtype membership in the preschool years?

Methods and Procedures

The subjects include 72 children, all of whom had been identified as DLD between the ages of 3 and 4 and had been enrolled in an early intervention program for preschool children with primary DLD for at least one year. Each had been identified by a neuropsychologist and a language pathologist. None came from a bilingual home, none showed evidence of frank brain damage or evidence of deficits in hearing acuity. None of the children had IQs below the average range. All of the preschool graduates are invited back for

TABLE I
Subtest Composition of Clinically Specified Factors and Constructs

Constructs	Factors	Subtests*
Auditory Perception (AP)	AP1	ITPA Auditory Closure[c]
	AP2	ITPA Sound Blending[c]
Auditory Discrimination (AD)	AD-Q	GFW Quiet[c]
	AD-N	GFW Noise[c]
Auditory Cognitive (AC)	AC1	WPPSI Similarities
		ITPA Auditory Association[a,b]
	AC2	WPPSI Information
		ITPA Auditory Reception[a,b]
	AC3	WPPSI Vocabulary[a]
		WPPSI Comprehension
Auditory Memory (AM)	AM1	WPPSI Sentences[a]
		McC Verbal Memory 1[b]
	AM2	McC Verbal Memory 2[b]
	AM3	ITPA Auditory Sequential Memory[b]
Retrieval (RET)	RS	McC Verbal Fluency[b]
Visual Discrimination (VD)	VD1	HN Picture Identification
		PTI Form Discrimination[a,c]
Visual Spatial (VSp)	VSp1	WPPSI Block Design[a]
		HN Block Patterns
	VSp2	McC Puzzle Solving[c]
Visual Cognitive (VC)	VC1	WPPSI Picture Completion
		ITPA Visual Reception[a,b]
	VC2	ITPA Visual Association[a,b]
		HN Picture Association
		PTI Similarities
	VC3	ITPA Manual Expression[b]
Visual Memory (VM)	VM1	HN Visual Attention Span[b]
	VM2	HN Memory for Color
		ITPA Visual Sequential Memory[a,b]
	VM3	PTI Immediate Recall[b]

Abbreviations:
ITPA — Illinois Test of Psycholinguistic Abilities (Kirk, McCarthy and Kirk 1968)
GFW — Goldman-Fristoe-Woodcock Test of Auditory Discrimination (Goldman, Fristoe and Woodcock 1970)
WPPSI— Wechsler Preschool and Primary Scales of Intelligence (Wechsler 1967)
McC — McCarthy Scales of Children's Abilities (McCarthy 1970)
HN — Hiskey-Nebraska Test of Learning Aptitude (Hiskey 1966)
PTI — Pictorial Test of Intelligence (French 1964)
[a]These subtests were given preference when scores were discrepant within a factor.
[b]These subtests were utilized in the cluster analyses.
[c]These subtests served as external variables for validation purposes.

TABLE II
Hypothetical Framework for the Classification of Developmental Language Disorders

Developmental Language Disorders	Subtype	Description of Neuropsychological Profiles	Quantitative Rules for Inclusion
Receptive-Expressive	C[a]	Auditory Semantic Comprehension Disorder	2/3AC ↓ relative to VC
	H[a]	Auditory & Visual Semantic Comprehension Disorder	2/3AC ↓, 2/3VC ↓
Expressive-Receptive	B[a]	Auditory Semantic Comprehension & Auditory & Visual Short-Term Memory Disorder	2/3AC ↓, AM1 ↓, AM3 ↓, 2/3VM ↓
	P[a]	Expressive and/or Receptive Disorder	2/3AC ↓, 2/3AM
	W	Global Language & Memory Disorder	2/3AC ↓, 2/3VC ↓, 2/3AM ↓, 2/3VM ↓
Expressive	F	Auditory Memory & Retrieval Disorder	AM1 ↓, AM3 ↓, RS ↓
	A[b]	Expressive Disorder	AC3 ↓, AM2 ↓
	S[b]	Expressive Disorder	AM2 ↓, RS ↓
	N	No Deficits	No more than 1 score ↓
Short-Term Memory	G[c]	Auditory & Visual Short-Term Memory Disorder	AM1 ↓, AM3 ↓, 2/3VM ↓
Auditory Processing	K[c]	Auditory Processing Disorder	2/2AP ↓ and/or 2/2AD ↓

[a]These subtypes were combined for validation purposes, to represent the "Receptive" subgroup.
[b]These subtypes were combined to represent the "Expressive" subgroup.
[c]This subtype was excluded from validity analyses.

annual follow-up testing; those in the study had returned for follow-up testing at least once after having entered grade school. In the
current sample, 62 children were in first or second grade and 40
were seen in third or fourth grade. A total of 27 were represented in
both grade level ranges.

Upon entrance into the preschool program, a comprehensive
assessment of each child was completed that included standardized
measures of cognitive ability, auditory and visual short term memory and perception, auditory discrimination, and receptive and expressive language. This assessment was repeated at least once prior
to the child's completion of the program. A similar assessment was
conducted each time the child returned for a re-evaluation; different
measures were substituted to tap the same functions as a child out-
grew norms. Measures of reading, arithmetic, and written expression were introduced at grade appropriate intervals.

For purposes of data analysis, one preschool evaluation was
selected for each child for profiling and classification. These profiles
were assigned, by visual inspection related to the rules for inclusion,
to subgroups that had been previously validated (Risucci 1984;
Rosati 1985; Wilson and Risucci 1986). The first analysis was aimed at
determining which variables that were assessed during the preschool evaluation could be used to predict later performance on the
four reading subtests. Pearson correlations were used for this purpose. A second analysis involved tabulation of the number of children in each preschool subtype who later obtained scores below either the 5th or the 16th percentile of the WI, WA, and/or PC subtests.
These percentile scores were chosen to represent two commonly
used cut-off points, one and two standard deviations below the
mean, for the definition of reading deficits.

Results and Discussion

Table III presents the results of the correlation analyses between preschool assessment measures and later reading subtest
scores. The coefficients reported in the table are only those that were
significant at the .01 level or less. As shown in the table, the significant correlations at the two grade level ranges differ; for the lower
grades, the preschool measures with the highest correlations are
those that place heavier demands on visual spatial abilities, while for
the higher grades, preschool measures of auditory, cognitive, memory, and retrieval factors correlate more highly, especially with the
PC subtest.

While each of the auditory-verbal constructs correlated significantly with Passage Comprehension in the third and fourth

TABLE III
Statistically Significant Correlations* between Preschool Assessment Constructs and Reading Measures at Grades 1–2 and 3–4

	Woodcock Reading Subtests	Auditory-Verbal Constructs							Visual-Perceptual Motor Constructs							
		AC 1	AC 2	AC 3	AM 1	AM 2	AM 3	RS	V Sp1	V Sp2	VC 1	VC 2	VC 3	VM 1	VM 2	VM 3
1st	LI								.47	.37						
&	WI						.37		.46							
2nd	WA				.39				.49	.38						
Grades	PC						.38		.49						.49	
3rd	LI															
&	WI									.50						
4th	WA					.58										
Grades	PC	.63	.63	.57	.58	.64	.53	.50	.53						.54	

*All correlations are significant at p < .01 or better

grades, it is interesting to note that the AM2 factor measured during the preschool evaluation was the only predictor variable that correlated significantly with both Word Attack and Passage Comprehension in the third and fourth grades. The subtest used to measure this factor—McCarthy Verbal Memory, Part 2—requires the child to recall a story read to him/her. This involves both receptive and expressive language, as well as memory and retrieval. In this sense, it is probably the most complex auditory-verbal measure included in the preschool battery. Thus, it may be appropriate to infer that later reading ability, in general, is best predicted by a child's ability to integrate these separate aspects of auditory-verbal function during the preschool years.

In contrast, the only significant correlations with first and second grade reading subtest scores were with preschool measures of memory and visual spatial abilities. These data suggest that the reading acquisition of a child with DLD is largely dependent on his/her ability to utilize visual spatial analysis and constructional and memory skills. It would seem then, that one could argue that a shift in reading strategy—at some time during the second or third grade—from primarily visual spatial (or right hemisphere based) to primarily auditory-verbal (or left hemisphere based), may be beneficial for children with DLD, as has been hypothesized by Bakker (1979) as being beneficial for normal children, but that many children with DLD have a great deal of difficulty making the shift.[1] Looking at first and second grade data provides substantiation of early findings of visual-spatial disorders in early poor readers (Fletcher and Satz 1980). The task demands in first and second grades involve the acquisition of the mechanics of reading, that is, those skills associated with the ability to decode. Although this group of children is identified as DLD, it is aspects of visual-spatial abilities, visual memory, and auditory memory that are correlated with reading in the first two grades.

In the third and fourth grades, on the other hand, the correlations between reading and visually mediated functions are minimal; it is the auditorily mediated functions that are significantly correlated, particularly with Passage Comprehension.

Table IV provides a summary of the proportion of children in each preschool subgroup who later obtained reading subtest scores in the deficit ranges.

As expected from the correlational analyses, the data presented in this table suggest that overall, preschool children with

---

[1]Editor's note: See Chapter 9, this volume.

TABLE IV
Percentage of Children with Below Average Reading Scores on Woodcock Word Identification,
Word Attack and/or Passage Comprehension Subtests in Relation to Subtype Membership

Preschool Subtype	WI		WA		PC	
	Below 5th %ile	6–16th %ile	Below 5th %ile	6–16th %ile	Below 5th %ile	6–16th %ile
Grades 1 & 2						
Receptive (N = 16)	37.5	0.0	31.3	18.7	31.3	0.0
Auditory Mem. & Retrieval (N = 6)	33.3	16.7	50.0	16.7	16.7	16.7
Expressive Formulation (N = 8)	0.0	25.0	0.0	12.5	0.0	0.0
Organizational (N = 25)	8.3	8.3	13.0	8.6	4.2	4.2
Grades 3 & 4						
Receptive (N = 10)	20.0	10.0	10.0	10.0	20.0	20.0
Auditory Mem. & Retrieval (N = 6)	50.0	0.0	33.3	0.0	50.0	0.0
Expressive Formulation (N = 8)	25.0	12.5	0.0	25.0	25.0	0.0
Organizational (N = 12)	0.0	0.0	0.0	0.0	0.0	0.0

DLD that is related to disordered receptive language and/or auditory memory and retrieval are most likely to experience later reading disabilities. As expected, based on overall performance levels, the organizational subgroup appears least likely to experience reading disabilities. In fact, in the third and fourth grades, none of the children in this subgroup had reading subtest scores in the deficit ranges. In contrast, reading subtest scores in the deficit range may occur in as many as 50% of children with receptive and/or auditory memory and retrieval disorders, at both grade levels. These proportions were not subjected to statistical comparisons due to the presence of large differences in the number of children in each subgroup at each grade level, and between grade levels. However, these data provide a basis for hypotheses related to the development of reading disabilities. Future studies will utilize longitudinal data for these purposes. While not statistically confirmed, it appears quite clear that there is a higher incidence of reading disability among children with DLD than would be expected in the normal population.

Overall, the results suggest that even among preschoolers with DLD, measures of visually mediated functions are better predictors of early decoding abilities while measures of auditory processing, comprehension, memory, and retrieval are better predictors of reading comprehension in the later grades when comprehension demands increase. Further, the data suggest that preschool children with receptive and/or auditory memory and retrieval disorders are at greatest risk for later reading disabilities.

These results support contemporary theories that relate disorders of language development and disorders of reading. The findings also support those of Satz and his colleagues (Fletcher and Satz 1980) which indicate a role for visually mediated deficits in the early acquisition of reading. The results provide additional support for the importance of specific aspects of early language for the prediction of later reading abilities and for the position that it is possible to predict reading disorders on the basis of selected constellations of preschool assessment data.

REFERENCES

Allen, D. V., and Bliss, L. S. 1978. *Evaluation Procedures for Screening Preschool Children for Signs of Impaired Language Development. Report of Project No. N1-NMS-6-2355.* Bethesda, Md., National Institute of Neurological Diseases, Communication Disorders and Stroke, National Institutes of Health, Department of Health, Education, and Welfare.
Bakker, D. J. 1979. Hemispheric differences and reading strategies: Two dyslexias? *Bulletin of the Orton Society* 29:122–129.

Danto, J., Wilson, B. C., and Risucci, D. A. 1987. Brainstem auditory evoked responses in preschool children with language disorders. Paper presented at the International Neuropsychological Society Conference, Barcelona, July, 1987. Abs. in *Journal of Clinical and Experimental Neuropsychology* 12 (2).

Fletcher, J. M. 1981. Linguistic factors in reading acquisition: Evidence for developmental changes. *In* F. Pirozzolo and M. Wittrock (eds.) *Neuropsychological and Cognitive Processes in Reading*. New York: Academic Press.

Fletcher, J. M., and Satz, P. 1980. Developmental changes in the neuropsychological correlates of reading achievement: A six-year longitudinal follow-up. *Journal of Clinical Neuropsychology* 2:23–37.

Gibson, E. J., and Levin, H. 1975. *The Psychology of Reading*. Cambridge, Mass: MIT Press.

Liberman, I. 1983. A language oriented view of reading and its disabilities. *In* H. R. Myklebust (ed.) *Progress in Learning Disabilities Vol. V*, pp. 81–102. New York: Grune and Stratton.

Ludlow, C. L. 1980. Children's language disorders: Recent research advances. *Annals of Neurology* 7:497–507.

Mattis, S., French, J. H., and Rapin, I. 1975. Dyslexia in children and adults: Three independent neuropsychological syndromes. *Developmental Medicines and Child Neurology* 17:150–163.

Rapin, I., and Wilson, B. C. 1978. Children with developmental language disorders: Neurologic aspects and assessments. *In* M. Wyke (ed.) *The Dysphasic Child*, pp. 13–41. Academic Press: New York.

Risucci, D. 1984. Empirical validation of a typology of language impaired preschool children. Doctoral dissertation, Hofstra University, Hempstead, NY.

Rosati, R. 1985. External validation of neuropsychological subtypes of preschool children with language disorders. Doctoral dissertation, Hofstra University, Hempstead, NY.

Satz, P., Taylor, H. G., Friel, J., and Fletcher, J. M. 1978. Some developmental and predictive precursors of reading disabilities: A six year follow-up. *In* A. L. Benton and D. Pearl (eds.) *Dyslexia: An Appraisal of Current Knowledge*. New York and London: Oxford University Press.

Vellutino, F. R. 1979. *Dyslexia: Theory and Research*. Cambridge, Mass: MIT Press.

Wiig, E. H., and Semel, E. M. 1976. *Language Disabilities in Children and Adolescents*. Columbus, Ohio: Merrill.

Wilson, B. C. and Risucci, D. A. 1986. A model for clinical-quantitative classification. Generation I: Application to language-disordered preschool children. *Brain and Language*, 27:281–309.

Wilson, B. C., 1987. An approach to the neuropsychological assessment of the preschool child with developmental deficits. *In* S. B. Filskov and T. J. Boll (eds.) *Handbook of Clinical Neuropsychology*. New York: John Wiley & Sons.

Wolpaw, T., Nation, J. E., and Aram, D. M. 1977. Developmental language disorders: A follow-up study. *In* M. S. Burns, and J. R. Anderson (eds.) *Selected Papers in Language and Phonology: Vol. 1. Identification and Diagnosis of Language Disorders*. Evanston, IL. Institute for Continuing Professional Education.

11

Phonological Precursors to Reading Acquisition

Susan A. Brady and Anne E. Fowler

The research presented in this volume emphasizes the role of language processes in reading acquisition. Our paper complements this theme and has three goals. We first review research on reading disability in school-age children, with a focus on what is currently known about the language deficiencies in this population. Second, we identify those questions about the nature of the language impairment and its role in reading disability that remain unanswered. And third, we share with you plans for a longitudinal training study extending from the beginning of kindergarten to the end of second grade which was designed to address these questions. In particular, the proposed study is intended to examine the question of whether the language abilities that have been found to be closely associated with reading ability in school-age children are in fact causal factors in reading success. A central premise of this approach is that an understanding of the causal factors in reading acquisition will point the way toward effective strategies for the early identification and remediation of reading problems.

This research was supported by NIH-HD-01994.

BACKGROUND RESEARCH

Research with School-Age Children

The emphasis on the role of language processes in the reading skills of school-age children has emerged from a coherent theoretical framework and a large supporting body of research. The theory, now widely held, contends that learning to read and to write depends in large part on special language-related abilities that include, and go beyond, those required in the use of spoken language (see Liberman and Shankweiler 1985, for discussion). A central line of evidence supporting this position comes from the numerous studies demonstrating that elementary school children who are poor readers perform consistently below good readers on a variety of language measures, but perform comparably to good readers on nonlinguistic control tasks. Attempts to isolate the source of the language difficulties have focussed on phonological processes for two reasons. First, the writing system we employ—the alphabet—represents the phonology. Therefore, in order for a child to have a conceptual grasp of what letters stand for, the child must be aware that language contains phoneme-sized elements. Second, both written and spoken language processing require phonological encoding of the message. Subsequent syntactic and semantic processing consequently will pivot on the adequacy of the phonological representation of the information.

Research examining the phonological abilities of school children who differ in reading ability has confirmed that poor readers are deficient in at least four areas of phonological processing:

1. *Phonological awareness.* Poor readers lack explicit awareness that spoken language is comprised of phonemes. Thus at a metalinguistic level, they are not consciously aware of the phonological structure of language. This is demonstrated by their poor performance on a large variety of tasks requiring phonological analysis of words into phonemes or syllables. Comparisons of good readers and poor readers have shown differences in phonological awareness to account for as much as 70% of the variance between reading groups. This, in combination with evidence that instruction in metalinguistic awareness facilitates learning to read, indicates that phonological awareness has a causal role in reading acquisition. At this time the cognitive basis for achieving phonological awareness and the barriers preventing it are unknown. There are tentative suggestions

that it may be related to other phonological processes described below.

2. *Phonetic coding to maintain information in working memory.* It has long been observed that poor readers have deficits in verbal memory. They generally recall fewer items from short lists of linguistic material than do children who are good readers. Close examination of the coding strategy of poor readers reveals that they are less efficient at creating and maintaining the necessary phonological code for storing verbal information. Deficits in memory may contribute to the difficulty in performing phonological awareness tasks as well as to the decoding and comprehension problems typical of poor readers.

3. *Phonetic perception to create a phonological code.* In word repetition tasks, poor readers make more errors if the words are somewhat difficult to perceive. For example, we found that by putting words in noise or by making them longer or less familiar, we have been able to discern differences in accuracy between good readers and poor readers. Good readers are affected, but poor readers much more so, pointing to an impairment in the ability to encode phonological information on the part of poor readers.

4. *Phonological recoding in lexical access.* Poor readers tend to be slower on tasks requiring the rapid naming of familiar objects, colors, or numbers. They also make more errors in retrieving phonologically complex labels (i.e., words such as thermometer or stethoscope). It is hypothesized that poor readers are less able to access the phonological representation of words in the lexicon.

These four areas of research have developed in relative isolation and have relied mostly on correlational studies with children in the second or third grade of elementary school. The findings from prediction and training studies generally converge with this pattern, as we note next.

Prediction Studies

Prediction studies are a potentially valuable way to study the factors ostensibly associated with reading performance. The development of cognitive abilities can be tracked prior to reading instruction, thus permitting evaluation of their predictive power and study of the developmental interrelationships of different factors. Studies conducted in kindergarten generally have been in agreement with research with school-age children, the conclusion being that reading performance is tied to language abilities, particularly in the phonological domain. Kindergarten skill in three of the four areas reviewed has been found to presage later expertise in reading (e.g., phonological awareness [Lundberg, Olofsson, and Wall 1980]; working memory [Share et al. 1984]; lexical access [Wolf 1984]). Indeed, several studies have now found that phonological awareness is the best kindergarten predictor of reading success, tied only with letter knowledge. However, because of several methodological problems, it is questionable whether this line of research has advanced our understanding beyond the correlational technique. For example, failure to assess and compare all measures at repeated points in the study prohibits distinguishing precursor from correlate. Wagner and Torgesen (1987) make this point persuasively by reanalyzing one of the most sophisticated prediction studies to date (Lundberg et al. 1980). Partialling out initial differences in reading skill rendered insignificant almost all other correlations in that study. Another frequent problem is a failure to be analytic; major predictors such as letter naming or complicated phonological awareness tasks have typically been accepted at face value as measuring one underlying construct.

Although no study has incorporated all the desired features to define unambiguously the phonological precursors to reading, recent research efforts have attempted to rectify these problems and point the direction for future research (Stanovich, Cunningham, and Cramer 1984; Share et al. 1984; Bradley and Bryant 1985).

Training Research

While phonological processing skills are important correlates and useful predictors of reading skill, whether proficiency in the phonological areas under study are causally related to reading skill has yet to be determined. It has been argued that the ideal way to investigate this question is to isolate the skill in question, train a preliterate population in that skill, and look for specific effects of that training on reading acquisition by including appropriate control conditions.

No study has attained that ideal in all respects. Indeed, the training approach suffers from many of the same problems found in prediction studies, and has the additional problem of needing good control groups for the training program. Nonetheless, the technique has been used to great advantage. Several studies have successfully demonstrated that preliterate children as young as four or five years of age can be taught to perform tasks requiring some level of phonological awareness; that is, their performance improves as a result of instruction. Other studies have found that training in phonological analysis skills does improve subsequent reading performance. These studies are valuable for considering the design of future training programs, but, because of methodological shortcomings, have been of limited use in addressing questions of causality.

One of the better training studies was conducted by Bradley and Bryant (1985). Children who received intensive training in categorizing sounds (i.e., noting that "hill" starts with a different first sound than "pin" or "pig") were significantly more advanced in reading at the close of the study than were children who received practice categorizing the same words on conceptual groupings (i.e., pig and hen are animals) or who had received no training at all. However, even higher reading and spelling scores were attained by a fourth group that had received auditory training with the additional aid of plastic letters. Bradley and Bryant concluded that "training in sound categorization is more effective when it also involves an explicit connection with the alphabet."

To summarize, training studies investigating the causal status of phonological processes in reading are few and mostly flawed. However, the Bradley and Bryant study has demonstrated the value of training studies in this endeavor and sets the standard for further research (see also Lundberg this volume).

On the basis of research to date, we now know a great deal about the role of phonological processes in reading. We know that skill in the four areas outlined above is associated with higher reading performance; we know that performance in phonological skill in kindergarten is predictive of later reading success; and, for phonological awareness at least, it appears that training of preliterates is specifically tied to later reading success.

DIRECTIONS FOR FUTURE RESEARCH

As current work in the field attests, further questions about the role of phonological processes in reading acquisition and reading disability need to be addressed. A central issue concerns which, if any, of the phonological processes are causal factors for reading success. A related question pertains to the interrelationships between the various phonological processes linked with reading performance: is there a unitary phonological deficit responsible for reading difficulty, or are there multiple, distinct components of phonological processing that may independently contribute to reading failure? Lastly, what is the relationship between training and phonological processing: can children be trained in the neccessary phonological abilities; do individual differences predict who can benefit from such training; and does reading experience contribute to the efficacy of phonological processing?

Causality: What Is the Role of Phonological Processes in Reading Disability?

We noted earlier that the research identifying the four areas of phonological processing associated with reading skill primarily has used correlational studies with school-age children. While the findings of individual correlational experiments are often ambiguous, the convergent pattern of results across many studies supports a theory tying reading to an explicit model of language processing. Further, the use of control groups and control tasks has permitted the evaluation of several hypotheses regarding the cause of reading problems. As noted, the empirical findings buttress the claim that the source of reading difficulties is in language, and specifically in phonological processes. It does not stem from a general deficit in perceiving visual or auditory patterns, or in using analytic strategies. However, a critical outstanding question concerns the details of the specific role of the individual phonological abilities in reading performance. Experiments using prediction and training designs are a potentially powerful way to examine this issue, though as discussed above, the existing studies have not supported strong conclusions.

What Are the Interrelationships of the Implicated Phonological Processes?

An extension of the causality question is to ask about the underlying relationship among the areas of phonological processes that have been implicated. We, like Wagner and Torgesen (1987), entertain three hypotheses.

Hypothesis 1. There is a single underlying deficit in the phonological domain. That is, the difficulties on the various language tasks mentioned above stem from a common factor. This hypothesis is attractive on grounds of parsimony, allowing us to tie together areas of weakness that seem very disparate. For example, there now is evidence that much of what have been seen as syntactic and comprehension problems in poor readers may derive from limitations in working memory (Fowler in press; Shankweiler and Crain 1987). A different line of evidence supporting the idea that reading ability is tied to a set of phonological abilities stems from research with hyperlexic children. These individuals perform poorly on intelligence measures, yet are precocious decoders. Against a backdrop of low intellectual abilities they have relative strengths in working memory and in phonological awareness (Healy, Aram, and Horowitz 1982; Pennington, Johnson, and Welsh 1987).

Hypothesis 2.   There are two separate factors: (1) metaphonological processes and (2) more basic (i.e., more "automatic") phonological processes involved in language activities such as perceiving, remembering, and naming.

We know that phonological awareness is strongly linked with reading ability, but this may be unrelated to the other, more basic, phonological processes that appear to play a role in reading performance. The link between metaphonological processes and more basic processes has not received much attention and those studies that have been conducted have yielded mixed results. Mann and Liberman (1984) and Goldstein (1976) reported significant correlations between awareness and other phonological tasks; on the other hand, Mann (1984) and Blachman (1983) found that the measures appeared to be tapping different aspects of language skill, each of which was predictive of later reading ability.

Nonetheless, a link appears to be justified among the more basic language tasks associated with reading disability. Verbal memory, phonological perception, and lexical access all require creation of an internal phonological representation, whether this representation is generated internally or through incoming stimuli. We, and others, have obtained significant correlations between the accuracy of phonological processes in perception and the capacity of working memory; this relationship obtains developmentally as well as in comparisons of good readers and poor readers. In contrast, these measures are not related to nonverbal memory (see Brady 1986 for a review). Thus, while we have evidence of correspondences between the underlying processes, these may or may not be distinct from phonological awareness.

Hypothesis 3.   Each of the tasks might tap separate deficits. Thus, not only would metaphonological abilities be distinct from more basic language processes, but deficits in naming, memory, and perception could, in turn, arise from independent factors. Although we have mentioned studies finding correlations among these tasks, other possibilities need to be considered. First, different groups of children may have different patterns of strengths and weaknesses. While performance on various phonological tasks has been found to be correlated in subjects who are identified using the usual exclusionary criteria, performance by subjects from more diverse populations may not conform to this pattern. Secondly, phonological tasks which correlate among themselves may differ in how strongly they relate to reading ability.

To reiterate, in asking how the phonological abilities relate to each other, three hypotheses emerge: (a) there is a single underlying deficit; (b) there are two factors (metaphonological and more basic phonological processes); and (c) different areas of phonological processing are themselves unrelated, but each contributes a component to reading success. One way to examine the nature of the interrelationships is to follow the development of these abilities prior to reading instruction, noting the degree of correspondence in their development.

What Is the Effect of Reading Experience on the Efficacy of Phonological Processing?

In addressing the issue of causality, a number of researchers have raised the possibility that the phonological abilities that distinguish good readers from poor readers may result from, rather than contribute to, experience in reading success. This argument has been most rigorously pursued with regard to metaphonological tasks (Morais et al. 1979). While it is now evident that the relationship between reading and phonological awareness is bidirectional, it is not clear what the mechanisms are for such a relationship and whether there are stages in both reading and awareness that build upon each other. The effects of reading skill on phonological processes (e.g. working memory) have yet to be explored.

What Is the Optimal Pre-Reading Training Procedure to Facilitate Reading Acquisition?

The most effective training studies have involved instruction in both phonological awareness and knowledge of the alphabet, each of which has been found to correlate highly with later reading ability. It remains to evaluate systematically whether the combination of methods is necessary, or whether training on phonological awareness alone or on the alphabet alone is equally beneficial.

What Are the Distinguishing Characteristics of Children Who Do Not Benefit From Pre-Reading Training Programs?

Individual differences in the effectiveness of pre-reading training programs are to be expected. Preliminary findings from phonological awareness training studies demonstrate that some children continue to have difficulty acquiring the metalinguistic concepts. An in-depth assessment of the cognitive abilities of such children at the pre-reading stage could be helpful for early identi-fication of children at risk as well as for a better understanding of the pre-reading requisites.

PROPOSED STUDY

To address the questions presented above, we believe that an appropriate and necessary project to build on the current state of knowledge is a longitudinal training study, extending from the be-ginning of kindergarten to the end of second grade. Our approach is not wholly novel. Rather, we have incorporated and built upon a number of methodological features that have appeared in individual studies, but have not yet been combined in this fashion.

In this study, 24 classes of children will be tested in the fall of their kindergarten year using a comprehensive battery of psycho-linguistic and cognitive measures that concentrate on phonological abilities but also include other major predictors and appropriate control measures. Multiple measures of the most important param-eters will be taken to provide more accurate estimates of the under-lying constructs for use in structural modeling analyses. For exam-ple, four measures of phonological awareness are to be given to allow differentiation of potentially distinct elements of this ability. In addition to a full range of phonological measures assessing memory, naming, and perception, we include a number of control tasks. First, to measure the contribution of general cognitive factors in ac-counting for the observed relationships, we intend to measure both verbal and nonverbal IQ. Second, for discriminant validation pur-poses we will measure arithmetic skill. This will allow us to contrast specific achievement in reading with school achievement in general. Third, to ascertain the specificity of phonological processes in read-ing acquisition, we include measures of articulation and of syntactic structure. Fourth, to evaluate whether nonlinguistic cognitive task requirements might be the basis for poor readers' difficulties on phonological awareness tasks, we plan to give an awareness task that is conceptually parallel to one of our phonological awareness measures, but that is nonlinguistic. And, lastly, it is essential to eval-uate reading. A complete reading evaluation will be administered to permit an analytic comparison of reading skills and of language abilities.

For the next 18 weeks, each classroom will participate in one of four training conditions; the methods to be used are drawn from those found to be most successful in previous research and are guided by our theoretical focus. The first experimental group (PHON) will receive training in phonological awareness, using the visual aid of colored tokens; several studies have found that visual aids facilitate learning about phonological units in spoken language. A second group (PHON/LETTER) will receive the same training with the introduction of letters as well. This was a condition that was maximally effective in the Bradley and Bryant (1985) study. A third group (LETTER) will receive training in letter naming alone. In this way we will be able to directly compare the value of letter knowledge and of phonological awareness ability for reading acquisition. By including the LETTER condition, we also expect to be able to address whether the possible superiority of the PHON/LETTER over the PHON condition can be accounted for simply because of the training in letter naming, or whether it is the combination of phonological awareness instruction and letter instruction that is particularly efficacious. A fourth group (CONTROL) will receive no training, serving to provide a baseline for assessment.

The actual training will be conducted by the classroom teachers who will attend workshops and will follow an explicit training manual. We shall design and monitor the training program and provide additional assistance to children encountering special difficulty. Classroom instruction was selected for its practical value. If, instead, training were conducted by research participants, it is very unlikely that the procedures would be adopted by school systems, even if they were proven effective.

The full assessment battery will again be administered at the completion of training, in April and May. This will allow us to assess the immediate impact of the training on the phonological measures of interest, and later to evaluate how those relate to learning to read. Follow-up assessment, using the identical battery, will be conducted at the end of the first and second grades.

At this point, we would like to highlight briefly the main features of this study, referring back to the questions raised earlier.

1. Causality. The combination of longitudinal and training designs will enable us to evaluate the causal relations between phonological abilities at kindergarten, the effectiveness of training, and later success at reading.
2. Interrelationships of phonological processes. The comprehensive nature of the assessment battery and its repeated administration will allow us to examine the developmental correspondence of the various language

abilities. Structural modeling techniques will be utilized to test the alternative hypotheses concerning the relationship among the various phonological processes.

3. The role of reading experience. Obtaining a full assessment of phonological skills and of reading skills before and after phonological training and subsequent reading instruction will enable us to specify the nature of the interaction between these areas.

4. The optimal training procedure. Here we shall find which of three training procedures, each strongly motivated, is most worthwhile in terms of both the impact on potentially related language abilities and the effect on reading acquisition.

5. Who will benefit from training. The use of both longitudinal and training designs will enable us to evaluate the causal relations between phonological abilities in kindergarten and the success of training. That is, if some children do not benefit from training, the longitudinal data on the cognitive abilities of those children may provide previously unavailable data concerning the abilities that are prerequisite to starting instruction relevant to reading.

CONCLUDING REMARKS

An ultimate aim of research in reading is to understand the basic disabilities that underlie reading difficulties. In this chapter we reviewed the evidence that problems in phonological processing are associated with poor reading skills, we identified several questions that remain for a better understanding of the role of phonological deficits, and we gave an overview of a proposed project designed to add to our knowledge about these issues. The proposed research should help appraise the causal relationships between phonological abilities at age five and reading performance at age seven. We see this as setting the stage for more effective early identification and intervention of children at risk and for determining which phonological abilities would be particularly valuable to study in initial language development.

REFERENCES

Blachman, B. 1983. Are we assessing the linguistic factors critical in early reading? *Annals of Dyslexia* 33:91–109.

Bradley, L., and Bryant, P. 1985. *Rhyme and Reason in Reading and Spelling*. Ann Arbor: The University of Michigan.

Brady, S. 1986. Short-term memory, phonological processing and reading ability. *Annals of Dyslexia* 36:138–153.

Fowler, A. Grammaticality judgments and reading skill in grade 2. *Annals of Dyslexia* (in press).

Goldstein, D. 1976. Cognitive-linguistic functioning and learning to read in preschoolers. *Journal of Educational Psychology* 68:680–688.

Healy, J., Aram, D., and Horowitz, S. 1982. A study of hyperlexia. *Brain and Language* 17:1–23.

Liberman, I. Y., and Shankweiler, D. 1985. Phonology and the problems of learning to read and write. *Topical Issues: Remedial and Special Education* 6:8–17.

Lundberg, I., Olofsson, Å., and Wall, S. 1980. Reading and spelling skills in the first school years predicted from phonemic skills in kindergarten. *Scandinavian Journal of Psychology* 21:159–173.

Mann, V. A. 1984. Longitudinal prediction and prevention of reading difficulty. *Annals of Dyslexia* 34:117–137.

Mann, V. A., and Liberman, I. Y. 1984. Phonological awareness and verbal short-term memory. *Journal of Learning Disabilities* 17:592–598.

Morais, J., Cary, L., Alegria, J., and Bertelson, T. 1979. Does awareness of speech as a sequence of phones arise spontaneously? *Cognition* 7:323–331.

Pennington, B. F., Johnson, C., and Welsh, M. C. 1987. Unexpected reading precocity in a normal preschooler: Implications for hyperlexia. *Brain and Language* 30:165–180.

Shankweiler, D., and Crain, S. 1987. Language mechanisms in reading disorders: A modular approach. *Cognition* 24:139–168.

Share, D., Jorm, A., Maclean, R., and Matthews, R. 1984. Sources of individual differences in reading acquisition. *Journal of Educational Psychology* 76:1309–1324.

Stanovich, K. E., Cunningham, A. E., and Cramer, B. B. 1984. Assessing phonological awareness in kindergarten children: Issues of task comparability. *Journal of Experimental Child Psychology* 38:175–190.

Wagner, R. K., and Torgesen, J. K. 1987. The nature of phonological processing and its causal role in the acquisition of reading skills. *Psychological Bulletin* 101:192–212.

Wolf, M. 1984. Naming, reading and the dyslexias: A longitudinal overview. *Annals of Dyslexia* 34:87–115.

Retrospect

Overview of Early Prediction and Intervention

Jeannette Jefferson Jansky

The papers in this book reflect advances in refinement and rigor in the various studies of prediction and intervention.

Prerequisites for participation in the symposium on which this book is based were that presentations be based on research results, and, as often as possible, the children studied be younger than kindergarten age. This selection process yielded an assortment of papers describing the functioning of children as young as a few months through the ages of 16 or 17.

Dr. Orton emphasized the importance of mature language functioning for success in reading, writing, and spelling. Mrs. de Hirsch and others elaborated this relationship in papers written in the 1950s, 60s, and 70s, and Frank Vellutino's recent studies have provided convincing documentation for this thesis of the earlier investigators. It is probably safe to say that nearly all current researchers work from a theoretical framework that accords language a central position as precursor for subsequent academic performance. Therefore language activities figure importantly in most predictive batteries and intervention programs.

In some of the studies reported at the symposium, the emphasis was on issues of theoretical interest: For example, Rachel

Stark questioned whether pre-linguistic measures might predict later academic status. Observations of 45 children were used to define stages of speech motor development from age 2 weeks through 20 months. Thirty of the children were followed up at ages six and seven by way of parent questionnaires. The three children who had been "off-stage" relative to expectation at the time they were first seen, had caught up in language status by the time they were six or seven years old. (And some children showed relatively mild problems with language for the first time as they approached school age.) One of the three children who had been "off-stage" linguistically when first examined (he had evidenced a lag in the development of speech motor skills) had a reading problem when he entered school. As it happened, this was the only study child who did have a later reading problem, and the presenter took it as a hopeful sign that the language measure identified that child as being at academic risk. These findings, of course, are in no way definitive, but they do reflect the attempts of one researcher, working from a theoretical framework that views oral language competence as the matrix from which reading develops, to reach back into the earliest years to find precursors of reading difficulty.

Katharine Butler described a study of 229 children that asked the question: To what extent does language processing ability, as examined upon entry to kindergarten, relate to reading as measured in Grades 3, 6, 8, and even 11? The poorest readers performed less well consistently across grades and had evidenced language difficulties early on (as compared with the good readers, who had evidenced no such early language difficulty).

Two studies (Nathlie Badian and Barbara Keogh) described cross-validation research of predictive batteries. The results of such studies were disappointing, regardless of age at time of prediction, and independent of predictive battery used. Badian, for example, undertook a 6-year follow-up study of 444 children to whom a predictive battery had been administered at age 4 years. In general, predictive batteries have been better at identifying good than poor readers, and such was the case in this study, where 95% of good readers were correctly identified. However, the battery failed to identify 61 percent of the boys and 50 percent of the girls who read poorly. It also misidentified many children who turned out to be good readers (two thirds of the low predictive test scorers subsequently read well). It was also found that test predictiveness differed for boys and girls. As did Keogh, Badian took a careful look at the failing readers. Specifically considered were certain background variables (family history of language or learning disability, birthweight, birth order), presence or absence of attention deficit disorder, and scores on the WPPSI, in combination with early print awareness and language variables. The data was then reorganized in such a way that various groupings of the predictive tests and background variables were developed retrospectively. This reorganization would account for all of the failing readers. What Badian did, essentially, was to ignore the battery cutting score, and to substitute membership in the various risk groups as a device for targeting individual children who were likely to fail. Badian noted that the procedure would have to be validated in subsequent studies in order to determine its prospective usefulness. The three cross-validation studies presented during the symposium went beyond test variables to consider possible background contributors. While the contribution of such variables and the fact that boys and girls require different sets of predictors had been reported years earlier, what is important here is that these contributors are now being more widely viewed as possible aids to prediction. Novel and most interesting is the notion that alternatives to the cutting-score may serve prediction better. Several investigators also remarked on the value of teachers' predictions. And however belately, many who are engaged in reading prediction research have come to view cross-validation procedures as requisite to battery development.

Three intervention studies were described. One investigated the value of a particular method, while the other two evaluated the general long range effectiveness of intervention.

Diane Sawyer's study, which investigated method, determined the reading achievement levels of 565 children who had been screened as kindergarteners or first graders to determine auditory segmentation ability. The early test of auditory segmentation purported to determine the size unit (phoneme, syllable, word) each child could segment. Based on that performance, children were provided with daily supplementary training that focused on the size unit suggested by test outcome. Among results reported was the finding that those children who had not yet mastered word segmentation when formal reading instruction began, seemed to enjoy greater long-term gains when taught by a whole language approach with a focus on whole words, than when taught by a highly structured sound-symbol approach. It was concluded that children may make greater gains in reading if the initial instructional materials are consistent with the level of segmenting competence and if training is provided to enhance improvement in segmenting at all levels: phoneme, syllable, and word.

In Yancey Padget's study, the speech, language and academic

status of 27 children who received individual speech therapy five days a week for either one or two years while in preschool, was followed for five years. Intervention notwithstanding, the majority (19) were classified as learning disabled five years later. The author noted the difficulties of having separate service delivery systems for preschool and school children, as well as the complex relationships between language development and academic skill development. The results suggest that intervention that is designed specifically to facilitate improvement in one area may not transfer to another. Barbara Wilson described a program in which more broadly based interventions were implemented as a long-term venture. The positive outcomes in such a setting confirm the value of cooperation among workers in various fields—early childhood, speech and language, and learning disabilities—to achieve better integrated and more effective programs for intervention.

The studies reflect a growing awareness of the complexity of the problems we must address in our efforts to intervene with young children. No doubt we were overly sanguine, if not downright naive, in our expectation that we could develop batteries that would enable us to accurately target all (and only) high-risk children, and in our expectation that early identification would lead the way to intervention that would virtually eliminate reading failure. Many of the difficulties in predicting for individuals have been discussed in the literature. Problems include the impact that the unexpected course children's lives take during the years between prediction and outcome may have on academic functioning. There is also the possibility that the child has behaved atypically on the day he was tested. Perhaps the investigator failed to select a wide enough range of acceptably reliable predictors. Or, there may have been errors in administering or scoring the tests. But the most important reason predictive tests can never be fully accurate is that "reading readiness" activities, including oral language facility, on the one hand, and reading, on the other, are simply not identical. Reading is truly a "new" acquisition in the child's repertoire of accomplishments. Therefore, it cannot be perfectly anticipated by the child's performance on precursor measures. Research makes it evident that we must understand both the limitations of the batteries we use, and the limitations inherent in the effort itself.

But is this realization to be taken as meaning that we should discard our imperfect batteries (about which we now know quite a lot as the result of cross validation work) and the attempt to identify high-risk children? Should we really discontinue early intervention? I hardly think so. First of all, anyone with in-classroom experience with early identification programs knows that most of the children who are identified do need the interventions they receive. In actual practice, teachers have the sense to combine their knowledge of the child with predictive battery results. When there are errors, adjustments are made either by eliminating the special pre-reading work if the child does not need it, or by implementing it when a child is discovered to be struggling with the readiness activities that his classmates manage with ease.

Even though reading precursors are not identical with reading, their general relevance for reading is not in doubt. Significant correlations of predictor measures with reading have come up consistently over time and across studies. Therefore, administering such tests to young children can be informative, not only about the childs later prospects for success, but also about his needs at the moment, especially when the results are used in conjunction with teacher's observations. The testing process provides the educator with a procedure for making structured observations and directs her attention to critical areas. It is unlikely that teachers would continue to use test results that were useless to them. It is possible that the researcher has not yet been able to capture whatever it is that has made screening valuable to the practitioner. There is, moreover, the very real danger that negative preliminary research results may lead to the premature abandonment of hard-won and useful programs designed to identify and intervene for at-risk children. While we want to be aware of the limitations of predictive tests, prediction as a broadly based effort may yet be shown to be as valuable as its proponents believe it is.

These papers describe work that is bringing the teacher and the researcher closer together. The result is that each seems ready to look to the other for help in elucidating realities that both are trying to uncover.

Discussion and Reactions to Prevention of Reading Failure

Doris J. Johnson

All of the papers in this volume should make us keenly aware of the relationships between oral and written language and the need for integrated services. They should also make us aware of several important directions for the future.

First, the findings from these studies highlight the need for changes in our school readiness tests. Typically, reading readiness tests include measures of word meaning, listening comprehension, auditory discrimination, and various visual and visual motor skills. Most, however, do not include tests for phonological awareness, segmenting, and auditory analysis. Furthermore, most group tests provide no information regarding oral expressive language. Hence, children with problems of word retrieval, sequencing, syntax, and organization may not be identified. This is an important issue since studies on prediction (Jansky and deHirsch 1972) indicated that letter naming, picture naming, and sentence repetition are among the best predictors of later reading failure. Problems of word recall and syntax often interfere with oral reading and with prediction of words in context.

The reports of progress of children with speech and language impairments necessitate a review of the type of intervention that is provided. Some of the early therapy programs for articulation disorders emphasized "ear training" for defective consonant sounds. These procedures fostered phonemic awareness in that children were asked to listen for particular sounds at the beginning, middle, and end of words. More recent approaches emphasize production. In the future, it may be beneficial to investigate the bases of the articulation errors more carefully in order to provide the most precise remediation. Some children with developmental apraxias have good linguistic awareness but they cannot learn the motor patterns for speaking.

While there is strong evidence for the importance of phonological awareness in early reading, we also need to do more extensive longitudinal studies of semantics and comprehension. Many of the current vocabulary tests are inadequate for detecting subtle problems of conceptualization and understanding. In some respects, they are primarily tests of memory; they assess words the child already knows but they do not provide information about the child's conceptual understanding. Thus, many children score within the average range on vocabulary tests but they may not be able to identify the criterial attributes of the object or experience. Some have overly general meanings whereas others have too restricted concepts. For example, a child with auditory receptive language disorders identified all women with white hats as nurses. Conversely, he thought that a person was not a nurse unless he or she had a white hat. Some of these problems are not unlike those described by Strauss and Lehtinen (1947) in their chapter on thinking disorders.

Research on sub-types of reading disorders should, in the future, examine more closely those individuals who have good phonological awareness and good decoding skills with poor comprehension. Further diagnostic teaching and research should also be done to examine possible sub-types of poor comprehenders. Some have generalized comprehension disorders whereas others have primarily receptive language disorders. We also find that some with very low nonverbal abilities may have "gaps" in their comprehension. In particular, they have problems understanding spatial, number, and temporal words.

While the research in our field is steadily improving we still need to clarify the population attributes in order to replicate findings. Many of the studies reported here have clearly specified the characteristics of the populations. Generally, it is important to state the criteria for both inclusion and exclusion of all subjects. Control groups drawn from regular nursery schools or classrooms often have children with a wide range of ability, including the gifted. Therefore, both upper and lower levels of ability should be noted.

Researchers in the future also should specify the attributes of tests, experimental procedures, and media used (Johnson 1987). In order to achieve a replicable body of literature, studies should provide a description of the tasks, including content, format, directions, reinforcement, and other pertinent details. This is particularly important in cross-cultural research where the nomenclature and tests are unfamiliar.

Finally, the attributes of intervention methods should be provided in more detail. Most educators are aware of the ambiguity of terms such as "phonics," or "whole word" approaches. Often methods are classified according to a single attribute with little regard for other significant variables. For instance, methods classified as "multisensory" such as the Orton-Gillingham and Fernald are very different with regard to vocabulary, sentence structure, and other important features.

New research in the areas of adult-child interaction also should be incorporated into future studies of prediction. Observations of parents and teachers of handicapped children can provide considerable insight into both problems and progress. Above all, we need to examine the patterns of communication and interaction that produce the greatest change. Our ultimate goal is to create an environment in which children thrive and learn.

REFERENCES

Johnson, D. 1987. Assessment issues in learning disabilities research. *In* S. Vaugh and C. Bos (eds.), *Research in Learning Disabilities*. San Diego: College-Hill.

Jansky, J., and deHirsch, K. 1972. *Preventing Reading Failure*. New York: Harper & Row.

Strauss, A., and Lehtinen, L. 1947. *Psychopathology of the Brain Injured Child*. New York: Grune & Stratton.

Appendix

Speech and Hearing Checklist

This checklist outlines behavior which may be expected of a child at various age levels. If he consistently fails to respond as the checklist suggests, he may have a problem which requires further evaluation.

Average Age	Question	Average Behavior
3–6 Months	What does he do when you talk to him?	He awakens or quiets to the sound of his mother's voice.
	Does he react to your voice even when he cannot see you?	He typically turns eyes and head in the direction of the source of sound.
7–10 Months	When he can't see what is happening, what does he do when he hears familiar footsteps . . . the dog barking . . . the telephone ringing . . . candy paper rattling . . . someone's voice . . . his own name?	He turns his head and shoulders toward familiar sounds, even when he cannot see what is happening. Such sounds do not have to be loud to cause him to respond.
11–15 Months	Can he point to or find familiar objects or people, when he is asked to? *Example:* "Where is Jimmy?" "Find the ball."	He shows his understanding of some words by appropriate behavior; for example, he points to or looks at familiar objects or people, on request.
	Does he respond differently to different sounds?	He jabbers in response to a human voice, is apt to cry when there is thunder, or may frown when he is scolded.
	Does he enjoy listening to some sounds and imitating them?	Imitation indicates that he can hear the sounds and match them with his own sound production.

Average Age	Question	Average Behavior
1½ Years	Can he point to parts of his body when you ask him to? *Example:* "Show me your eyes." "Show me your nose."	Some children begin to identify parts of the body. He should be able to show his nose or eyes.
	How many understandable words does he use—words you are sure *really* mean something?	He should be using a few single words. They are not complete or pronounced perfectly but are clearly meaningful.
2 Years	Can he follow simple verbal commands when you are careful not to give him any help, such as looking at the object or pointing in the right direction? *Example:* "Johnny, get your hat and give it to daddy." "Debby, bring me your ball."	He should be able to follow a few simple commands without visual clues.
	Does he enjoy being read to? Does he point out pictures of familiar objects in a book when asked to? *Example:* "Show me the baby." "Where's the rabbit?"	Most 2-year-olds enjoy being "read to" and shown simple pictures in a book or magazine, and will point out pictures when you ask them to.
	Does he use the names of familiar people, and things such as *Mommy, milk, ball* and *hat*?	He should be using a variety of everyday words heard in his home and neighborhood.
	What does he call himself?	He refers to himself by name.
	Is he beginning to show interest in the sound of radio or TV commercials?	Many 2-year-olds do show such interest, by word or action.
	Is he putting a few words together to make little "sentences"? *Example:* "Go bye-bye car." "Milk all gone."	These "sentences" are not usually complete or grammatically correct.
2½ Years	Does he know a few rhymes or songs? Does he enjoy hearing them?	Many children can say or sing short rhymes or songs and enjoy listening to records or to mother singing.
	What does he do when the ice cream man's bell rings, out of his sight, or when a car door or house door closes at a time when someone in the family usually comes home?	If a child has good hearing, and these are events that bring him pleasure, he usually reacts to the sound by running to look or telling someone what he hears.

Average Age	Question	Average Behavior
3 Years	Can he show that he understands the meaning of some words besides the names of things? *Example:* "Make the car go." "Give me the ball." "Put the block in your pocket." "Find the big doll."	He should be able to understand and use some simple verbs, pronouns, prepositions, and adjectives, such as *go, me, in,* and *big*.
	Can he find you when you call him from another room?	He should be able to locate the source of a sound.
	Does he sometimes use complete sentences?	He should be using complete sentences some of the time.
4 Years	Can he tell about events that have happened recently?	He should be able to give a connected account of some recent experiences.
	Can he carry out two directions, one after the other? *Example:* "Bobby, find Susie and tell her dinner's ready."	He should be able to carry out a sequence of two simple directions.
5 Years	Do neighbors and others outside the family understand most of what he says?	His speech should be intelligible, although some sounds may still be mispronounced.
	Can he carry on a conversation with other children or familiar grown-ups?	Most children of this age can carry on a conversation if the vocabulary is within their experience.
	Does he begin a sentence with "I" instead of "me"; "he" instead of "him"?	He should use some pronouns correctly.
	Is his grammar almost as good as his parents?	Most of the time, it should match the patterns of grammar used by the adults of his family and neighborhood.

This Checklist was compiled by Mary Wootton Masland for the purpose of finding preschool children who were delayed in speech, language, or hearing development. The project was completed while Mrs. Masland was a consultant to the Montgomery County, Maryland Department of Health and was sponsored by that agency.

The Checklist was published in 1969 in *Learning to Talk* (Superintendent of Documents, U.S. Government Printing Office, Washington, DC 20402) and in January 1970 in the *Volta Review* (Alexander Graham Bell Association for the Deaf, 3417 Volta Place, N.W., Washington, DC 20007.)

Index

Absenteeism, 43

Academic failure, early screening and, 107–109

Academic performance, prediction and, 78–79

Academic skill acquisition and speech/language problems: early studies of, 52–55; elementary school years study and, 62–73; evaluation of studies of, 73–76; preschool years study and, 55–61, 73–75

Acquisition. *See* Reading acquisition

Age: DLDs study subject, 195; dyslexia preventive study subject, 82; language processing test subject, 22–23, 29; reading deficiency precursor study subject, 177, 178; rhyme recognition study subject, 145, 150, 157–58, 161; speech motor development subject, 4, 5–6, 9–16. *See also* Speech-impaired three and four year olds

Alliteration, 144

Anton Brenner Developmental Gestalt Test, 126, 134, 138

Apraxia, 191–92

Aram, D., 53, 54, 69, 73

Arithmetic: phonological awareness program and, 170, 174; Slingerland screening and, 111, 112, 113, 116; speech/language-impaired children and, 67

Articulation disorders, 226

Articulation problems, language-impaired students and, 70

Attentional deficits, 22; dyslexia predictive study and, 86, 93, 97, 98, 99

Attentiveness (language processing test analysis), 26, 27, 28, 34, 38, 43, 44

Audio recordings, 6; language processing test and, 24–25, 44

Auditory cognition, 190, 191, 192. *See also* Cognition *entries*

Auditory comprehension: language processing test and late reading performance and, 23–24, 44; reading and, 3–6

Auditory memory, 190, 191, 192, 202. *See also* Memory

Auditory perception: developmental language disorders (DLDs) and, 190, 191, 192; Slingerland screening and, 116

Auditory processing disorders, 22

Auditory segmenting, 164, 221; correlates of poor reading and reading achievement and, 134, 140; data sources (tests administered), 124–26; disabled reader profile and, 138–39; poor phonemic segmenters and reading achievement and, 131–32; prediction and (kindergarten measures), 139; reading acquisition and, 121–22; reading program and, 123–24; segmenting ability and reading achievement and, 127–31; study subjects and, 123; syllable awareness and, 124, 125, 134, 139; word awareness and, 124, 125, 131, 134, 139

Babbling: consonants use and, 4, 8; speech motor development predictive study and, 8–9, 11, 12, 14, 15

Badian, N. A., 96

Badian, Nathlie, 220, 221

Bajuniemi, L. E., 80
Bakker, D. J., 183, 200
Bashir, A. S., 20–21
Behavioral checklist, 231–33
Behavioral competencies, 118
Behavioral disturbances, 20
Bilingualism, 41, 43, 82
Blachman, B., 210
Bradley, L., 174, 208, 213
Brown, F. G., 32
Bryant, P., 174, 208, 213
Butler, Katharine, 220

Catts, H. W., 21, 47
Cerebral hemispheres, 177, 178, 179, 180, 181, 182, 183
Checklist, Speech and Hearing, 231–33
Chukovsky, K., 144, 148
Cognition: DLDs and auditory, 190, 191, 192; language and, 187–88
Cognitive Abilities Test, 125, 138
Cognitive linguistic classification, 189, 193–94
Colligan, R. C., 80
Comprehension delay, 70
Comprehensive Test of Basic Skills (CTBS), 32–33, 34, 37, 45
Computer analysis (speech motor development study), 7–9
Consonants: babbling and, 4, 8; early use of, 4; speech motor development predictive study and, 8, 9, 12, 14–15, 17
Cross, L., 108

Daley, S., 108
de Hirsch, K., 219
Developmental language disorders (DLDs): cognition and language and, 187–88; cognitive linguistic classification of, 189, 193–94; identifying (screening for), 189–90; incidence of, 187; language and reading and, 195; neuropsychological assessment and, 190–93; predictive study of, 195–202
Diagnostic classification (speech/language problems study), 56–60, 62–66
Dichotic listening, 177, 178
Distar, 123, 124, 131, 139
Dougherty, C., 139
Dyslexia, 17, 47; accuracy of predictive analysis and, 79, 85, 89, 92–93; biographical information (subjects in predictive study), 85–86, 89–90, 96, 97, 98, 100, 102; cerebral hemispheres and, 177, 178, 179, 180, 181, 182, 183; defined, 85; dichotic listening tests and, 177, 178; early intervention and, 86, 94–95,

100–101; false negatives (predictive study) and, 90, 94, 100; false positives (predictive study) and, 85, 90, 94, 99, 100; follow-up measures (predictive study), and, 84; good readers and, 79, 85, 89, 92, 94, 97, 100; learning-to-read intervention and, 180–83; longitudinal study to discover deficient readers and, 177–78; L- and P-types, 178, 179–80; methods and procedures in predictive study of, 81–86; poor readers and, 80, 85, 86–88, 90–94, 95–96, 97, 98, 99, 101, 102; phonemic unit segmentation and, 121; predetermination and prevention of L- and P-types, 183–84; prediction improvement and, 85, 90–94; prediction for individual children and, 96–99; predictive measures (preschool test scores study) and, 82–84; reading at grade six and, 84–85, 86; reading tests and, 177, 178; special help and, 86, 94–95, 100–101; subjects in predictive study and, 81–82; submorphemic segments and (case example), 165; subtyping and subgrouping and, 22
Dysphasia, 47

Education. *See* Academic performance; Academic skill acquisition and speech/language problems; Placement; Special education; Training
Eisenberg, L., 80
Elementary school years study of speech/language problems: academic progress and, 67–68; current status related to early diagnosis of problem in, 69–70; diagnostic classifications, 62–66; duration of early intervention and, 73; educational placement and, 66–67; follow-up and, 68–69; intelligence measures and, 70–73; subjects in, 62, 69, 70
Emotional disturbances, 20
Ethnicity: dyslexia predictive study subject, 82; language processing test subject, 23, 29, 38, 41

Familial influence, school performance and, 117
Finucci, J. M., 80
Fletcher, J., 79
Florida Kindergarten Screening Battery (FKSB), 183

Garvey, M., 52
Gates MacGinitie Reading Tests—Readiness Skills, 125, 134
Goins, K. W., 108

Goldstein, D., 210
Gordon, N., 52
Griffiths, C., 52
Gualtieri, T., 99

Halliday, N. A. K., 7
Hall, P., 53, 54, 68
Handedness, 83, 96
"Have We Prepared the Language Disordered Child for School?" (Snyder), 54
Hearing, DLDs screening and, 189
Hearing problems, speech/language-impaired children and, 69
Hicks, R. E., 99
Holbrook Screening Battery, 81, 82–83, 84, 85, 86, 89, 90, 93, 94, 96, 97, 98, 99, 100
Horn, W. F., 79
Houghton-Mifflin basal reading series, 123
Hyperactivity, 16

Information-processing difficulties, 21–22
Intervention. *See* Training
Iowa Tests of Basic Skills, 125, 126–27, 129, 132, 134, 138, 141

Jansky, J. J., 20, 46–47
Jargon, 9, 13
Jones, C., 53, 68

Kamhi, A. G., 21, 47
Kaufman, A., 72
Keogh, Barbara, 220
Keogh, B. K., 47, 108, 111
King, R., 53, 68

Language acquisition (preschool). *See* Preschool language processing performance
Language delay: intervention and, 226–27; reading difficulty and, 3–5. *See also* Developmental language disorders (DLDs)
Language experience approach (LEA), 123, 131, 139
Language-impaired three and four year olds: early studies of, 52–55; elementary school years study and, 62–73; evaluation of studies of, 73–76; preschool years study and, 55–61, 73–75
Language processing performance (preschool). *See* Preschool language processing performance
Lasky, E., 53, 68
Learning disorders, language skills deficiency and, 188
Lehtinen, L., 226
Leong, C. K., 22
Letter Names (test), 126, 134

Letters: phonemic level of language and, 168; reading acquisition and, 213
Letter strings: rhyme and, 149, 150, 151; rhymes and training in, 157–60
Lexical access, phonological process and reading acquisition and, 206
Liberman, I. Y., 210
Licht, R., 177, 178
Liebergott, J., 4, 17
Lindquist, G. T., 78
Lindsay, G. A., 78
Lundberg, I., 164

Mann, V. A., 210
Margolis, J. S., 47
Mathematics: phonological awareness program and, 170, 174; Slingerland screening and, 111, 112, 113, 116; speech/language-impaired children and, 67
Mattis, S., 98
Memory, 22; DLDs and auditory, 190, 191, 192, 202; DLDs and visual, 200; letter strings and, 150, 151; reading acquisition study and, 206, 210
Mental retardation, 71
Menyuk, P., 4, 17
Metalinguistic skills, 75
Metaphonological processes, 210
Mobility (parental), 43
Morais, J., 172

Naming: dyslexia predictive study and, 98; phonological process and reading acquisition and, 206, 213; prediction and, 225
Nation, J., 53, 54, 69, 73
Neuropsychological assessment, developmental language disorders (DLDs) and, 190–93
Nursery rhyme groups, 161. *See also* Rhyme recognition

O'Donnell, J. P., 79
Oller, D. K., 8
Oral language, written language and, 225
Oral language disorder: general background on, 19–22, 47–48; general discussion of, 44–47; language processing test (preschool) and, 22–31; language processing test follow-up (grades 3, 6, and 8) and, 32–37; language processing test follow-up (13 years after preschool testing), 37–44; language processing test used in related studies and, 29–31, 45. *See also* Developmental language disorders (DLDs); Speech-impaired three and four year olds
Orton, Samuel T., 219

Padget, Yancey, 221–22
Peabody Picture Vocabulary Test, 125–26, 134
Phonemic unit segmentation. *See* Auditory segmentation
Phonetic coding, 206
Phonological awareness: effects of extensive training in, 170–74; effects of training in, 167–70, 175; importance in early reading, 226; longitudinal predictive study and, 166–67; poor and normal readers (cross-sectional study) comparison and, 164–66; preventive actions (for reading-disabled children) and screening for, 163–64, 175; reading acquisition and, 205–206, 207, 208–214; rhyme recognition study and, 144, 147–48, 160–61
Placement: Slingerland screening and, 109–110; speech/language problems studies and, 60–61, 66–67, 74
Pragmatics of language, learning-disabled and, 70
Prediction: accuracy for good readers and poor readers and, 79, 85, 89, 92–93; developmental language disorders (DLDs) and, 195–202; important issues in study of, 225; language development and, 163; language processing test background and general discussion and, 19–22, 44–48; language processing test follow-up (grades 3, 6, and 8) and, 32–37; language processing test follow-up (13 years after preschool testing), 37–44; language processing test (preschool) and, 22–31; language processing test used in related studies and, 29–31; longitudinal poor reader study and dyslexia, 177–78, 183–84; misclassification of at-risk children and, 118; naming and, 225; phonological awareness and, 163–64, 166–67, 175; phonological precursors to reading acquisition and, 204, 206–207; preschool test scores and dyslexia (discussion of study), 95–101; preschool test scores and dyslexia (results of study), 84–95; preschool test scores and dyslexia (test methods and procedures), 81–86; reading as focus of studies, 79–81; research and, 220–23; school achievement and, 78–79; Slingerland screening and, 109–119; sound categorization test and, 161; speech and language delay and learning impairment, 3–4; speech motor development study and, 4, 5, 9–17; studies and, 219–20
Prelinguistic abilities, prediction and, 220

Preschool language processing performance, 220; general background and discussion of, 19–22, 44–47; language processing test follow-up (grades 3, 6, and 8), 32–37; language processing test follow-up (13 years after preschool testing), 37–44; language processing test (preschool) and, 22–31; language processing test used in related studies and, 29–31, 45
Preschool years study of speech/language problems: diagnostic profile and, 56–60; educational placement and, 60–61; evaluation of, 73–75; subjects in, 55–56
Public Law for Education of All Handicapped (P.L. 94-142), 45–46

Questionnaire: parent (dyslexia predictive study), 83–84, 97; parent and prelinguistic measures, 220; speech motor development study and, 16

Reading: developmental language disorders (DLDs) and, 195; as focus of predictive studies, 79–81; language activities and, 219; metalinguistic skills and, 75; Slingerland screening and, 111, 112, 116
Reading acquisition: auditory segmentation and, 121–22; auditory segmentation study methods and, 123–26; auditory segmentation study results and, 127–39; background research on phonological precursors to, 204, 205–206; future research on phonological precursors to, 208–214; language development as predictor of, 163; language processes and, 204, 205, 209; phonological training and, 204, 206–207, 207–208, 211–12, 212–14; prediction and, 204, 206–207; rhyme and, 147–50, 152, 154–55, 160–61; sound categories and, 208; writing and, 205
Reading deficiency precursor study: cerebral hemispheres and, 177, 178, 179, 180, 181, 182, 183; dichotic listening tests and, 177, 178; L- and P-type dyslexia and, 179–80; learning-to-read intervention and, 180–83; predetermination and prevention of L- and P-type dyslexia and, 183–84
Reading difficulty: DLDs and, 195; language processing test background and general discussion and, 19–22, 44–48; language processing test and related studies and, 29–31, 45; language processing test (time 1, preschool) and,

22–29; language processing test (time 2, 3, and 4, 3rd, 6th, and 8th grades follow-up), 32–37; language processing test (time 5, 13 years after preschool testing), 37–41; phonological process and, 205–206, 208–209; related to speech and language delay, 3–5; rhyme recognition and, 145–47; speech motor development study methods and, 5–9; speech motor development study results and, 9–17

Reading failure prevention program (phonological awareness training): cross-sectional study comparison and, 164–66; effects of training and, 167–74, 175; longitudinal predictive study and, 166–67; preventive action and screening and, 163–64, 175; research on, 225–27

Reading intervention. See Training

Reichmuth, M., 80

Rhyme recognition: alliteration and, 144; categorizing words by first sound and, 144; children with reading problems and, 145–47; as helpful learning tool (reading and spelling), 147–50, 152, 154–55, 160–61; identifying difficulty in, 157–60; phonological awareness training and, 172; as preschool skill, 143–44; sound categories and spelling patterns and, 150–53; sound category training and, 155–57; spontaneous rhyme as, 144

Richardson, A., 22

Ritalin, 16

Rutter, M., 80, 96, 99

Satz, P., 20, 79, 99, 101, 119, 202

Sawyer, Diane, 221

Scanning process, prediction of reading problems and preschool, 20

School achievement. See Academic performance

School readiness tests, 225. See also Tests

Schonhaut, S., 101

Schultz, M., 4, 17

Screening process, 79; academic failure and early, 107–109; DLDs and, 189–90; language processing test and, 24, 30. See also Tests

Second language use, 41, 43, 82

Shephard, Margaret, 161

Silver, A. A., 20, 79, 81

Slingerland screening: discussion of, 113–17; generalizations and implications of, 117–19; methods of (subjects and procedures), 109–111; results of, 111–13

Smith, R., 119

Snyder, L., 54, 55

Social influence, school performance and, 117

Socioeconomic status (SES): dyslexia predictive study test subjects and, 82, 86, 90, 98; language processing test subjects and, 23, 30, 34, 41, 46; phonological awareness training study and, 170; reading disorder prediction and, 20; Slingerland screening and, 117, 118

Sound categories: prediction of reading difficulty and, 161; reading acquisition and, 208; spelling patterns and, 150–53; training in, 155–57, 160

Special education: dyslexia predictive study and, 86, 94–95, 100–101; P.L. 94-142 and, 45–46; Slingerland screening and, 110; speech/language-impaired children and, initial, 60, 61, 73–75

Speech and Hearing Checklist, 231–33

Speech delay: intervention and, 226–27; reading difficulty and, 3–5

Speech-impaired three and four year olds: early studies of, 52–55; elementary school years study and, 62–73; evaluation of studies of, 73–76; preschool years study and, 55–61, 73–75

Speech motor development study: computer analysis and, 7–9; reading difficulty prediction and, 4, 5, 9–17; study methods and, 5–9; subject age range and, 4, 5–6, 9–16; test protocol and, 6–7

Spelling: language activities and, 219; learning-to-read treatment and, 182; phonological awareness study and, 166, 167; phonological awareness training and, 168, 173; poor and normal readers and, 165–66; poor reading prediction and, 93; prediction and, 175; rhyme and learning, 147–50, 152, 154–55, 160–61; rhyme and sound categories and patterns in, 150–53

Spoken language comprehension, DLDs and, 188, 202

Stanford Achievement Test, 84

Stark, Rachel, 220

Strauss, A., 226

Submorphemic segment analysis, 164–65

Superphonemic segment manipulation, 172

"Supplementary Language Program," 123

Swanson, H. L., 21–22, 47

Syllable awareness, 124, 125, 134, 139

Tallal, P., 47

Temperment, school performance and, 118

Test of Auditory Comprehension of Language,
126, 134
Test of Awareness of Language Segments, 126
Tests: academic progress (speech/language
impaired studies), 67, 69; auditory segmenting study and, 123, 124, 125,
126–27, 129, 132, 134, 138, 141; content
validity (CTBS), 32; DLDs predictive,
189–90, 195–98; dyslexia predictive and
IQ, 88, 98, 99; dyslexia predictive and
SAT, 84; *Holbrook Screening Battery* and
dyslexia predictive study and, 81,
82–83, 84, 85, 86, 89, 90, 93, 94, 96, 97,
98, 99, 100; intelligence (speech/lan-
guage problems study), 56, 57, 69,
70–73; language processing, 22–31;
phonological study (reading acquisition)
and, 212–13; poor reader evaluation
and, 43; prediction and, 79; reading deficiency (dyslexia study), 177, 178, 183;
"reading readiness," 80; rhyme recognition study and, 158; school readiness
and, 225; Slingerland screening,
109–119; speech motor development
study and, 6–7. *See also* Prediction
Tomblin, B., 53, 54, 68
Torgesen, J. K., 207, 209
Training: decision to provide, 4; learning-
to-read (dyslexia study), 180–83; letter
string and sound categories and,
157–60; phonological awareness,
167–74, 175; phonological (reading acquisition), 204, 206–207, 207–208,
211–12, 212–14; preschool predictive
dyslexia study and, 86, 94–95, 100–101,
221–22; sound category, 155–57; speech
and language impairment and, 226–27

van Kleeck, A., 22
Vellutino, F. R., 85, 219
Videotape recordings, 6, 189
Vihman, M. M., 4, 17, 143, 148
Vinke, J., 183
Visual perception, Slingerland screening
and, 116
Vocabulary development, 70
Vocalization behavior (speech and motor
development study): computer analysis
and, 7–9; reading difficulty prediction
and, 4, 5, 9–17; study methods and,
5–9; subject age range and, 4, 5–6,
9–16; test protocol and, 6–7
Vowels, speech motor development pre-
dictive study and, 8, 9, 11–12, 14–15

Wagner, R. K., 207, 209
Wedell, K., 78
Werner, E. E., 119
Wilson, B. J., 80
Word attack skills deficits, 188
Word awareness, 124, 125, 131, 134, 139
Word formation, 4
Word retrieval, DLDs analysis and, 190
Words, longitudinal study to discover dys-
lexia and normal and degraded, 177
Writing: language activities and, 219; oral
language and, 225; reading acquisition
and, 205; rhyme recognition and, 154;
speech and language impairment stud-
ies and, 54

Yule, W., 99